China's Crony Capitalism

China's Crony Capitalism

The Dynamics of Regime Decay

Minxin Pei

Harvard University Press

Cambridge, Massachusetts

London, England

2016

Second printing

Library of Congress Cataloging-in-Publication Data

Names: Pei, Minxin, author.

Title: China's crony capitalism : the dynamics of regime decay / Minxin Pei.

Description: Cambridge, Massachusetts : Harvard University Press, 2016. | Includes bibliographical references and index.

Identifiers: LCCN 2016002392 | ISBN 9780674737297 (alk. paper)

Subjects: LCSH: Political corruption—China. | Capitalism—China. | Elite (Social sciences)—China. | Power (Social sciences)—China. | China—Economic conditions—1976–2000. | China—Economic conditions—2000– | China—Politics and government—1976–2002. | China—Politics and government—2002– | Zhongguo gong chan dang.

Classification: LCC JQ1509.5.C6 P45 2016 | DDC 330.951—dc23

LC record available at http://lccn.loc.gov/2016002392

To Roderick MacFarquhar
Teacher, mentor, and friend

Contents

China's Crony Capitalism

Introduction

> Corruption in regions and sectors is interwoven; cases of corruption through collusion are increasing; abuse of personnel authority and abuse of executive authority overlap; the exchange of power for power, power for money, and power for sex is frequent; collusion between officials and businessmen and collusion between superiors and subordinates have become intertwined; the methods of transferring benefits to each other are concealed and various.
>
> —Xi Jinping, October 16, 2014

XI JINPING, the general secretary of the Chinese Communist Party (CCP), obviously has good reason to worry. The symptoms of corruption he described graphically after listening to the reports of inspection teams dispatched to investigate high-level misconduct in the provinces in 2014 are those of a Leninist regime in late-stage decay. Immediately after assuming his position in November 2012, Xi launched the most ferocious anticorruption campaign in the post-Mao era to expunge the rot from the party—and purge his rivals in the process. Tens of thousands of party and government officials, including dozens of "tigers" (provincial- or ministerial-level officials), were sent to jail. While it is uncertain whether his effort will save the CCP, the lurid details of looting, debauchery, and utter lawlessness that have emerged during the campaign only confirm, albeit with fresher empirical evidence, the prevailing view that, instead of building Deng Xiaoping's "socialism with Chinese characteristics," modernization under one-party rule has produced a form of rapacious crony capitalism, the defining features of which are neatly summarized in Xi's brief remarks above.

To appreciate how predatory, pervasive, and entrenched China's crony capitalism has become, we need look no farther than at some of the tigers and their cronies felled in Xi's war on corruption. Exhibit A is Zhou Yongkang, the former Politburo Standing Committee (PSC) member responsible for internal security and undoubtedly the biggest fallen tiger.[1] The case against Zhou, who received a life sentence in 2015 after a secret trial, is remarkable not only because the prosecution of a top leader of his stature effectively broke the taboo against jailing PSC members on corruption charges in the post-Mao era, but also because the network of corruption Zhou and his family members had woven together reveals what Xi called the interconnection of "collusion between officials and businessmen and collusion between superiors and subordinates." Prior to his rise to the PSC in 2007, Zhou had served as the head of China National Petroleum Corporation (CNPC, the country's largest state-owned oil company), the party chief of Sichuan, and the minister of public security. Besides strengthening his power base inside the CCP, Zhou's extensive network of loyalists—eight ministerial and provincial officials and several dozen bureau- or prefecture-level officials—was essential to his family members' thriving business ventures.[2] According to an investigation by *Caixin,* a highly respected business publication, his two brothers and sister owned an Audi dealership, mines in Sichuan and Xinjiang, real estate projects in Sichuan, a liquefied natural gas (LNG) business, and a franchise selling one of China's most famous spirits. Zhou Bin, Zhou's elder son, specialized in securing contracts from CNPC and flipping assets cheaply bought from the oil giant. In one deal alone, he sold an oil block bought for 10 million yuan from CNPC to a private businessman for 500 million yuan.[3]

Among Zhou Bin's business partners, Liu Han, a crime boss executed for involvement in multiple murders after Zhou Yongkang's fall, merits special mention. Liu, a Sichuan-based mining mogul who controlled a listed conglomerate with assets of over 40 billion yuan, paid Zhou Bin 20 million yuan in 2004 for an undeveloped tourism project with a fair market value of under 6 million yuan. Liu should be grateful to the Zhou family. After all, it was Zhou Yongkang who, as the party chief of Sichuan, took his name off a list of mafia bosses the Ministry of Public Security was about to arrest in 2001.[4] Later, it turned out that Liu's favor to Zhou Bin was fully reciprocated—and more. In 2006, Zhou Bin helped him obtain approval from Sichuan's regulatory authorities to construct three hydro-power stations and get a 600 million yuan loan from state-owned banks. Shortly before his arrest in March 2013, Liu sold his power company for 1.7 billion yuan. Among those connected with Zhou Yongkang, the most unusual is Cao Yongzheng, his personal fortune-teller allegedly endowed with supernatural abilities. The CCP charged that Zhou gave Cao top-secret documents in his office, and *Caixin*'s investigation shows that a company owned by Cao became a partner in an oil-production joint venture with a subsidiary of CNPC. At the end of 2012, Cao's company recorded undistributed profits of 1.1 billion yuan. At Zhou's sentencing in June 2015, the court alleged that Zhou's wife and his elder son took bribes worth 129 million yuan from four businessmen and informed Zhou after the fact, and that Zhou used his power to help Zhou Bin, his brother, a nephew, Cao, and a businesswoman reap illegal profits of 2.136 billion yuan, causing the state to suffer 1.486 billion yuan in losses.[5]

The Zhou family case may be extreme, but it is not exceptional. Consider the case of Ling Jihua, the powerful director of the General Office of the CCP Central Committee and longtime aide to Hu Jintao, the CCP general secretary from 2002 to 2012. Although not part of Zhou's network, Ling made a fatal mistake in March 2012 by asking him to cover up a traffic accident in which Ling's Ferrari-driving playboy son was killed, a scandal that led directly to his removal from his position a few months later. In a separate case against Ling officially launched in 2014, the party quickly dismantled his network of corruption based in Shanxi, his native province, where eight provincial-level officials and over thirty prefecture- and bureau-level officials were arrested. According to media reports, Ling's family members had amassed an impressive fortune. His youngest brother, Ling Wancheng, owner of a private equity firm, made 1.2 billion yuan with well-timed investments in high-tech and media firms (Ling Wancheng later fled to the United States after his brother's fall). Ling's sister-in-law and nephew owned a successful advertising and public relations firm that got contracts for the 2008 Beijing Olympics and the Shanghai 2010 World Expo. Ling's wife was the legal owner of several media and Internet companies.[6]

Had Lou Zhongfu not tried to ingratiate himself into Ling's family circle by putting up 10 million yuan—nearly all the upfront cash capital—for an Internet start-up jointly owned with Ling's wife, the real estate tycoon in Zhejiang probably would have been left alone in the purge of Ling. Until then, Lou had gained national fame for buying the People's Liberation Army (PLA) basketball team of the Shenyang Military Region in 2005 and erecting his own version of the Eiffel Tower on one of his (never-completed) real estate projects. But betting on the wrong horse landed Lou in jail. In a country where princelings (children of senior officials) seem to rule, Lou's is a rags-to-riches story.

A construction worker who never finished middle school, Lou took over a tiny township-owned construction company in 1984 and, during the wave of privatization of collectively owned enterprises, turned it into his family business. In little over two decades, he built it into China's ninth-largest private company, with 120,000 employees and annual sales of 98.6 billion yuan (and 6.49 billion yuan in profits) in 2014. An entrepreneur who knew the value of political connections, Lou paid top value to lure over one hundred local officials, either away from their mid-level positions or out of retirement. The list of executives who worked for him included a former vice president and a former chief of the civil tribunal in the Zhejiang high court, a former president of an intermediate court, and a former chairman of the Zhejiang securities regulatory commission. Lou's biggest political coup in Zhejiang was to become a close friend of Si Xinliang, a director of the provincial CCP organization department who wielded enormous influence in the appointment and promotion of local officials during his eight-year tenure (2001–2009). Shortly after Lou was detained at the end of 2015, the CCP's Central Commission for Discipline Inspection (CCDI) arrested Si on charges of taking bribery and trading power for sex—the same offenses allegedly committed by Zhou and Ling.[7]

Like Lou, Wang Chuncheng, a coal-mining mogul from Liaoning, was a big dreamer from a humble background. Wang stumbled into the coal business in the early 1990s when he became unemployed after his state-owned employer went bankrupt. To feed his family, Wang pilfered coal from a local mine and sold it to a local power plant in a push-cart. Through grit, smarts, and luck, he built his business into a major supplier of coal for Liaoning's power plants. Along the way, Wang bribed a succession of local officials in Inner Mongolia into giving him the right to mine giant coal fields in the resource-rich province. For a while, Wang was riding high. His car had a PLA license plate, exempting him from paying highway tolls and traffic tickets. A member of the People's Armed Police chauffeured him around. Based on press reports, Wang was undone by two events. One was his ill-fated decision in 2006 to build a multibillion yuan railway to connect his coal fields in Inner Mongolia to the power plants in Liaoning. Years behind schedule and over budget, the project brought him to the brink of financial ruin. The other event was his son's responsibility for the death of an individual killed in a barroom brawl. To get his son off the hook, Wang allegedly bribed one of the China's most powerful generals, the vice chairman of the Central Military Commission and Politburo member Xu Caihou. According to the official indictment against Xu and press reports, Xu amassed a fortune, mostly in bribes from fellow PLA officers seeking promotion. It took several trucks to cart away his loot—a ton of cash (roughly 100 million yuan), gold bars, jewelry, rare jade, and valuable artwork. In conducting its investigation against Xu, the Chinese Military Procuratorate arrested Wang in April 2014 as well.[8]

These are but a few examples of the looting, lawlessness, and collusion in the upper reaches of China's crony capitalist order. In the remainder of the book, we will encounter various, albeit lesser, versions of Zhou, Ling, Lou, Wang, and Xu who populate the less lofty realms of the Chinese party-state and hybrid economy. Of course, the cases we will be examining, like the more infamous tales told above, differ in important details, such as the perpetrators' rank, status, wealth, and means of looting. However, the central plot remains the same. The story, and the theory behind it, is one of the rise and entrenchment of crony capitalism in a one-party regime that happened to preside over one of history's economic "miracles." The defining character of this strain of crony capitalism, as Xi helpfully notes in the quotation at the beginning of this chapter, is collusion among elites in the perpetration of corrupt activities aimed primarily, though not exclusively, at enriching themselves.

Crony Capitalism and Elite Collusion in Post-Tiananmen China

The conventional and popular definition of crony capitalism, as conveyed in the *Economist,* is that it is a system in which capitalists gain valuable rents from politicians.[9] A broader definition of crony capitalism may treat the phenomenon as an instrumental union between capitalists and politicians designed to allow the former to acquire wealth, legally or otherwise, and the latter to seek and retain power. The illuminating portrayal of crony capitalism in Russia in Karen Dawisha's *Putin's Kleptocracy* confirms that this marriage is, indeed, a key feature of crony capitalism.[10] However, recognizing the defining feature of crony capitalism is only the first step toward understanding the phenomenon. While crony capitalism has become a popular term, conducting research on crony capitalism presents at least two difficult challenges to academics.

The first challenge is to develop an analytical concept that can distill the essence of crony capitalism and be applied to an empirical investigation of this phenomenon. Here we propose such a concept, "collusion among elites," with which to study crony capitalism. The use of this concept can be justified by the simple but basic fact that such collusion, both legal and illicit, lies at the heart of crony capitalism in all societies regardless of the nature of their political regimes. In addition, the adoption of this concept can help us understand both the origins of crony capitalism and its real-life manifestations. Evidence indicating the emergence of such collusion is likely to help us establish the genesis of crony capitalism, while evidence of the behavioral characteristics of collusion among elites should reveal the economic and sociological dynamics of crony capitalism.

The application of the analytical concept of collusion among elites to a study of crony capitalism in China is likely to yield important insights because collusion among elites, now prevalent throughout key sectors and public institutions, was not observed until the early 1990s. By analyzing the most important institutional differences between the 1980s and the subsequent two and one-half decades, we should be able to trace the most likely origins of elite collusion and its salient behavioral patterns. Empirically, the evidence that collusion among elites did not emerge in a meaningful sense until the early 1990s can be seen in the rise, since the 1990s, of particular types of corruption cases—*wo'an* and *chuan'an*—that involve multiple officials, either in the same public institution or across several institutions or even several geographical jurisdictions.[11] Of course, official corruption existed in the 1980s, but collusive corruption, *wo'an* and *chuan'an* in Chinese parlance, was extremely rare.[12] Published reports of corruption cases that were prosecuted in the 1980s and newspaper stories of official misconduct in the same decade contained no references to collusive corruption.[13] A keyword search for *"wo'an"* and *"chuan'an"* in the China Knowledge Resource Integrated Database (cnki.net, an electronic database of newspapers, magazines, official documents, and scholarly journals) finds no reference to these two terms until 1992.[14] Since the 1990s, however, official collusion in corruption and other types of criminal activities have become increasingly common. A small number of researchers who have studied this development share the view that collusive corruption is more sophisticated, destructive, and difficult to detect.[15]

Although China's anticorruption authorities do not publish systemic data on *wo'an* and *chuan'an,* senior officials, including Xi Jinping, have admitted publicly that such cases are common. Liu Liying, a deputy director of the CCDI who presided over some of the most notorious corruption cases in the late 1990s and early 2000s, said in an interview published in 2003 that the number of *chuan'an, wo'an,* and *anzhong'an* (case within a case) had risen and corrupt officials had formed, in her words, "interest-based alliances," and their corrupt activities resembled those of "cliques."[16] Sporadic disclosure by provincial and municipal procuratorates also offers some empirical confirmation of the pervasiveness of the collusive corruption Liu identified. On average, should the data from the jurisdictions in Table I.1 be representative, roughly half of the individuals apprehended for corruption are involved in *wo'an* or *chuan'an.* Such cases account for 45 percent of all prosecuted corruption cases.

Collusive corruption, in theory as well as in practice, is more destructive than individual corruption because such behavior destroys the organizational and normative fabric of the state, increases the difficulty of detection, and produces greater financial gains for its perpetrators. Due to the greater predatory capabilities possessed by elites engaged in collusive corruption, local governments penetrated by these elites unavoidably experience degradation in their capacity for providing public goods. In the worst case, corruption networks, consisting of officials, businessmen, and gangsters, seize control of these jurisdictions and turn them into local mafia states. Another harmful effect of collusive corruption by local elites is that such behavior fuels the conflict between the state and society. In jurisdictions that have fallen prey to collusive elites who systematically abuse their power, tensions between the public and local authorities are more likely to arise and result in more frequent riots and violent clashes between the public and the local authorities.[17]

Although collusive corruption poses a serious threat to the sustainability of China's economic development and the survival of the

CCP, this phenomenon has largely been overlooked in the abundant literature on "red capitalism" and corruption. Research on red capitalism, pioneered by Bruce Dickson, focuses exclusively on shared political values and policy priorities between private entrepreneurs and local officials, but does not explore how their close political

Table I.1. Percentage of *wo'an* and *chuan'an* reported by the National Audit Office, provinces, and municipalities

Jurisdiction	Period	Individuals involved in *wo'an* and *chuan'an* as percent of all prosecuted for corruption	*Wo'an* and *chuan'an* as percent of all prosecuted corruption cases
National data			
National audit conducted by National Audit Agency	2013	69	35.7
Provincial data			
Shanghai	2000		32
Jiangsu	2000		36
Jiangxi	2003		Above 20
Hubei	2003		43
Guizhou	2004		42
Jiangxi	2007–2009		55.4
Sichuan	2007–2010		45
Zhejiang	2009–2013		Around 50
Guizhou	2012		58
Shanghai	2011	39	
Shanghai	2012	49.5	
Shanghai	2014 (Jan.–May)	35	27
Municipalities			
Hangzhou	2001		42
Guangzhou	2003		71
Hangzhou	2004		63
Chongqing	2008	39	34

Jurisdiction	Period	Individuals involved in *wo'an* and *chuan'an* as percent of all prosecuted for corruption	*Wo'an* and *chuan'an* as percent of all prosecuted corruption cases
Dalian	2011	53	39
Shenzhen	2012	70	
Fuzhou	2012 (Jan.–June)	63	50
Guangzhou	2012–2013		Above 70
Mean		52	45
Median		51	42

Data sources: National Audit Office, "2013 年度审计报告" [Annual audit report 2013], http://www.audit.gov.cn/n1992130/n1992165/n2032598/n2376391/3602645.html; "江西三年查处职务犯罪案 700 件" [Jiangxi prosecuted 700 cases of using public office to commit crime in three years], *PD*, October 13, 2010; "行贿犯罪工程建设领域最多" [Bribery most prevalent in construction sector], *PD*, February 9, 2011; 中国改革报, August 7, 2003; "江苏今年职务犯罪案件中窝案串案占三成六" [*Wo'an* and *chuan'an* account for 36 percent of all cases of using public office to commit crime in Jiangsu this year], *CNN*; http://review.jcrb.com.cn/ournews/asp/readNews.asp?id-=13942; "湖北公开典型腐败窝案" [Hubei publicizes representative cases of *wo'an*], 湖北日报, February 25, 2004; "贵州去年侦查贪污贿赂案 984 件" [Guizhou investigated 984 cases of embezzlement and bribery last year], *XHN*, February 16, 2005, http://news.sina.com.cn/c/2005 -02-16/10325115766s.shtml; "贵州 2012 年查办涉农贪污贿赂犯罪 223 件" [Guizhou investigated 223 agriculture-related cases of embezzlement and bribery in 2012], *PD*, January 15, 2013; "上海5 年内 14 名局级干部落马" [Fourteen bureau-level officials arrested for corruption in five years in Shanghai], *CNN*, http://www.chinanews.com/fz/2013/01-24/4518728.shtml; "沪检方贪贿立案今 年增 17.4%" [Shanghai prosecutors report a 17.4 percent increase in the number of embezzlement and bribery cases filed], *OMN*, June 24, 2014; "受贿滥用职权等五宗罪占浙江职务犯罪 9 成" [Bribery, abuse of power, and three other kinds of crimes account for 90 percent of crimes committed by using public office], *CNN*, http://news.sina.com.cn/o/2014-07-10/180430500807 .shtml; "7成腐败案为窝案串案" [70 percent of all corruption cases are *wo'an* and *chuan'an*], 广州日报, February 21, 2003; "广州两年查处 24 名厅局级 窝串案占立案数七成" [Guangzhou investigated twenty-four bureau-level officials; *wo'an* and *chuan'an* make up 70 percent of all corruption cases filed], 大洋网, http://news.dayoo.com/guangzhou/201403/18/73437_35529435 .htm; "深圳检察院: 窝案串案占 70%以上" [The Shenzhen procuratorate reports *wo'an* and *chuan'an* account for over 70 percent of all cases], 第一财经日报, January 23, 2013; "大连检察机 关去年查办职务犯罪案 193 件" [The Dalian procuratorate prosecuted 193 cases of using public office to commit crimes last year], 正义网, http://news.jcrb.com/jxsw/201201/t20120105_785840 .html; "查办行业系统窝案串案" [Prosecuting *wo'an* and *chuan'an* in various sectors], 人民检察 10 (2005); "重庆: 深挖窝串案" [Chongqing digs up *wo'an* and *chuan'an*], *PD*, December 29, 2008; "福州查办职务犯罪 122 件" [122 cases of using public office to commit crimes were prosecuted in Fuzhou], *PD*, August 5, 2012.

relationship is exploited to generate mutual economic benefits.[18] Research on corruption since 1989 has covered the types, participants, intensity, empirical measurements and causes of corruption, efforts to fight corruption, and effects of corruption on economic growth.[19] To be sure, some scholars have produced informative case studies of collusive corruption, such as *maiguan maiguan* (buying and selling office) and protection of organized crime. But these studies fail to explore its theoretical and substantive importance in the Chinese context.[20] Among the few researchers who have studied collusive corruption, Ting Gong provides the first systematic analysis of the phenomenon.[21] However, Gong does not address a critical question: why collusive corruption was rare before the 1990s but has become prevalent since then.

The lack of attention in the existing literature to the institutional origins of collusive corruption and its behavioral characteristics means that we do not have a good understanding of how "reform and opening" in the post-Mao era has engendered a destructive combination of authoritarian rule and crony capitalism. Equally important, our insufficient understanding of the dynamics of collusion may deprive us of knowledge about the internal process of decay in China's late-Leninist regime.

Methodological Challenges in the Study of Crony Capitalism

The second challenge facing researchers attempting to investigate the world of crony capitalism is methodological: how to gather evidence to support their hypothesis. Identifying the symptoms of crony capitalism is relatively easy. One can, as the *Economist* does, look at unusual connections between the concentration of wealth among billionaires operating in heavily regulated industries (the implication is that the higher such a concentration, the more intense the rent-seeking activities, and hence the greater the influence of crony capitalism).[22] But this approach is both too simplistic and uninformative since an index so constructed tells us nothing about whether or how political and economic elites actually collude with each other to produce such outcomes.

An alternative approach is to use data from corruption involving multiple officials and businessmen. Because practically all the acts of collusion that constitute crony capitalism are generally concealed from public view, the empirical evidence researchers gather to study crony capitalism can only come from cases of corruption exposed by investigative journalists or public authorities. To be sure, this approach has its limitations, the most serious of which is the nonrandom nature of the evidence since the researcher must rely on the media and government authorities as sources of the original cases of corruption. The problem of selection bias is real. However, on balance, a methodological approach based on a relatively large but still manageable sample of exposed cases of corruption has its advantages. First, such cases, typically collected from official media and court documents, contain colorful and illuminating details that provide valuable insights into the micro-level dynamics of collusion among elites, thus correcting a major flaw in purely quantitative studies of corruption based on large samples. Typically, studies using aggregate quantitative data present no micro-level details that can shed light on the motivations and tactics of the perpetrators. Second, a sample containing a sufficiently large number of cases permitting some basic quantitative calculations also remedies the flaws of single-case studies or research based on a very small number of cases, which may provide rich descriptions of individual incidents but do not paint a bigger picture.

We thus opt for a hybrid approach, one that is not ideal but may be the best alternative under the circumstances. By analyzing a sufficiently large, but still manageable, dataset of 260 cases, we extract from this sample important information on individual characteristics and activities. Analysis of such information helps derive useful insights into the world of crony capitalism in China. This hybrid approach does not claim to be "representative" in the same sense as a randomized large-N sample, but it does provide more robust empirical evidence than case studies based on a single or a very small number of cases. Unlike large-N studies that miss many crucial micro-level details, the hybrid approach can yield illuminating information on the behavioral characteristics of collusive corruption.

The 260 cases used in this study are highly publicized cases in the official press. A likely selection bias resulting from the high profile of these cases is that they may overrepresent officials with higher ranks since their arrests and prosecutions tend to attract more media coverage. While this may be the case, such overrepresentation does not pose a serious problem for a project on crony capitalism. Since, in the world of crony capitalism, only those with sufficient political power can trade it for wealth, any study of crony capitalism has no choice but to focus on political elites in possession of sufficient amounts of power. In selecting these cases, our most important criterion is that they must contain sufficient information on the individual characteristics of the collusion this study seeks to analyze. All the cases have been reported in the official press and highly respected publications: newspapers, magazines, news agency reports, government documents, official press releases, and court documents. All cases involve three or more individuals, the official definition of collusive corruption. Of course, in an ideal world, access to the CCDI's own files would give researchers the opportunity to construct a random sample based on a large number of detailed cases. But this opportunity clearly does not exist at the moment.

Crony Capitalism in Comparative Perspective

China, to be sure, is not the only victim of crony capitalism. Collusion between power and money is a universal phenomenon varying only in its manifestations and degrees. This form of capitalism is particularly prevalent in postcommunist societies, most prominently Russia, Ukraine, and the former Soviet Central Asian republics. As in the Chinese case, the defining feature of crony capitalism in the former Soviet republics is collusion among elites and between elites and organized crime.[23] However, it must be noted that crony capitalism is not an inevitable outcome in the transition from communism in the former Soviet bloc. As shown by studies on diverging transitions in Russia and Eastern Europe, the configuration of political power and the pattern of regime change jointly determine the outcome of economic transition.[24]

Among the origins of crony capitalism in the former Soviet republics, the most obvious is the privatization of state-owned assets, an event that motivated collusion among elites. Collusive corruption takes place during the privatization of state-owned assets when political and economic elites collude to underprice such assets or seize them for free, either through outright theft or by ostensibly legitimate procedures they can manipulate or control. As a result, collusive corruption during privatization has given rise to the concentration of wealth and power in the hands of a small number of well-connected elites, or "oligarchs."[25] Although the privatization of state-owned assets has attracted most of the scholarly attention, another form of privatization, perhaps even more insidious in breeding collusive corruption is the privatization of the power of the state, the second likely origin of crony capitalism. On the surface, this might be related to the decentralization of power that takes place during economic transition. In reality, decentralization of power and privatization of the power of the state are distinct phenomena. While decentralization may lead to devolution of greater authority and discretion to local officials, this process does not necessarily lead to the use of such power for private gain (although decentralization without accountability definitely creates more opportunities for corruption). In comparison, the privatization of the power of the state occurs when local officials appropriate the administrative power of the state and establish independent monopolies to advance their private interests.[26] The most visible symptoms of the privatization of the power of the state include extracting private revenue streams by selling government services (such as protection and judicial relief). In the worst cases, local officials can even sell government appointments for huge personal gain, a widespread practice in China. A variation on the theme of the privatization of the power of the state is "state capture." By influencing politicians and bureaucrats, powerful business interests can make parliaments and regulatory agencies produce legislation and regulations that favor the particularistic interests of these businesses. State capture can stifle competition and increase the economic rents to the "captors" of the state. At the same time, this phenomenon also increases the level of collusive corruption within the political system.[27]

Systematic decentralization during economic transition, the third suspect in the rise of crony capitalism, is also believed to facilitate collusion at the local level. Decentralization has resulted in giving local elites control of previously centralized property rights (such as the disposal of state-owned assets or the income from such assets) and greater discretion in the delivery of public services.[28] Although the debate over the relationship between decentralization and corruption remains inconclusive, one area of consensus is quite clear: Decentralization without accountability can greatly exacerbate corruption at the local level.[29] Indeed, evidence from the former Soviet Union appears to support this observation. While corruption is lower in countries such as the Baltic states, which pushed through thorough decentralization that was complemented by democratic reforms, decentralization followed by stagnant institutional reform is found to be especially conducive to collusive corruption.[30] Decentralization without accountability can fuel collusive corruption in several ways. Local political elites can collude to steal the assets of the state in the privatization program. Through the abuse of their newly granted discretionary authority, they can extract payments for government services that should be provided free of charge, thus effectively running an extortionist state.[31]

Finally, crony capitalism, albeit of a violent variety, can be traced to the breakdown of the central authority, the weakness of the state, and the subsequent emergence of local mafia states in the former Soviet republics.[32] This line of argument stresses the fragmentation of state authority as a result of the collapse of the communist party-state. Discipline of the agents of the state, especially those in the security apparatus, declines precipitously. Besides encouraging the looting of the state's assets, the decline of the state creates power vacuums that are quickly filled by unsavory political and social forces.[33] In Central Asia, for example, powerful clans have captured the state and used its power to acquire vast wealth and political influence.[34] In other former Soviet republics, the political power vacuum has attracted organized crime, which has penetrated law enforcement and the military. The economic hardships brought about by recessions during the transition further reduce the state's capacity to fund its police and military adequately or to invest in recruitment and training. Consequently, the state's security forces become less capable of fighting organized crime. In many instances, they even collude with organized crime or perpetrate crimes themselves.[35]

Crony capitalism, of course, exists outside postcommunist societies. However, the symptoms of crony capitalism in noncommunist societies are qualitatively different from those in postcommunist societies. If the essence of the strain of crony capitalism that emerged from the wreckage of communism is about seizing unclaimed or ill-defined state-owned property or reconstructing a new predatory order during a period of political chaos and state failure, crony capitalism in other societies is mostly about rent-seeking and entrenching the power and privileges of the established elites in a relatively stable political environment.[36] Companies owned by cronies of autocratic elites, as one study of Indonesia shows, enjoy higher stock valuations.[37] Even in some of the more established democratic societies, political connections can give corporations significant economic benefits.[38] In the more extreme versions of crony capitalism in developing countries, such as the case of the Philippines under the rule of Ferdinand Marcos in the 1970s and early 1980s, oligarchs directly control the power of the state.[39] Although crony capitalism, as a rule, is more prevalent in nondemocratic countries where political power can more easily be employed as an instrument of looting and the ruling elites are unaccountable, crony capitalism can also take root in newly democratized regimes and can both undermine the democratic process and breed corruption.[40]

From a comparative perspective, China's crony capitalism has far more in common with its cousin in the former Soviet Union because they are both products of the transition away from communism despite their different paths. Compared with crony capitalism in noncommunist countries, China's crony capitalism, it may be argued, is qualitatively different because the state continues to own most of the property in the economy and the surviving Leninist regime has far greater repressive capacity and willingness to use it to defend its privileges. However, while the post-Soviet transitions can offer useful insights into the origins of China's crony capitalism, especially the seizure of state-owned property by colluding elites, a closer look at the circumstances under which such property was looted in the former USSR during the chaotic 1990s reveals crucial differences between the crony capitalism that emerged in the immediate aftermath of the collapse of the Soviet bloc and its variant in China today.

The most obvious difference is that the looting of nominally state-owned property in the former USSR and some parts of Eastern Europe occurred *after* the collapse of the communist regimes in those countries, whereas the appropriation of such assets by the ruling elites in China is taking place while the post-totalitarian regime remains securely in control. In the former case, the vacuum of state authority, political chaos, legal loopholes, and lack of experience and knowledge of privatization were the culprits. In the latter case, the Chinese ruling elites made deliberate policy choices that subsequently helped to create an environment enabling them to convert state-owned assets into their private property.

Another key difference is the degree of centralization in the looting of state-owned assets. In the former USSR and Eastern Europe, looting occurred in a highly centralized manner. This may seem to be a strange phenomenon considering the evaporation of political authority following the collapse of communism, but it happened most probably because the concentrated characteristics of the rights to state-owned property, such as natural resource assets and gigantic heavy manufacturing facilities, made centralized looting possible. As a result, in these countries a small group of entrepreneurs, through either their business acumen or political ties, managed to amass huge fortunes built on formerly state-owned assets acquired at ludicrously low prices.[41] The reason for this is not hard to fathom. Weak political authority in those countries facilitated the seizure of large stocks of state-owned assets by well-connected tycoons. By comparison, looting in China is a far more decentralized affair, with local elites, as shown by data on corruption, participating in the process of seizing state-owned assets alongside senior officials at the center of power. Decentralized looting is not only necessitated by the diverse nature of China's manufacturing-based economy, but also is determined by the decentralization of the control of property rights and administrative power that has given local elites a competitive edge, relative to their political status, in the seizure of state-owned property.

The last key difference between crony capitalism in China and that in many parts of the former Soviet bloc is that the theft of state-owned property by those connected with the ruling elites was a one-time event in the latter, whereas the illicit seizure of such property is an ongoing process in the former. This is mainly because the rapidity of the mass privatization process in the wake of the collapse of communism in the early 1990s succeeded in converting the bulk of state-owned assets into private ownership.[42] By comparison, no such rapid mass privatization has taken place in China and, as a result, the state continues to own the most valuable assets—land, mines, monopolistic state-owned enterprises (SOEs)—that are subject to systematic theft by the ruling elites. According to an estimate of the net worth of China's total assets produced by the Chinese Academy of Social Sciences in 2015, the assets owned by the Chinese state were valued at 181 trillion yuan, 51 percent of the country's total net worth.[43]

Moreover, the sustained economic growth in China since the early 1990s has created enormous new wealth and added to the stock of state-owned property through high rates of investment. Consequently, the economic value of political power has appreciated dramatically, as reflected in the huge increase in the amount of bribery paid to officials. Even if we take into account the residual assets owned by the state that were spared from privatization in many of the former Soviet bloc countries, looting becomes more difficult after they become democratic and the power of the political elites is more constrained. In contrast, the possibility of remediation through the democratic process simply does not exist in China, where the CCP has successfully maintained its political monopoly and faces no constraints on the use of its power in pursuit of self-enrichment.

To probe the key differences between China's crony capitalism and its variants in other parts of the world, especially the former Soviet bloc, this study proposes a theoretical framework to understand the origins and dynamics of collusion among elites. This framework, centered on the consequences of the partial reform of property rights and the decentralization of administrative authority, fills an important gap in the research on crony capitalism in general, and its emergence in China in particular. In Chapter 1, we develop this framework and identify the incentives, means, patterns, and determinants of the success of collusive corruption carried out by elites. Chapter 2 retraces the most consequential changes in property rights and administrative decentralization in post-Mao China to provide the historical and institutional contexts in which favorable conditions for collusion are created. Chapter 3 studies the practice of buying and selling public office in an illicit market for political power. This chapter attempts to illustrate how political power itself has become a tradable commodity under crony capitalism and how this trade facilitates the construction of networks of collusion. Chapter 4 examines how local political elites exchange favors for bribes from private businessmen in the latter's efforts to acquire undervalued state-owned assets and to pursue economic rents. Chapter 5 probes systematic theft in SOEs by executives through collusive corruption. Chapter 6 investigates how local law enforcement officials provide protection to organized crime in exchange for bribes and other payoffs. Chapter 7 focuses on the spread of collusion to key state institutions, such as the judiciary and regulatory agencies, and on "collapse-style" corruption cases that have turned large jurisdictions into virtual local mafia states. This chapter underscores the argument that one of the inevitable consequences of crony capitalism in China is the decay of its Leninist regime. In the concluding chapter, we briefly discuss the implications and consequences of China's crony capitalism and the decay of the CCP.

1

The Origins of Crony Capitalism:
How Institutional Changes Incentivize Corruption

> We must concentrate our crackdown on corruption in critical sectors such as mining resources, land transfers, and real estate development.
>
> —Xi Jinping, January 23, 2014

WHAT MAKES the areas singled out by Xi—land and mines— unique and worthy of special attention in his anticorruption drive is that these assets are publicly owned. The connection between corruption and public ownership of assets should not come as a surprise since the defining feature of crony capitalism is the looting of nominally state-owned assets by colluding elites. While the consequences of China's crony capitalism are highly visible, the institutional origins of crony capitalism are poorly understood. In this chapter, we explore the rise of crony capitalism in China since the early 1990s. Empirically, this task is made easier by the fact that endemic collusive corruption by elites—the heart and soul of crony capitalism—was not observed before the 1990s. Thus, the emergence of crony capitalism since then is most likely the result of some critical changes in the political and economic institutions of China and the subsequent behavioral response by the elites to these changes. Probing the connection between institutions and collusion among elites should help us understand the likely origins of crony capitalism.

Briefly summarized, our argument is that partial and incremental reforms of the property rights associated with nominally state-owned assets in the post-Tiananmen era have decentralized control over these assets without clarifying their real ownership. This combination has created previously unavailable opportunities for political and economic elites to acquire these valuable assets at steep discounts or at no cost. But because of the unclear ownership and the resultant competing claims over these assets, elites must collude to share the spoils in order to avoid mutual vetoes. Besides the opportunities and incentives, local elites require the necessary means—in this case political power—to carry out collusion. Fortuitously, such power became readily available in the post-Tiananmen era, due to radical decentralization of administrative authority, particularly of that over the appointment of local officials. Understanding the opportunities, incentives, and means of collusion is only the first step toward developing a theory of this phenomenon. The second step is to explore possible mechanisms of coordination that enable individuals sharing similar incentives to cooperate with each other illicitly. This we accomplish by formulating three possible models of collusion to allow us to grasp how, in real life, collusion is carried out. As a theory of collusion is incomplete without identifying the critical determinants of its success, we analyze pertinent factors, such as bonding, commitment, and prevention of defection. We hope that this theory of collusion, encompassing opportunities, incentives, means, mechanisms, and determinants, will help us achieve a deeper understanding of the origins and dynamics of crony capitalism, especially in the Chinese context.

Collusion and Corruption

Conceptually, corruption and collusion are distinct concepts. While corruption is generally defined as the abuse of public authority for private gain, collusion—illicit or unauthorized cooperation among agents or between supervisors and agents—does not necessarily result in private gain or economic benefit and may not be explicitly criminal. Generally speaking, collusion is a practice that benefits a small number of perpetrators at the expense of the general welfare of an organization or society. When carried out in an organization, it destroys its discipline, norms, and capacity. Politically, pervasive collusion can subvert the authority hierarchy of the state and lead to regime decay. Murrell and Olson speculate that rampant collusion among managers of enterprises in the former Soviet Union generated institutional sclerosis and made the Soviet economy extremely unproductive.[1] Economically, unchecked collusion, which allows cartels to artificially raise prices or depress offered bids, can lead to severe price distortions and rampant rent-seeking. Economies plagued with endemic collusion are hobbled by chronic inefficient allocation of resources due to the oligarchical power wielded by the collusive elites.[2] Unfortunately, theories of collusion developed by economists have focused narrowly on only two dominant motives. The first is profit maximization through price-fixing.[3] This typically occurs when a small number of sellers form a price cartel to eliminate competition and keep prices high. Bidders in an auction can also collude with each other to eliminate competition and force the seller to accept a lower price. The resulting behavior is called horizontal collusion since the participants are more or less equal in terms of their hierarchical status. The second motive behind collusion is shirking, a classical principal-agent problem. Collusion allows agents to be less productive with impunity.[4] Collusion is sometimes rephrased as a problem of "side-contracting," which entails a supervisor striking an unsanctioned deal with a subordinate agent without the authorization or knowledge of the principal.[5]

These insights may provide two valuable perspectives, but they do not help us understand collusion when no such motives seem to exist. Another shortcoming in the existing literature on collusion is the dominance of mathematical modeling and the absence of theory-testing based on empirical evidence. As a result, there are few case studies that illuminate the complex dynamics of collusion, whether horizontal or vertical. A rare exception is an original study of local government behavior by Xueguang Zhou, who advances a theory of organizational adaptation to explain widespread collusion among local governments.[6] In his view, local governments collude with each other to avoid implementing the policies of the central government that are impractical or harmful to their organizational interests.

Adding organizational adaptation as a cause of collusion offers a useful perspective on collusion among organizational actors. But this theory does not explain collusion among individuals seeking benefits beyond profit maximization for their companies or shirking. Most critically, conventional theories of collusion do not explain the phenomenon of "collusive corruption"—the participation by a group of public officials in acts of collusion with the explicit purpose of reaping private material gains. Attempts to understand this puzzle were first made by scholars of corruption. In one of the first studies on collusive corruption among individual officials, Ting Gong attempts to identify the dominant motives.[7] She attributes the rise of collusive corruption in China to profit maximization and risk reduction. Although the profit-maximizing motive is well known, the idea that collusion helps reduce the risks of detection is original. In Gong's formulation, colluding officials can not only jointly increase the amount of corrupt income for themselves; they can also greatly reduce the risks of detection because they provide cover for each other. Even though Gong does not elaborate on its dynamics or provide specific examples, this risk-management perspective is useful because, as illuminated by econometric modeling, corruption is difficult to detect in an environment where a very large number of officials engage in corruption.[8] To the extent that collusion involves a greater number of officials, collusive corruption is, in theory, harder to detect. Intriguingly, there is some empirical evidence that implies collusive corruption in post-1992 China might have increased income and reduced risks for its perpetrators.[9] The coincidence of pervasive collusive corruption and a rapid rise in corrupt income could support the profit-maximization hypothesis.

Nevertheless, the two motives identified by the existing literature on collusion—profit maximization and shirking—and the motive for collusive corruption (risk reduction) overlook a critical factor responsible for collusive corruption: Individual officials control only a particular department or part of the decision-making process and need to collude in order to overcome the threat of a mutual veto. Thus, a plausible explanation for collusion among government officials engaging in corruption is that they possess individual veto power that can block each other from realizing any benefits from such power unless they collude. For instance, government bureaucracies are divided into functional departments, each of which exercises monopolistic control over a specific part of the process in granting regulatory approval (such as zoning, licensing, and so forth) or allocating public funds. With collusion, officials working in separate departments can help a bribe-paying individual obtain all the necessary permits quickly, thus gaining pecuniary benefits from the use of their power. Without collusion, any single official is unlikely to obtain support from his colleagues and help the bribe-paying individual to secure his desired permits, thus failing to realize any income from his power. This dynamic—colluding to overcome a mutual veto—can be understood by looking at corruption from the industrial organization perspective. Shleifer and Vishny argue that decentralized corruption resulting from independent monopolists produces greater efficiency losses than centralized corruption because each independent monopolist (in reality, officials who control a particular department in a bureaucracy and have incentives to extract maximum amounts of bribe money) has an incentive to maximize the amount of his bribes, regardless of the consequences of his action.[10] In the worst case, an independent monopoly will result in a total cessation of transactions if the bribe payers refuse to pay. A completely different situation would be perfect competition, which drives corruption profits to zero. However, between these two extremes, one can think of a compromise that overcomes the coordination problem caused by independent monopolies. Such a compromise would entail illicit cooperation among those independent monopolists who, in an exchange of guaranteed corruption income, are willing to share the spoils. As a result, equilibrium is reached, benefiting everyone involved—bribe payers and colluding bribe takers alike.

Of course, collusion in real life is more complicated and cannot occur without coordination, trust, knowledge, and commitment. Motives alone cannot lead to successful collusion. For instance, officials inclined to collude with each other must overcome practical difficulties in coordination. They may lack knowledge about other officials' intentions, vulnerabilities, and the price for cooperation. They may also fear that their overtures may be rejected or, worse still, reported to the anticorruption authorities. In explaining the rise of crony capitalism, we need to incorporate the powerful insights of the industrial organization perspective and enrich them with an understanding of the institutional and sociological contexts unique to a transition economy and to contemporary China's political system.

Opportunities and Incentives for Collusion

To understand the emergence of crony capitalism in China in general, and collusive corruption since the 1990s in particular, we need to examine changes in micro-level incentives and the overall institutional and policy contexts. We have to explain why a type of behavior rarely seen in the 1980s gradually became prevalent in the 1990s. The existing literature on collusion helps us understand only part of the puzzle. For instance, profit maximization and risk reduction are plausible explanations, and we should expect to find evidence showing that collusive corruption allows its perpetrators to increase their income and avoid detection for an extended period of time. However, in light of the dramatic difference in the nature of corruption—individual versus collusive—between the 1980s and the 1990s, these two motives are not very useful to probe the most important causes of collusion among corrupt officials. Framed differently, to the extent that corrupt officials always seek to maximize bribes and minimize the risk of detection, why did they not engage in collusion before the 1990s?

The answer to this puzzle can be found in policy and institutional changes that occurred in the early 1990s, significantly altering the incentives, risk–reward calculations, and ability to collude among Chinese officials. Of the most important policy and institutional developments that have occurred since the 1990s, we argue that partial and incremental changes in property rights created the initial opportunities and incentives for collusion.[11]

After Deng Xiaoping's historic 1992 southern tour, China's economic reforms accelerated. Although liberalization constituted the dominant thrust of the reforms of the early 1990s, full or partial privatization, euphemistically called "property rights reform" due to lingering ideological opposition, quickly became an essential part of the post-1992 reforms. Of course, small and cautious experiments in property rights reform began in the mid-1980s, but the Chinese government did not expand these experiments because of conservative opposition. After Deng's southern tour, such opposition weakened and property rights reform picked up speed. However, China adopted a less radical approach to property rights reform. Instead of complete privatization, the government sought to disentangle control rights from ownership. The economic thinking behind this move was straightforward: Separating ownership rights from control rights would give managers more incentives and create a market for control rights (although the standard term used in China for the equivalent of control rights is "use rights"). However, given the complex reality in China, property rights reform was carried out in a dizzying array of forms, and the term privatization does not really capture the diversity of property rights reform. To be sure, privatization—the outright transfer of ownership rights and/or use rights from the state to private individuals as real owners—did occur in this process. But many transfers of property rights involved only use rights (in the case of land and mines). And some property rights reform simply resulted in the transfer of control between governments (from central to local). To complicate matters even further, decentralization of administrative power, particularly the authority to allocate capital, award large contracts, and determine land use, granted local officials and managers in SOEs unprecedented control rights.

Despite the varying forms and degrees of property rights reform, two characteristics of the post-1992 changes in Chinese property rights stand out. The first is a significant devolution of the power to define property rights and dispose of state-owned property. As a result of this devolution, property that was inaccessible to private control could be effectively privatized or utilized to generate income for private individuals. The second is that property rights remained highly contested during this process. The contestation over property rights originated from multiple sources.

Incomplete Property Rights Reform

One clear culprit of the contestation was the incomplete nature of most of the property rights reforms, which separated control (use) rights from ownership rights but failed to clarify ownership rights, the more important component of property rights. This change did result in the creation of a market for partial property rights, but the incomplete nature of such reforms engendered conflicts between those who nominally owned the property and those who effectively controlled it. In China, the conflict between the nominal owner of such property (the state) and those with effective control rights (mostly members of the party) is much more difficult to resolve than in a market economy. In a market economy, private property rights are not only more clearly defined, but also they can be asserted through a more competitive and open corporate governance system, capital markets, and large private institutional owners. In China, the fact that a monopolistic political party is in control of the state, which nominally owns such property, means that the interests of the party diverge fundamentally from those of the state. The party's interests lie in self-perpetuation in power, which requires the loyalty of its followers, who exercise control rights over state property. This discussion suggests two types of conflict over property in post-1992 China: contests over property rights between the state and the CCP and contests between the CCP and its agents. To the extent that the CCP's interest in retaining power diverges from the state's interest in protecting the income, value, and security of its property, the party will appropriate for its own use the benefits generated by nominally state-owned property. In reality, such acts of appropriation create a conflict with the real owner of the property of the state—the Chinese people. In the case of conflicts between the party and its agents, similar dynamics are at play. Although the party regards the assets of the state as its own property, its members, all self-interested individuals, do not share this belief. The CCP members' interest is to exercise their control rights over these assets to divert some of the income to themselves and/or to seize legal control of these assets. This divergence inevitably leads to a conflict between the party and its members over state-owned property and explains the party's motives in punishing those members who may take too much from the party.

Conflicting Claims

Another cause of the contestation of property rights is conflicting claims over the assets of the state that are being made accessible to private ownership or utilization. One type of claim results from the poor definition of property ownership. For instance, the vague nature of land ownership in China is a major cause of contested land rights. Another source of contested claims is the presence of residual rights—workers in state-owned enterprises, residents in housing built on publicly owned land, and farmers tilling leased land all consider that they are entitled to some of the benefits generated by any changes in the rights of state-owned property. Government officials and SOE executives who possess effective control rights over the assets of the state have claims as well since they strongly believe that, due to their management of these assets, they are entitled to the benefits generated by any changes in the redefinition of the rights over these assets. A third source of contestation originates in society. As the rights to these assets are poorly defined and there are no real owners, the transfer of substantive ownership rights from a nominal owner to a real owner will be seen by certain elements in society as a process in which they are entitled to participate. In particular, one social group—private entrepreneurs who sense the enormous profit potential of gaining control of these assets and who have the ability to realize such potential—will be motivated to contest the property rights of these assets. In the Chinese case, since private entrepreneurs lack political power, they will resort to the most effective means available—bribery—to help them gain an advantage to seize such assets. Another social group, organized criminals, will also be tempted to profit from this process. In addition to bribery, such elements can resort to violence and intimidation to help them contest the rights to control nominally state-owned assets.

Mutual Veto

The presence of several contestants in the reform of property rights makes the process of redefining these rights inherently a political contest among competing groups. However, in this contentious process, those in direct control of the bureaucratic or administrative power needed to redefine the rights over state-owned property have an enormous advantage. Yet, even for individuals in this group, they face the threat of a mutual veto, which is mostly procedural but can also be informal (exercised through bureaucratic subterfuge). A mutual veto may be overcome if an individual official, such as a local party chief, possesses dictatorial power and can order his subordinates to comply with his wishes. Absent such power, a local official will need the cooperation of his colleagues, who, by the division of bureaucratic authority, control part of this process. Without their cooperation, an individual bureaucrat will face enormous difficulties in trying to gain access to the coveted state-owned assets. Even though collusion offers the benefits of profit maximization and risk reduction, its most important advantage in the case under discussion here is that, in complex transactions involving multiple vetoers in a bureaucratic system, collusion is required to overcome a mutual veto.[12] This is one of the principal drivers behind collusion among more or less equally empowered Chinese officials.[13]

Administrative Decentralization

Incentives and opportunities may not necessarily lead to collusion if its perpetrators lack the capacity to do so. Colluding officials must be endowed with sufficient means, specifically formal political authority, to carry out their schemes. In the reform era in general, and in the post-Tiananmen era in particular, radical administrative decentralization has empowered local elites and granted them the political means of committing collusive corruption. In China's unitary state, such decentralization encompasses all aspects of governance, such as legislative interpretation, fiscal management, investment approval, control rights over state-owned property, and regulatory enforcement.[14] Decentralization of such administrative authority, carried out as part of the CCP's economic reforms, grants local officials new powers and capacities to extract bribes, making them prime targets for rent-seeking private entrepreneurs. But the most important aspect of decentralization is undoubtedly that of personnel management—the power to appoint and promote officials inside the hierarchy of the party-state.[15] Conventional collusion usually involves individuals or corporate entities more or less equally endowed with power and resources. In this type of horizontal collusion, commitment and coordination are critical. Vertical collusion, an act involving parties with unequal power and resources, depends on both coercion and an alignment of interests. A superior who needs to collude with his subordinates, in theory, will more likely get his way if he has credible means to reward or penalize them. In a bureaucratic organization, such means are embodied in the personnel management system. Clearly, a superior will find it much easier to persuade or coerce his subordinates to collude if he controls their job security and career prospects.

As we have seen, local officials (almost exclusively party chiefs) were granted the power to appoint and promote their immediate subordinates in the reform of cadre management in 1984, but the full institutionalization of this far-reaching reform probably did not occur until the early to mid-1990s.[16] This unique combination—vertical decentralization of power accompanied by horizontal concentration of personnel power in the hands of local party chiefs—has a profound impact on the incentives and dynamics of collusion at the local level. It immediately strengthens the bargaining position of a local party boss who needs the illicit cooperation of his subordinates. His newly granted power over their careers provides him with the coercive capacity to ensure that his subordinates comply with his wishes. An even more profound, albeit subtle, impact of the new system is that it drastically alters the dynamics of competition for career advancement inside the local party-state. As the local party chief has a near monopoly over personnel matters, his underlings are all motivated to seek to please him, either with outstanding performance or (more likely) bribes. The introduction of bribery as a means of career advancement, in turn, results in two closely connected developments. One is a virtual "arms race" among subordinates eager to bribe the local party chief for a desired promotion. In this race, the logic of "bad money driving out good money" prevails, rewarding those with fewer scruples but greater capacity to fund their bribes. The other is that the need to bribe their superiors for career advancement makes these subordinates more likely to seek bribes from businessmen. The combined effect of these two developments is collusion begetting collusion *and* corruption: vertical collusion motivated by career advancement leading to collusion with outsiders (businessmen).

The last piece of the puzzle in this complicated tale of the origins of collusion are the economic calculations of officials seeking better positions inside the party-state. Other than prestige and security, the potential for extracting bribes from businessmen is the most powerful motive because, due to the administrative decentralization and the economic boom that began in the 1990s, local officials possess a much greater capacity to dole out favors in exchange for bribes. Naturally, positions in the local party-state that have such power have grown more desirable. Not surprisingly, almost immediately after the promulgation of the new rules on cadre management, the CCP issued regulations prohibiting behaviors that violate these rules, specifically those related to using bribes and other means to please superiors and seek promotions. Judging by the persistence of *maiguan maiguan* (buying and selling office), these regulations and subsequent attempts to enforce them have had no real effect.[17]

Modes and Dynamics of Collusion

Collusion may give its perpetrators many benefits, but this activity cannot occur without overcoming the coordination problem and preventing free riding. Under normal circumstances, the existence of an opportunity to gain income from corruption may not enable several officials to participate in collusion. They will need coordination to engage in this illicit cooperative activity. In the Chinese case, the coordination role is played by two groups of individuals—government officials wielding enormous influence inside the bureaucracy and private businessmen, including crime bosses, who use bribes to buy off officials in various departments. In reporting incidents of *wo'an* or *chuan'an,* the Chinese authorities provide skimpy details on how collusion actually takes place in local governments and SOEs, or whether those allegedly involved in *wo'an* or *chuan'an* actually conspire directly with each other to commit their crimes. Close examination of the cases published in the official media and theoretical insights from the social sciences enable us to construct and explore the three principal modes and underlying dynamics of collusion in these public institutions. Though conceptually distinct, in reality these modes may occasionally overlap and produce cases in which all of them are observed.

Vertical Collusion

In this pattern of collusion, a powerful superior, typically the local party chief, plays the central role, both as coordinator and enforcer, in weaving together a corruption network spanning multiple government agencies within his jurisdiction. Local party chiefs, called *yibashou* in Chinese and the most powerful officials in Chinese localities and state institutions, are entrusted by the CCP with unconstrained power and enormous discretion in its exercise.[18] As we will see, local party chiefs possess a near monopoly on the appointment and promotion of subordinate officials within their jurisdictions, thus giving them a credible coercive capacity to impose their will on their subordinates and a unique ability to build a network of coconspirators.

The principal means of vertical coordination by *yibashou* is *maiguan maiguan*.[19] The value of an executive position in the Chinese state appreciates as the bribe-extracting capacity of such a position increases with rising wealth and administrative decentralization, thus raising the demand for such a position among aspiring officials and further strengthening the hand of the monopolistic seller—the local party chief. For a local party chief, *maiguan maiguan* generates both financial and political benefits. The direct profits from these transactions are substantial but less lucrative than bribes from private businessmen. Politically, this practice allows a *yibashou* to build up a local power base filled with loyalists.[20] Arguably, a *yibashou* should find a subordinate more trustworthy and reliable as a coconspirator if that individual has paid him a significant bribe for his position.[21] However, the greatest potential payoff from *maiguan maiguan* is that it will facilitate collusion coordinated by a *yibashou*. Since in most cases officials willing to pay bribes for office rationally seek positions with substantive executive authority and greater bribe-generating potential, those who succeed in purchasing them are likely to be appointed party chiefs in a lower-level jurisdiction or heads of powerful government departments that oversee zoning, land resources, mining rights, finance, or SOE assets. In the event that a *yibashou* has to deliver a favor to a businessman who has bribed him, he can easily utilize his network of loyalists inside the government to do so. Indeed, the empirical evidence in Chapters 4–7 supports this hypothesis. Of course, a *yibashou* also relies on his near-dictatorial power to coerce his subordinates in these departments into delivering his promised favors to businessmen. But this practice, while common, carries greater risk for the *yibashou* because it easily arouses resentment among his subordinates and makes them suspicious of his motives.

The existence of *yibashous* who have a network of loyalists or who can coerce uncooperative subordinates into compliance greatly simplifies the challenge of coordination for favor-seeking private entrepreneurs. Instead of trying to coordinate officials in multiple agencies through time-consuming socializing activities and bribes, these entrepreneurs can focus their energy and resources on local party chiefs to obtain the desired favors. Corrupt deals with these *yibashous* thus entail much lower transaction costs than those with his under-lings, justifying a significant premium in bribes. The risks of a coordi-nation failure become negligible since, once bribed with a handsome amount, local party chiefs usually act with vigor and speed to ensure that their bureaucratic minions comply with their edicts.

Buying off *yibashous* may be the most efficient path for private businessmen, but in real life not all of them can actually succeed. *Yibashous* are selective in taking on clients. Characteristically, they will favor well-established moguls who have already acquired a cer-tain commercial prestige, social status, and who have proven their ability to pay substantial bribes. Moreover, reckless and indiscrimi-nate bribe-taking is too risky, even for powerful *yibashous*. Practi-cally speaking, their time constraints also force them to limit their circle of friends in the private sector to a select group. Of course, busi-nessmen of lesser means are not left helpless. If a *yibashou* is unavail-able, they still can try to bribe veto-wielding individual officials dispersed among key government agencies. This approach entails greater transaction costs and risks of coordination failure, but still promises reasonable chances of success.

Corruption by a boss in general, and collusion coordinated by a *yibashou* in particular, produces substantial externalities that, in and of themselves, can create a vicious cycle of corruption. One form of externality is obviously the contagion effect of corruption. Subordinates knowledgeable about or suspicious of corruption by their superiors, particularly *yibashous,* are more likely to follow their example and start accepting or demanding bribes. A more subtle but probably more serious form of an externality is a general reduction in the risks of detection of corruption for all. A *yibashou* on the take has weak incentives to crack down on corruption by subordinate officials in close bureaucratic proximity because exposing their misconduct will attract unwanted attention from higher authorities. Worse still, should these officials possess credible information about a *yibashou*'s own corruption, they are almost certain to denounce him to the investigators in the hope of receiving leniency. This line of reasoning may explain why a large number of officials tend to be exposed, along with their *yibashou* boss, in a Chinese jurisdiction or bureaucratic agency even though they have no direct collusive ties with each other. Empirically, we can find evidence supporting this hypothesis. A study of 142 cases of corruption featuring prefecture-level *yibashous* as the chief perpetrators shows that 83 of them were involved in *wo'an.*[22] Of the fifty cases of collusion involving local officials and private businessmen examined in Chapter 5, the overwhelming majority of the chief perpetrators (nearly 80 percent) were local party chiefs or former local party chiefs, even though many of the subordinate officials who were caught did not collude with them directly (Table A.2 in the Appendix).

Outsider–Insider Collusion

This pattern of collusion involves an outsider, typically a private businessman, and a group of insiders—officials in a number of key government agencies. As we hypothesize above, businessmen lower on the food chain of crony capitalism, particularly those who may lack the resources or flamboyance to impress and befriend *yibashous,* have to perform the critical role of coordinator-in-chief themselves. Even in cases where businessmen have succeeded in buying off *yibashou* bosses, they may still have to bribe their subordinates because the *yibashou* bosses are unable or unwilling to coordinate through coercion or because the businessmen, unsure about the ability of *yibashou* bosses to deliver, want to invest extra bribes to increase their chances of success. If a transaction requires approval across several large jurisdictions, the businessmen also need to bribe officials in these jurisdictions.

In outsider–insider collusion, private businessmen are more favorably positioned than officials in playing the role of coordinator-in-chief. They are not political competitors, and can thus more easily gain the trust of the officials they want to approach. Their private wealth can easily finance the risk capital—costs of expensive entertainment, visits to "massage parlors," and bribes—needed to ensnare officials, individually, into their network. Once these networks are established, the coordinating businessman functions as a spider weaving and maintaining a web. Normally only he has direct contact with the officials involved, but the officials themselves have no direct contacts or dealings with each other. It can be argued that explicit knowledge of the participation by their colleagues is not necessary for officials to participate in collusion. Coordination can occur indirectly, through a participant's own educated guesses and signals or coded language conveyed by the outsiders. Officials who suspect that their colleagues are involved in these shady schemes are likely to agree to participate when approached. Their calculation is that if their colleagues are on the take, they should not miss the same opportunity. More importantly, indirect knowledge of their colleagues' participation may reassure an official that their collusive enterprise is more likely to be fruitful and detection risks may be reduced by mutual protection. As we explain above, the final factor facilitating outsider–insider collusion is the externalities of the misconduct by senior officials on their subordinates. In local governments or agencies in which the *yibashou* boss is corrupt, a private entrepreneur attempting to entice his subordinates to collude is pushing on a figurative open door.

Horizontal Collusion among Insiders

This mode of collusion is more likely to occur in specialized government agencies or public institutions, such as regulatory agencies, SOEs, and law enforcement agencies.[23] In the case of regulatory and law enforcement agencies, the dynamics of this type of collusion resemble the outsider–insider mode of collusion only in one crucial respect: A private entrepreneur typically bribes his way into these public agencies or institutions, either directly or through intermediaries. But in other respects, this type of collusion has its own characteristics, the most important of which is that its successful execution depends totally on the cooperation of a small number of insiders in the same government agency in which administrative authority is shared, colleagues have direct knowledge of each other's work, and bureaucratic procedures are clearly specified. In these functional agencies, lower-level officials sharing a wide range of administrative responsibilities collude and split the spoils mainly because they need each other's cooperation.

In government agencies that control no state-owned assets, outsiders' bribes motivate insiders to collude primarily to seek rents. For example, collusion inside the judiciary and law enforcement agencies in our case studies is prompted by bribes from litigants and crime bosses. The reward for the coconspirators is a share of the bribe. Unless the coconspirators have other streams of corruption income, the amount of the bribe they collect is relatively small because the service they provide is not as valuable as that of state-owned assets. By comparison, SOE executives colluding with each other can generate far more corruption income because they directly control state-owned assets and can award lucrative contracts to private businessmen. When a private businessman is involved in an SOE collusion case, typically he is willing to pay substantial bribes to secure large contracts or a piece of state-owned property at a deep discount. When a collusion case in an SOE involves only its key executives, the amount of theft through embezzlement can be significant since the SOEs have large cash flows. If these executives collude to illicitly privatize state-owned assets, they can expect windfall profits.

Besides the prospect of earning income from corruption, the key to the success of horizontal collusion among insiders is their interpersonal relationship and trust. In local bureaucracies, courts, and law enforcement agencies, the relatively small size of these organizations can facilitate the development of these relationships and trust.[24] In addition, social interactions conducted in small circles and often involving unsavory activities (such as attending lavish entertainment hosted by private businessmen, gambling, or visiting "massage parlors") can further strengthen bonding and trust.

Determinants of Successful Collusion

Insights from the literature on collusion among cartels suggest that the success of collusion is largely influenced by the number of coconspirators, product homogeneity, the effective enforcement of their commitment, and the absence of external shocks.[25] In this section, we briefly analyze whether the success of collusion among officials is determined by similar factors.

Generally, collusion is more likely to succeed if the number of coconspirators is small. Obviously, the risks of coordination failure and detection are reduced and enforcement against cheating and free riding is more effective when a small number of actors are involved. The survey of price-fixing cartels by Levenstein and Suslow finds that in the majority of such cases the median number of firms involved is under ten.[26] Evidence from our sampled cases confirms this observation. Overall, the number of officials directly involved in a scandal or arrested after investigations into the initial scandal uncovered their separate misconduct is relatively small, making coordination possible and enforcement effective. The median number of officials involved or implicated in collusive corruption cases in regulatory agencies and the judiciary is six, the same as that in collusion between organized crime and local government and law enforcement officials (Tables A.4–A.6 in the Appendix). In cases of collusion between officials and businessmen and among SOE executives, the median number of officials involved is eleven (Tables A.2 and A.3). The larger number of individuals involved in these two types of cases can be explained by the impact of *maiguan maiguan,* a practice prevalent in local governments and SOEs that tends to implicate a larger number of officials. Besides the manageable number of colluding partners, the services provided by the coconspirators in our sample may appear diverse in form and execution, but in essence they are highly homogenous, involving the misuse of official power to help businessmen or themselves gain private benefits. This is another favorable factor for collusion.

As Stigler notes, collusion often fails because of cheating by coconspirators.[27] However, insights from research on organized crime and nuclear deterrence, and observations of bonding and trust-building among officials in contemporary China indicate that colluding officials may have successfully managed the enforcement challenge. The Chinese party-state, in personnel terms, is a closed labor market. Exit for officials is costly and, once they attain a certain seniority, extremely rare. This is a favorable factor in deterring potential cheaters since they have no realistic exit. Additional favorable factors such as personal friendship, bonds, and trust can be established through conventional channels and settings, such as the clan, hometown, college, and workplace.[28] In the Chinese case, party schools or mid-career training programs provide ideal settings for forming close personal ties among officials across different geographic areas and bureaucracies.[29] More noteworthy, however, are some of the unique rituals performed by Chinese officials to develop interpersonal trust. In some locations, officials will bring their mistresses to attend dinners together—in a perverse gesture to seek mutual trust that resembles giving a hostage as a demonstration of commitment.[30] Among the cases examined in this book there are numerous instances in which the coconspirators gambled and visited brothels together. They also collected bribes in each other's presence. While overt acts of dissolution and greed may be taken as evidence of deteriorating morality among China's ruling elites, these rituals are functionally critical in forging bonds of trust. Research on trust-building in criminal organizations indicates that initiation rites typically consist of acts of violence and depravity that signal the commitment of new recruits and bind them to the group.[31] This does not mean that degeneration of moral norms is not a factor in collusion. On the contrary, there is substantial evidence that the overall decline of such norms since the 1990s may have aided and abetted collusion among elites. One indicator of normative degeneration is the sexual misconduct of corrupt officials. Such behavior was less prevalent in the 1980s, but has become endemic since the 1990s.[32] Academic research and official reports suggest that a large percentage, if not a majority, of corrupt officials engage in adultery, patronize prostitutes, keep multiple mistresses, and even father illegitimate children. In some instances, the financial pressure to maintain mistresses is a major reason for officials to extract bribes from businessmen.[33]

The prevention of cheating and defection can be achieved through enforcement by coconspirators. If the lead perpetrator is a *yibashou* official, vertical enforcement is relatively easy because he can impose sanctions on opportunistic junior coconspirators. The bribing businessmen can also prevent defection because they pay their bribes in installments and can punish defectors by either withholding payment or ruining their careers or reputation by making their dishonorable conduct known to potential bribers. Worse still, they may blow the whistle.[34] A subtle mechanism of self-enforcement is also at work here: Once a coconspirator participates in a collusive crime, he has little hope of freeing himself from the corruption network. In addition to forgoing substantial corruption income, he faces ostracism and even blackmail. Of course, he can turn himself in to the CCDI and face the consequences, but in reality very few officials pick this unattractive option.

A striking oddity about collusion involving multiple but unrelated networks of officials is that such networks tend to survive for a considerable period but then unravel or collapse quickly after one of their members is ensnared in an anticorruption investigation. Odder still is the fact that these networks may be headed by bitter political rivals who have knowledge of each other's corruption but nevertheless choose not to denounce each other before their own arrests.[35] Overlapping modes of collusion ensure that multiple unrelated corruption networks can operate inside the same jurisdiction or government agency. Based on frequent press reports of how disgraced officials try to gain leniency by providing leads about their colleagues' corruption to the CCDI, as shown in several instances in this study, we can reasonably assume that some of these officials have knowledge of the corrupt acts of their colleagues even though they belong to different networks. Insights from the doctrine of mutually assured destruction (MAD) may help illuminate this puzzle. Such knowledge has two useful purposes.[36] In "peacetime," or before they fall into the CCDI's dragnet, such knowledge deters these rivals from harming each other. Until they hear the CCDI's dreaded knock on the door, preemption against one's rival makes no sense since he will certainly retaliate by providing information about your own corruption to the party. After they are arrested, belated preemption—providing such knowledge to the investigators—can help them gain more lenient treatment.[37]

The Chinese criminal code gives anticorruption investigators a powerful tool to uncover collusion. Because the penalty for embezzlement or bribery exceeding 100,000 yuan ranges from ten years of imprisonment to death (under particularly egregious circumstances), CCDI investigators and prosecutors can threaten coconspirators with severe penalties if they refuse to cooperate. Prosecutors claim that relying on the cooperation of coconspirators is the most effective method of uncovering collusion cases.[38] The authorities in Jiangsu reported in 2015 that 80 percent of all corruption cases were uncovered by deepening investigations into *wo'an* and *chuan'an*.[39] If such claims are true, we may conclude that there is little loyalty among colluders—despite the enormous effort they apparently have invested in building trust and friendship.

2

The Soil of Crony Capitalism: Where Corruption Thrives

The soil for breeding endemic corruption is present.

—Xi Jinping, November 19, 2013

ONE DOES NOT NEED to be an institutionalist to understand why corruption thrives in certain political and economic environments, the metaphoric "soil" in Xi's quote above. In charting the rise of China's crony capitalism, it is necessary to trace the key institutional changes, particularly those affecting property rights and control of appointments and promotions of local officials, that have occurred in the post-Tiananmen era. The evidence indicates that decentralization of control over state-owned assets without complete clarification of their ownership rights can create an ideal environment for looting by means of collusion among elites. Additionally, in the context of the decentralization of cadre management that grants local officials total control over personnel matters, changes in property rights and administrative decentralization can interact with each other and further facilitate the looting of state-owned property that, as we argue, is the origin of crony capitalism in China.

A striking difference between China's economic reforms in the 1980s and in the post-Tiananmen era is the degree to which the state's control of property rights has been decentralized.[1] In the 1980s, conservative opposition blocked any substantive efforts to loosen this control. However, in the 1990s, control was significantly liberalized. As a result, local government officials and managers of state-owned enterprises (SOEs) gradually acquired the ability to dispose of state-owned assets with growing ease and decreasing scrutiny. Yet, despite dramatic decentralization of control over property rights, most of these rights remain poorly defined or clarified. In particular, land rights and mining rights remain, both legally and nominally, in the hands of the state. Even more importantly, the question of who actually exercises effective control over these rights has never been resolved. One result of the partial reform of property rights—radical decentralization without clarification—is that the ruling elites and their friends in the private sector are presented with abundant opportunities to acquire state-owned assets—mainly land and natural resources—at below-market prices or for free.

The Evolution of Land Rights

It is no accident that the real estate sector has become a hotbed of crony capitalism in China. Data on the incidence of corruption consistently show that real estate, which generates most of its profits from obtaining cheap land, is one of the two most corrupt sectors (the other is infrastructure, which also involves acquisition of state-owned land).[2] Obviously, the value of land in a country undergoing rapid urbanization and industrialization tends to rise rapidly, attracting private entrepreneurs who must pay bribes in navigating China's bureaucratic maze to develop their projects. But a more important cause of the pervasive corruption in the real estate sector is the partial reform of the property rights of land. As discussed earlier, partial property rights reform that decentralizes control without clarifying ownership breeds collusive corruption. In this section, we trace the institutional changes in China's land rights since the mid-1980s and provide a historical context for understanding the connection between crony capitalism and state ownership of land in contemporary China.

The incremental reform of land rights began in the mid-1980s. The most important legislation governing China's land use is the Land Administration Law, first passed in June 1986 and amended in 1988, 1998, and 2004. Cumulatively, these amendments have significantly liberalized the state's control over land use, even as the ownership of the land remains unchanged. In the first version of the Land Administration Law, the singular legal breakthrough was the separation of ownership rights from use rights. This paved the way for the Chinese government to permit the sale and transfer of land without having to change its legal ownership. However, the 1986 Land Administration Law did not explicitly authorize the sale or transfer of use rights. Its stipulation of land ownership also left land ownership rights poorly defined. According to this stipulation, the state owns the land in urban areas and villagers collectively own the land in rural areas (except for land explicitly owned by the state in these areas). Following passage of the law, the central government established the State Land Management Bureau.

Despite the absence of a formal legal basis for selling land use rights, the State Council indicated in April 1987 that land use rights could be transferred for a fee. In November 1987, it formally approved the State Land Management Bureau's proposal to start pilot projects to reform the land use systems in Shenzhen, Shanghai, Tianjin, Guangzhou, Xiamen, and Fuzhou. In 1988, land use rights were further liberalized after the National People's Congress amended the constitution in April, abolishing the ban on leasing land. The amendment added a provision that "land use rights can be transferred according to law." In December 1988, the Land Administration Law was amended to authorize the legal transfer of use rights to state-owned and collectively owned land and to establish a system of fee-based land use. In May 1990, the State Council issued the "Interim Rules on the Sale and Transfer of Use Rights of State-Owned Land in Urban Areas," providing detailed regulations for fee-based sales and transfers of land use rights in urban areas. (Such rules were unnecessary in the rural areas because the use rights of collectively owned land could not, and still cannot, be freely sold and transferred. Only the state is allowed to first acquire land in rural areas, assume its ownership, and then sell or transfer its use rights.)

Following the revision of the Land Administration Law in 1988, the Chinese government promulgated additional laws and rules to regulate land use. In 1994, it passed the Urban Real Estate Management Law, allowing the auction, tender, and negotiation of land transfers. In 1998, the Land Administration Law was revised again to liberalize the process. As most land transactions were conducted through secret negotiations, not market-based channels, the Ministry of Land Resources in 1999 issued regulations on "Furthering the Implementation of the Sale of User Rights of State-Owned Land through Bidding and Auctions." In 2001, the State Council also issued a "Notice on Strengthening the Administration of State-Owned Land Assets," tightening rules on the transfer of land use rights. However, steps taken by the Chinese government to ensure that land use rights would not be sold too cheaply to well-connected individuals and firms did not appear to be effective since the government repeatedly had to issue regulations to address problems of corruption and underpricing in land transactions. In May 2002, the Ministry of Land Resources promulgated the

"Rules on the Sale of State-Owned Construction Land through Bidding, Auctions, and Public Announcements," mandating that use rights for all state-owned land slotted for construction purposes must be sold through auctions, bidding, or public notices, instead of by secret agreements between the seller (the government) and the purchaser. As the practice of using underpriced land to lure investment became widespread among local governments, in October 2004 the State Council issued another document, the "Resolution on Deepening Reform and Tightening Land Administration," prohibiting this practice. In 2004, the Land Administration Law underwent another revision, permitting the government to acquire land for the public interest.

These incremental changes greatly loosened the state's control over land use and gave birth to China's two decades of real estate and infrastructure boom. However, China's approach to reforming land rights may have created more problems than it provided solutions. On the surface, the separation of use rights from ownership rights seems an ingenious reform that allows the state to create a market for land use without giving up its ownership. Unfortunately, experience since the early 1990s shows that a genuine market for land use is all but impossible if ownership rights remain firmly in the hands of the state. As long as the state owns the land and can determine the supply of land, a primary market for land use cannot exist. In addition, absent a real market for land transfer systems, cronyism and corruption are certain to be pervasive in a hybrid system in which political power sets the price.

The Rise of a Land-Based, Local Fiscal System

The modest steps in reforming land rights had a negligible impact on land transactions in the late 1980s. Between 1986 and 1990, in the twenty-eight cities where pilot projects involving transfers of land use rights were launched, only 2,000 hectares were transferred, generating 1 billion yuan in income.[3] It was not until 1991 that the sale of land use rights started its spectacular takeoff. In 1991 alone, about 22,000 hectares were sold, 7.3 times more than the total sold in the previous five years. The number of real estate developers exploded as well. At the end of 1992, China had 12,000 real estate developers, three times more than in the previous year.[4] In 1993, the amount of land sold, in terms of size, was 57,338 hectares, more than twice that sold in 1992.[5]

Revenue from the sale of land use rights soared correspondingly. Partial statistics put the total amount of revenue from such transactions in the period since land user rights could be sold at 123 billion yuan as of the end of 1993.[6] Between 1990 and 2005, cumulative income from land sales was 2.19 trillion yuan.[7] In subsequent years, the volume of land sales continued to skyrocket, making revenue from land sales increasingly important in local public finance. In 1999, revenue from land sales amounted to 9.2 percent of local fiscal revenue and 5.7 percent of the expenditures of local governments. By 2007, the figures were 52 percent of revenue and 32 percent of spending.[8] In the period 2008–2011, such revenue varied between 36 and 71 percent of ordinary local fiscal income.[9]

The growing dependence of local governments on land-sale revenue has been traced to the 1994 fiscal reform, which instituted a new revenue-sharing system that successfully recentralized fiscal revenue and instantly enabled Beijing to claim the bulk of the country's fiscal receipts.[10] Although the 1994 fiscal recentralization is now widely viewed as the principal factor responsible for driving local governments toward a fiscal system heavily dependent on land-sale income, the reality is perhaps more complex. The rising importance of land sales to local public finance was gradual, indicating that revenue-hungry local governments slowly learned to tap into the land they controlled. More importantly, when the actual use of land-sale revenue by local governments is scrutinized, it is evident that it is not spent on on-budget expenses (such as social services and salaries for government employees) but on fixed-asset investments. In fact, the massive increase in the amount of land sold by local governments during 2000–2010 was driven by financial leveraging by local governments, which used land as collateral for bank loans spent on fixed-asset investments.[11]

The most likely explanation is that there was a tacit agreement between Beijing and the local governments in 1993 over ownership of land-sale revenue in order to overcome opposition by provincial governments to fiscal recentralization. Though there is no documentary evidence proving such a deal, it strains credulity that the central government, which traditionally preferred to have direct control over major macroeconomic policies and tax revenue, would passively allow local governments to turn land into a source of abundant revenue. According to one newspaper article, government regulations in force in 1992 required that 5 percent of the proceeds from land sales should be paid to the central government (local governments could decide what to do with the rest).[12] Another scholar noted that in 1994, when the fiscal reform occurred, it was decided that local governments would be given all the income from land transfers. He revealed that the rule in 1989 stipulated that land-sale proceeds should be split 40/60 between the central government and the local governments. However, because it was impossible to verify the exact amount of such income (which in those days was very small), the central government actually received very little. Starting in 1994, local governments were allowed to keep all the receipts from land sales.[13]

In retrospect, the resulting arrangement, although never formalized, between the central government and local governments concerning the use of revenue generated by land sales has benefited both parties. For the central government, it merely traded a revenue source it would have had great difficulty in tapping for acceptance by local governments of a new fiscal system that channels the bulk of tax revenue to the center. Local governments were given authority over a vast new revenue source—land sales. In subsequent years, the new fiscal system did indeed channel most of the taxes to Beijing while local governments raised prodigious amounts of new revenue from land sales. However, the land-based local fiscal system is one of the most important factors contributing to crony capitalism. As our case studies in the rest of the book show, land-related collusive corruption is widespread, and revenue generated by land sales, which fund the bulk of local infrastructure projects, can be easily stolen by local officials and their business cronies.

Contested Land Rights and Rent-Seeking

With the substantial liberalization of the state's control over land use since the early 1990s, local governments quickly acquired the ability to monetize a previously illiquid asset—land. However, like other key reforms in China, the reform of property rights in land was instrumental in purpose, partial in nature, and incremental in pace. Despite the reformist rhetoric, making land use more efficient through market-based allocations, let alone a complete privatization of the property rights of land, was never the ultimate objective of land rights reform. Instead, the goal was instrumental and narrow—solving practical difficulties generated by excessively tight control over land transfers and, later, generating revenue from land sales for local governments. Unwilling to give up its control over China's most valuable assets, the CCP had no desire to privatize land ownership. The combination of its distrust of the market in allocating resources and its desire to maximize private benefits from the liberalization of control over land meant that the regulatory framework and the actual process of allocating land were heavily tilted toward maximizing government control and official discretion. The result was a combination of deliberately ambiguous property rights and rich rent-seeking land use opportunities.[14]

Initially, rent-seeking opportunities emerged, logically, from the continuation of the state's ownership rights in land. Obviously, as legal owners, the government could decide how to dispose of the land. The discretion given to local government officials for transactions in land use rights easily created opportunities for corruption and cronyism. During the initial stage of the commercialization of land use rights, most transactions occurred through nonpublic "agreements" (*xieyi*) between sellers and purchasers. In 1993, for example, only 5 percent of land use rights transactions were conducted through public auctions. In 2000, 13 percent of such transactions were conducted through public auctions. In 2002, only 15 percent of these transactions were conducted through public auctions.[15] Worried that local officials were giving away land too cheaply, in May 2002 the central government issued the "Rules on the Sale of State-Owned Construction Land through Bidding, Auctions, and Public Announcements," requiring that land use rights be sold through public auctions and bidding. Consequently, an increasing number of transactions in land use rights were conducted via auctions and public bidding. In 2003, in terms of the amount of land involved, 28 percent of the transactions were conducted through auctions and bidding. In 2008, the number rose to 84 percent.[16] However, these numbers should be viewed with skepticism. As revealed in the exposed corruption cases, the process of public auctions and bidding is rigged to favor buyers who have bribed local officials.

Because local governments can acquire land cheaply through co-ercion, they can make a significant profit by selling land use rights to real estate developers. Based on data provided by the Ministry of Finance, local governments enjoyed profit margins averaging 42 to 45 percent during the period 2008–2010.[17] In many ways, however, such high profit margins are a reflection of a highly distorted market for land use rights in China. If the government does not artificially restrict supply, land prices will likely fall, thus reducing its income. At the same time, acquisition costs are deliberately depressed by un-derpaying farmers and urban residents. Finally, given the wide-spread practice of underpricing land to benefit favored businesses and real estate developers, local governments must have lost signifi-cant revenue from land sales. Indeed, Chinese press reports indicate that government rules are routinely violated in the process of selling land use rights, resulting in an enormous loss of revenue. For ex-ample, between 2003 and June 2005, 60 of the 87 development zones investigated by the government were found to have violated the rules and to have leased 7,873 hectares of land below mandated prices, failing to collect 5.565 billion yuan in revenue.[18] Based on the National Audit Agency's audits of eleven provinces in 2009, 38.1 billion yuan in land-sale income that should have been paid was not collected.[19]

From a bureaucratic perspective, rich rent-seeking opportunities inevitably mean the competitive involvement of myriad local govern-ment agencies in land-sale transactions and in activities in the down-stream real estate industry, where most of the final profits are realized. Based on a study by the Ministry of Land Resources, the real cost of land accounts, on average, for only 23 percent of housing prices na-tionwide, whereas the gross profit margin for developers is generally 30–50 percent.[20] The prospect of huge profits motivates developers to bribe local officials whose decisions can determine the price of the land they want to acquire as well as the regulatory approvals they must obtain to develop their projects. At the same time, local officials also have an incentive to turn their power into opportunities for extracting bribes from developers. Since ten government agencies have jurisdiction or regulatory approval authority over land use, it is often necessary for the developer to bribe multiple individuals.[21] In order to obtain approval from these agencies, developers have to take the lead. Typically, they first identify the desired plot of land, negotiate with its current user to strike an agreement, and afterwards they go to each agency to gain approval. Whether they can get the land depends on whether they have "dependable connections" in these agencies.[22] In this process, a private developer colludes with a group of officials who may have no personal or collusive relationships with each other.

The driver of collusion in the discussion above is the existence of complementary authority over land use in general, and over the real estate industry in particular. In the case of land use, however, collusion is also necessitated by the contested nature of land rights. First, a local government official trying to seize a particular plot of land from its current users (farmers or urban residents) must collude with officials in other agencies (the police, for instance) and with the real estate developer to dispossess the current users. Second, since several real estate developers are competing for the same underpriced plot of land, the potential winner must collude with the most powerful local official (in many cases, the party boss). Finally, because multiple government agencies all have some claim to the land and its use, officials must collude with each other (even the all-powerful local party boss must gain the cooperation of his junior colleagues in various government departments) in order to complete the process of allowing their favored real estate developer to gain the use rights to the land.

The Evolution of Mining Rights

Many of the large private fortunes made during China's boom years, as the cases of Liu Han and Wang Chuncheng show, can be traced to the mining sector. In our studies of corruption in SOEs, local governments, and law enforcement agencies in the remainder of this book, we will also encounter lesser versions of Lius and Wangs who struck gold in the natural resources sector. The puzzle about the origins of their wealth is how these elites, some from humble backgrounds while others were well connected, were able to acquire mining rights that, according to Chinese law, the state has never fully relinquished. In this section, we briefly trace how, as in the case of reforming the property rights of SOEs, the Chinese state progressively decentralized control of mining without actually relinquishing its ownership rights, thus allowing local elites to collude with each other to exploit these valuable resources and enrich themselves in the process.

One of the structural features of China's mining sector that has likely enabled local elites to appropriate nominally state-owned natural resource wealth is the existence of an abundance of small-scale mines that account for a significant share of Chinese mineral products.[23] Based on data collected in the late 1990s, artisanal and other small mines contributed between 30 and 76 percent of the country's output of various mineral products.[24] The decentralization and diversity of China's mining sector, a product of the country's vast size and geological conditions (low mineral content, small reserves, and remote locations make large-scale mining uneconomical, if not altogether impossible) means a ceaseless contest among various claimants (private individuals, village collectives, local governments, state-owned enterprises, and the central government) over these resources.[25] A study by a government research group reported that as of the end of 1990, China had 8,000 state-owned mining firms, 115,000 collective mines, and 114,000 individually operated mines. According to this study, most disputes revolved around mining rights between SOEs and local firms owned by different entities (such as township collectives or local governments). Local government-run mines were also embroiled in mining disputes with collectively operated mines that were owned by townships.[26] In Yunnan, for example, 55 percent of the mines operated by township collective firms and individuals in the early 1990s did not have licenses.[27] Thus, in a strict sense, mining rights in China are more ambiguously defined than land rights.

Changes in mining rights in China since the late 1970s have reflected a recognition of this complex reality on the part of the central government, which proceeded to pass laws and regulations to legalize this informal mining sector. Besides this pragmatic approach, there were two additional drivers to redefine the property rights of China's mines. One was obviously the country's growing demand for mineral resources. Meeting this demand without liberalizing the mining sector would be impossible.[28] The other driver was a deliberate government policy of gradual liberalization without full privatization. As in the case of land rights, the Chinese state continues to assert legal ownership of mineral resources, but it has formulated a legal and regulatory framework separating exploration, mining, and production rights from ownership rights. The first step in this direction was taken in April 1984 when the State Council issued "Eight Measures on Accelerating the Development of Township and Village Coal Mines," permitting collectives and individuals to invest in small coal mines.[29] The effect of the liberalization of the coal sector was instant. Within two years, output from township and village coal mines reached one-third of the nationwide total. The coal output of the small mines contributed one-third of the country's total production in 1985.[30]

After liberalization began in the mid-1980s, the government took additional measures to accelerate the reform of mining rights. The most important legislation was the Mineral Resources Law, passed by the National People's Congress in March 1986. While continuing to maintain state ownership of mineral rights, the law nevertheless affirmed the limited rights of collectives and individuals to mine mineral resources. Specifically, the law encouraged collective mines and individuals to explore and produce small quantities in state-designated areas for their own use. In 1994, the State Council issued specific implementation rules to further clarify the 1986 law, stipulating that collective and private mines could operate in areas not suitable for large and medium-sized mines owned by the state. By establishing a legal framework for diverse property rights, the first version of the Mineral Resources Law and its implementation rules paved the way for a further loosening of the state's control of mining rights in subsequent years.

In 1996, the Mineral Resources Law was revised to allow the transfer of mining rights, removing a significant constraint imposed by the 1986 version that explicitly forbade such transfers. With legal sanctions for buying and selling mining rights, a market for such rights emerged in no time. Of course, some of the restrictions on the transfer of mining rights remained in place under the revised law. The most prominent restriction prohibited the transfer of production rights unless the transaction was the result of a merger, acquisition, joint venture, or sale of assets. In February 1998 the State Council issued specific rules governing the transfer of exploration and production rights. The most important feature of these rules was the delegation of approval authority to lower levels of government. Each level of government was granted the power to decide to whom to transfer these rights on behalf of the "state." Following the State Council's promulgation of the regulation, many provinces issued their own regulations on transfers of mining rights. Another critical feature of the regulation was its huge loophole: The regulation put fewer restrictions on transfers of exploration rights than on production rights. In reality, the rules significantly loosened the transfer of both exploration and production rights. Since it is difficult to distinguish the two types of rights (especially after exploration finds proven reserves), this loophole could be exploited to facilitate the transfer of the more tightly controlled production rights.[31] Furthermore, since provincial departments were empowered to approve the transfer of both rights, it became easier for those seeking to sell or purchase such rights to get the desired approvals. Most importantly, the rules permitted the transfer of the rights in state-owned mines after a fair-value assessment.

The state's control over the mining sector was further loosened in 1998 with the State Council's "Administrative Rules on Exploration of Mineral Resources." While reserving the approval of exploration and production of oil and natural gas to departments designated by the State Council, this regulation granted provincial authorities the power to approve medium-sized to small mines in mining areas not designated by the national government as "valuable to the national economy." In addition, departments in charge of mineral resource management above the county level were authorized to issue production permits. Immediately after the issuance of this regulation, the Ministry of Geology and Mineral Production announced the "Regulation on Authorizing the Issuance of Licenses for Mineral Exploration and Production," which established that licenses for projects requiring exploration expenditures of less than 5 million yuan could be granted by provincial departments and production licenses for medium and small mines could be approved by provincial authorities.

The combined effect of the three regulations issued in 1998 on the exploration and production of mineral resources was to significantly liberalize property rights in the mining sector and to decentralize approval authority to provincial departments. Among other things, the most consequential regulatory change was a substantial loosening of the prohibition against transfers of production rights. In the revised Mineral Resources Law (1996), the government prohibited the transfer of production rights except as a result of a merger, acquisition, joint venture, or sale of assets. The same law also forbade the sale of exploration and production rights for profiteering purposes. However, the State Council's "Administrative Rules on Transfers of Exploration and Production Rights," issued in February 1998, effectively abolished the ban and permitted such sales.

Given the importance of coal in China's mining and energy sectors, it is worth briefly mentioning the evolution of property rights in this sector. As discussed earlier, the Chinese government recognized the necessity of mobilizing the production capacity of nonstate-owned coal mines to meet the country's energy needs in the 1980s and it issued special rules to permit collective and private coal mines to operate (although transfers of mining rights remained illegal). In the 1990s, the coal mining sector also underwent significant liberalization. The two most important regulatory changes were liberalization of the rules governing transfers of production rights in coal mines and, as specified by the State Council's December 1994 "Administrative Rules for Township Coal Mines," devolution of approval authority to county-level governments. As a result of these liberalizing measures, private investment poured into coal mining.[32] While most of the capital came from private entrepreneurs, government officials also took advantage of the liberalization and became investors in these mines (although press reports indicated that many did not put up real money, but instead used their influence as capital).[33]

The Evolution of SOE Property Rights

The most noteworthy characteristic of the privatization of assets owned by SOEs during the reform era is that there has never been a formal privatization program, even though significant quantities of SOE assets have been effectively privatized, mostly since the 1990s, as a result of an incremental, evolutionary, and opaque process.[34] Throughout the 1980s, ideological opposition to privatization within the CCP was so strong that no official initiatives were undertaken to liberalize the state's control of SOE assets. Property rights reforms were restricted to pilot projects in selected areas, and only a few small SOEs were permitted to experiment with such reforms.[35] Only in the early 1990s did the CCP begin to take modest steps toward loosening the rules regarding disposal of SOE assets.

The first document implicitly allowing such disposal, the "Rules on Evaluating State-Owned Assets," was issued in November 1991. The new regulation, among other things, indirectly sanctioned the sale and transfer of assets owned by state entities to nonstate entities. The pace of such implicit or concealed privatization accelerated following Deng Xiaoping's tour of southern China in the spring of 1992. The State Council approved, in July 1992, the "Rules on Changing the Management Mechanisms of State-Owned Industrial Enterprises." Among the provisions granting SOE management more operational authority, this document allowed the leasing, mortgaging, and sale of SOE assets. SOE executives were also given the power to acquire other firms. A survey of Chinese SOE managers during this period indicated that, as a result of this reform program, executives in newly formed shareholding companies gained the right to dispose of assets.[36]

Property rights reform gained new momentum in November 1993 when the CCP's 14th Central Committee issued "The CCP Central Committee's Resolution on Several Issues Regarding the Establishment of a Socialist Market Economic System," which explicitly stated that small SOEs could be leased, restructured as joint-stock companies, or sold to collectives or individuals. This document, it can be argued, represents the first high-level official endorsement of the privatization of SOE assets. Following promulgation of the resolution, provincial governments began to formulate and issue their own regulations on the disposal of SOE assets.[37]

During the mid-1990s, the privatization of SOE assets was closely connected with the process of restructuring bankrupt SOEs. In the restructuring process, the Chinese government allowed, albeit on an experimental basis, the sale of their assets to private entities or individuals. The document authorizing this practice, the "State Council's Announcement of a Pilot Project on the Bankruptcy of SOEs in Selected Cities," was issued in October 1994. The focus of the announcement was the arrangements for unemployed workers following the bankruptcy of their enterprises. As a result, proceeds from the sale or disposal of the assets of these SOEs were earmarked for this purpose. Another important provision of the announcement was that SOEs on the verge of bankruptcy could be reorganized by changing the management, restructuring the management of the assets of the enterprise, or adjusting the organizational structure of the enterprises. Although the document did not specify what such "restructuring" or "adjusting" would entail, the language used typically refers to leasing, contracting, and partial privatization.

In the late 1990s, as the financial conditions of the SOEs continued to deteriorate, the Chinese government embraced more radical reforms. A central component of the new strategy was privatizing small and medium-sized SOEs and giving preference to large SOEs. Called *zhuada fangxiao* (grab the big and let go of the small), the strategy was enshrined in the "CCP Central Committee's Resolution on Several Major Issues Pertaining to the Reform and Development of SOEs," issued in September 1999. To be sure, the resolution insisted that the state-owned economic sector would be "the main component" of the Chinese economy and it focused chiefly on the strategic goal of turning large SOEs into competitive firms. Liberalizing and revitalizing small and medium-sized firms through a competitive process of picking winners and weeding out losers was the most radical part of the reform strategy. The resolution reiterated the continuation of a multipronged approach to revitalizing small SOEs, such as restructuring, merging, leasing, converting to joint-stock ownership, or selling. On paper, the resolution sanctioned the sale of small SOEs only as part of a multipronged approach. However, in practice, the resolution merely endorsed a widespread practice favored by local governments to dispose of loss-making small SOEs.

For local governments, quick disposal of loss-making SOEs produced multiple benefits. Besides reducing drains on local finances, this process allowed well-connected local businessmen and government officials to purchase SOE assets at steep discounts.[38] Indeed, in this process, the assets of SOEs were routinely undervalued and the tax liabilities and bank loans of bankrupt SOEs were left unpaid as neither the purchasers nor the local governments were willing to assume such liabilities. This practice was so widespread and serious that the State Economic and Trade Commission, the Ministry of Finance, and the People's Bank of China issued a joint document in February 1999, the "Notice on Issues Related to the Sale of Small SOEs," to tighten the privatization process. The document criticized "some localities" for "violating the spirit of the CCP's 15th Party Congress" and "treating the sale of small SOEs as the principal or the exclusive form of reform." As a result, "there were irregularities that led to the loss of state-owned assets, the failure to pay off bank loans and taxes, and infringements on the rights of employees." As is always the case with policies of the central government, this effort to regulate the sale of small SOEs failed. Following promulgation of the resolution, many local governments quickly began selling such firms, usually at deep discounts. Soon afterward, even profitable SOEs were put on the block as well.[39]

In the early 2000s, the Chinese government further decentralized approval authority for the disposal of SOE assets. Local governments were assigned responsibility to manage the assets of the SOEs they owned.[40] According to a key document, "On Regulating the Restructuring of SOEs," issued by the State-Owned Assets Supervision and Administration Commission (SASAC) and approved by the State Council in November 2003, there were considerable irregularities during the privatization process that resulted in the loss of state-owned assets. To tighten control over this process, SASAC proposed new restrictions on the approval procedure. Under the new SASAC rule, an SOE could be restructured into a non-SOE through multiple means, such as reorganization, merger, leasing, contracting, joint-venture, or transfer or sale of the SOE rights and shares. Plans for such restructuring must be approved by multiple government agencies (such as the local finance bureau, labor department, and local government agencies in charge of SOE assets). In addition, the assets of the SOEs being restructured must be valued and the SOEs' finances must be audited by licensed accounting firms. When SOE assets are transferred to nonstate investors, the direct owners of the SOE assets must retain asset-assessment firms to value the assets, which include patents, technology, brands, and intangible assets. A groundbreaking provision of the SASAC document was the permission for management to privatize SOE assets, although management was prohibited from selling SOE assets directly to themselves.

A revised and updated SASAC regulation in December 2005 imposed stricter regulations on privatization. The document, "On Further Regulating the Restructuring of SOEs," accentuated government concerns about the loss of state-owned assets during the privatization process. In particular, the regulation required that SOEs requesting restructuring of their ownership must make a strong case for their proposal and provide details on the new ownership structure, governance, their liabilities and assets, and a plan for resettling the workers. Restructuring plans must make explicit provisions to protect the SOE's financial assets and settle its liabilities. Additionally, the revised SASAC rules stipulated that the disposal of land and mining rights must follow the procedures specified by the relevant laws, most likely because such rights had been sold either too cheaply or in violation of the legal procedures.

Compared with changes in the property rights in land and natural resources, those affecting SOEs can be said to represent two extremes. On the one hand, small and medium-sized SOEs have been privatized despite the absence of a formal legal framework and explicit legal authorization by the only lawmaking body of the country, the National People's Congress, which has not passed any legislation authorizing the disposal of SOE assets by agents of the state. In a technical sense, such privatization has been accompanied by both decentralization of control and clarification of ownership rights. Rent-seeking and cronyism in this process is a one-time affair. In these instances, the looting of undervalued assets takes place in a single transition. The agents of the state—managers of SOEs and local officials responsible for liquidating these firms—have reaped lucrative personal gains mainly because of the vagueness and loopholes in the improvisational rules issued by the various ministry-level bureaucracies (although approved by the State Council). As analyzed above, these rules contained few key procedural provisions. They were designed to provide local authorities and SOE managers considerable discretion in carrying out the privatization program. Even though the rules characteristically emphasized the need to prevent the loss of state-owned assets in the privatization process, they consistently failed to set detailed operational restrictions to achieve this goal. This regulatory environment facilitated collusion among elites because the vagueness of the rules effectively dispersed approval authority among several government agencies and officials.

At the other extreme is the continuing state ownership (or majority ownership) of large SOEs, where collusive corruption, as our sample cases in Chapter 4 will reveal, has become endemic. The repeated efforts by the CCP to make these behemoths more efficient appear to have produced no real improvements in their competitiveness or financial performance even as senior managers are empowered to engage in collusive corruption.[41] We should not be surprised by this outcome by now. China's reform of its large SOEs has resulted in decentralization of control over state-owned assets without clarifying their real ownership—a perfect combination for generating opportunities for looting by insiders.

Administrative Decentralization: Cadre Management

As a Leninist regime, the CCP's most critical instrument of maintaining power is its *nomenklatura,* a term imported from the Soviet Union. During the reform era, this system of cadre management underwent significant changes. Among other things, the CCP imposed mandatory retirement, raised educational qualifications, specified rotations, and introduced detailed procedural rules, at least on paper, governing appointments and promotions.[42] These changes were designed to strengthen the party's ability to recruit more capable, better-educated, and more loyal officials.[43] In retrospect, however, the most consequential institutional change occurred in 1984, when the CCP decided to radically decentralize cadre management. Under the previous "managing two levels down" (*xiaguan liangji*) system, the central leadership controlled the appointment of cadres in provinces and prefectures while provincial CCP organizations controlled cadre appointments in counties. To give local leaders greater and more direct authority over cadres in their jurisdictions, the radical reform in 1984 replaced *xiaguan liangji* with *xiaguan yiji* (managing one level down). Under the new system, the central leadership managed provincial cadres who, in turn, supervised prefecture-level officials, who in turn monitored, evaluated, and appointed county-level officials, who, due to the reform, could manage township officials.

The 1984 reform significantly empowered local party chiefs by giving them unprecedented power to decide the political future of prefecture, county, and township officials. While provincial party chiefs gained considerable power at a reasonable cost (losing their

appointment authority over county-level cadres), the greatest beneficiaries were prefecture and county party chiefs who were granted
personnel power over substantial administrative positions (county
and subcounty officials, respectively). For example, prefecture party
bosses could henceforth appoint and promote county-level officials,
while county party chiefs, who had no substantial personnel management authority under the old system, could decide who to appoint for
subcounty and township leadership positions. Of course, in addition
to decentralization of cadre management, the Chinese government
also decentralized investment approval, fiscal management, and regulatory enforcement.[44] Parallel to this development was a similar empowerment of SOE executives as part of the restructuring of the state-
owned industrial sector.[45]

It is impossible to overstate the impact of the change from "managing down two levels" to "managing down one level" in facilitating
collusion between a local official and his immediate subordinates,
over whom he now had direct power of appointment and promotion. This dramatic change in the nature of his relationship with his
immediate subordinates gives a prefecture or county party chief the
ability to increase the incentives for his subordinates to collude with
him. Obviously, the emergence and spread of the buying and selling
of offices by local officials since the 1990s, a phenomenon we study in
the next chapter, can be traced to the 1984 reform. In addition, the
problem of out-of-control *yibashou* officials is also likely the result of
administrative decentralization without commensurate institutional
constraints on the use of newly delegated authority. Based on press
reports and academic research, the corruption of *yibashou* officials is
the most salient characteristic of corruption in contemporary China,
mainly because of their unchecked power.[46]

The challenge posed by this far-reaching decentralization was how to monitor newly empowered local elites.[47] Yet, despite devising numerous measures to evaluate and police local elites, the CCP has not been able to decentralize administrative authority without suffering the adverse consequences of the misalignment of interests.[48] The CCP should not be faulted for not trying hard enough to address the governance ills caused by the newly empowered but misbehaving local party chiefs. This agency problem is deeply embedded in the institutional structure of a Leninist party-state that prizes execution of the will of the top leadership above all other goals. In such a system, the party-state has no choice but to vest complete authority in local leaders with proven political loyalty. The cures that might moderate abuses of power by these officials, such as intraparty competition, checks and balances, transparency, and third-party monitoring and enforcement, are worse than the disease itself from the perspective of a Leninist regime because they can both make the trusted local party boss less effective and undercut his loyalty.

One puzzle is why the reckless abuse of power, collusion, and looting by local elites, particularly party chiefs, did not emerge immediately after the 1984 reform. Instead, such phenomena began to spread only after Deng Xiaoping's southern tour in 1992. The most obvious answer is that the decentralization of personnel power occurred nearly a decade before the decentralization of control of property rights. The empowerment of local elites met one favorable condition for looting state-owned property through collusion, but unfortunately for these elites in the mid- to late 1980s, the opportunities for looting were severely limited because they could not lay their hands on state-owned property. As a result, corruption in the late 1980s was largely confined to conventional forms of petty theft, bribery, and exploitation of rents in government licensing, and the system of dual-track pricing.[49] A second likely explanation is that the overall political ethos of the mid- and late 1980s was fundamentally different from that of the post-Tiananmen era. At the top of the party were reformers committed to both economic and political liberalization. Chinese society in general, and the media in particular, enjoyed greater freedom. Pressures from both the top and below effectively constrained the predation of local elites. A third reason is that, like all other milestone institutional changes, the decentralization of cadre management announced in 1984 took years to implement and, if we factor in the Tiananmen shock, the new system probably did not start functioning fully until the early 1990s.[50]

The only institution that could constrain the abuse of power by local party chiefs was the CCP's own commissions for discipline inspection (CDIs).[51] However, as academic research shows, these are largely toothless agencies in checking the abuse of local elites, especially the party chiefs.[52] These committees' investigative capacity has been severely limited by their small and nonprofessional staff. For example, in 1990 Fujian had 4,717 full-time staff in its discipline inspection system, which consisted of one provincial-level committee, five prefecture-level committees, eighty county-level committees, and 978 township-level committees, averaging fewer than five staff per committee. In 2014, according to a news report, a typical prefecture-level CDI had four offices, each staffed by three people (an average prefecture had 4 million people and about 275,000 CCP members). The Central Commission for Discipline Inspection (CCDI) had only 360 investigative staff.[53] The most fatal flaw in the CCP's discipline inspection system is its lack of autonomy and political stature inside the party itself.

In the CCP hierarchy, a local CDI is jointly under the leadership of the CDI one level above and the party committee at the same level, and the secretary of the CDI is outranked by the party secretary in a local party committee. His junior status effectively makes him subordinate to the party chief whom he is supposed to monitor and police. The committee also has limited power to investigate cases and determine outcomes. It has only "preliminary investigative authority." It cannot launch a formal investigation or determine a final resolution of a case without the approval of the party committee at the same level (which means approval by the party chief). Worse still, it is not required to report its investigations to the CDI at a higher level, thus making cover-ups relatively easy. It should surprise no one that, of the widely reported cases of corruption by eighty-three officials at or above the prefecture level arrested between November 2012 and October 2013, none was exposed or investigated by the CDI in his jurisdiction.[54] The institutional weakness of the CDIs is not unknown to the CCP top leadership. Xi Jinping remarked to a gathering of CCDI officials in January 2014, "It is an anathema for local committees of discipline inspection to monitor officials at the same level. Few of the corruption cases involving *yibashou* officials were reported by local CDIs on their own. In some localities, leaders of these committees would tell comrades blowing the whistle on officials of the party committees at the same level: Stop, I hear nothing."[55]

To be sure, after Xi Jinping began his crackdown on corruption, Wang Qishan, the head of the CCDI and Xi's political ally, introduced several measures to strengthen the political independence of the local CDIs and to prevent cover-ups. Among other things, the head of the provincial CDIs are now people from a different province and unlikely to be tied to local patronage networks. To make it more difficult for lower-level CDIs to cover up misconduct by local officials, the CCP now requires that all investigations formally launched by a local CDI must be reported to the CDI one level above.[56] While it is too early to tell whether these measures will make the CDIs more effective, these changes are likely to produce limited results because they do not address critical issues, such as under-staffing and the subordination of the CDI chief to the party boss. Cover-ups will also continue since local CDIs may simply stop filing formal investigations so as not to leave behind a paper trail.

In China during the reform era in general, and since the 1990s in par-ticular, an institutional environment highly conducive to collusion and looting began to emerge. Incremental and incomplete reforms of property rights starting in the 1990s made nominally state-owned property especially vulnerable to looting by colluding political and business elites. And the decentralization of cadre man-agement greatly empowered local party chiefs while reducing their accountability.

In terms of changes in property rights, we can observe similari-ties in the reform of the property rights of the three types of state-owned assets studied in this chapter. Such reforms were marked by deliberate vagueness in definitions, language, procedures, and reg-ulatory provisions. They were incremental in the scope, speed, and degree of reform. One inevitable result of such incrementalism is that, while the ruling elites have gained progressively greater dis-cretion and control over the disposal of the state-owned assets, the rights to these assets have consistently remained ill-defined, con-tested, and vulnerable. Another logical outcome of this process is the persistence of insecurity of rights in the property transferred from the state to private hands and of uncertainty about government pol-icies that affect these rights.

Without effective monitoring and policing, either by higher authorities in the CCP or by third parties, newly empowered local elites have irresistible temptations and abundant opportunities to enrich themselves through the seizure of state-owned assets, legally or otherwise. They can transfer undervalued assets or even give them away for free to their family members or to private businessmen who have bribed them. Colluding elites who control the coercive apparatus of the state or who have links with organized criminal gangs can also misappropriate private property that was previously or residually owned by the state (housing, land, and mines). In retrospect, it is difficult to imagine that China's crony capitalism would have emerged, let alone thrived, in the absence of these two institutional conditions.

3

Public Offices for Sale:
An Illicit Market for Political Power

> Corruption in personnel matters is a prominent problem;
> the practice of appointing officials in violation of the rules
> is widespread. Our system of cadre management is for show
> only. In some areas, the problems of bribing for votes, lob-
> bying for office, and *maiguan maiguan* are grave.
>
> —Xi Jinping, October 16, 2014

THE BUYING AND SELLING of office, or *maiguan maiguan*, has become such a serious problem that, in the eyes of the CCP's general secretary Xi Jinping, the party's system of personnel management is "for show only." On the surface, this practice may have little to do with conventional crony capitalism since it involves only political elites and not private businessmen. The link between partial property rights and the rise of crony capitalism seems to be missing in this type of transaction. While this observation may be true, a study of the rise and entrenchment of crony capitalism in China would be incomplete without an understanding of the connection between corruption inside the Leninist party-state and collusion among the agents of the regime and private businessmen. We have seen how a private businessman who has paid off a party chief can count on him to deliver on his promise of assorted favors. Typically, the delivery of such favors must involve the cooperation of the party chief's subordinates in a process of vertical collusion. Obviously, the party chief can use his power to coerce his underlings to carry out his orders to assist the private businessman. But an even better solution is for the party chief to entrust this chore to a subordinate who has bribed him for his position. As the evidence will show, such vertical collusion is a central feature of crony capitalism in contemporary China.

Additionally, it can be argued that *maiguan maiguan* is a contributing cause of crony capitalism since officials seeking promotions through bribery are more likely to engage in collusion with private businessmen. They need to accumulate sufficient funds to finance their purchases and they use the power granted by the offices they have bought to recoup their investments. As their meager salaries as local officials are inadequate sources of funding, they must rely on corrupt activities to generate the funds for their purchases and to recover their investments. Finally, exploring the illicit market for political power has another intellectual benefit—it can help us understand the political ecosystem in which crony capitalism thrives. Generally speaking, corruption involving government officials and private businessmen is a reflection of the corruption inside the state. Crony capitalism is far more likely to prosper in a country where the state itself is deeply corrupt and a large number of its agents resort to bribery to advance their careers.

As our brief review of changes in the CCP's cadre management system in Chapter 2 shows, *maiguan maiguan* is most likely the product of the radical decentralization of personnel management that started with the 1984 reform, though the practice did not evolve into a mature and illicit market for power until the 1990s. Indeed, available evidence indicates that the practice did not exist in the 1980s but it has become prevalent since the 1990s. A keyword search for *maiguan maiguan* in the China Knowledge Resource Integrated Database, the country's largest electronic database for newspapers and magazines, yields no results prior to 1990. A study of 142 heads of municipalities prosecuted for corruption between 1983 and 2012 also confirms that there were no such cases prior to 1990.[1] A study that examines more than 2,800 corruption cases prosecuted between 2000 and 2009 finds that 365, or 13 percent of all cases, involved so-called "organizational and personnel corruption," another code phrase for *maiguan maiguan*.[2] In all likelihood, the extent of *maiguan maiguan* in contemporary China is much greater than revealed because of underreporting. In official press reports describing the alleged corrupt acts committed by disgraced officials, we often come across references such as "gain benefits from helping others get jobs and official appointments," coded phrases for *maiguan maiguan* even though these officials were not explicitly charged with this crime.

Although collusion among elites through *maiguan maiguan* is a telling symptom of late-stage regime decay, it has received relatively little scholarly attention.[3] In this section, we probe its underlying political economy and the contexts in which the practice has thrived. We will rely on details gathered from fifty prosecuted cases in which the perpetrators were singled out for engaging in *maiguan maiguan*. These cases were chosen because they received extensive press coverage and they contain sufficient details to give us a deeper understanding of collusion among political elites.[4]

Key Findings

Even though the fifty cases (see the Appendix, Table A.1) in the sample were not randomly chosen, they provide useful clues for understanding how this form of collusion is carried out. Geographically, the fifty cases are drawn from twenty-two provinces, indicating the prevalence of this practice. Nine cases are from Anhui, a poor province with a high incidence of *maiguan maiguan,* at least according to press reports. Henan, a relatively poor agrarian province, and Guangdong, the booming manufacturing powerhouse, have five cases each. Hainan and Shandong have three cases each. As the sample includes both poor and prosperous regions, it appears that this practice exists in regions at all levels of economic development, although, without more data, it is impossible to determine its exact distribution.

A unique feature of *maiguan maiguan* is the dominance of local party secretaries in the illicit market for office. Of the fifty cases, thirty-one of the perpetrators were party secretaries in counties and prefectures (there was also one township party secretary). Six were directors of the CCP's organization department or deputy party secretaries in charge of personnel matters. They could influence the initial selection and screening of nominees for appointments and promotions. Nine were directors of administrative agencies (such as the commerce and land resources bureaus) or law enforcement agencies (bureaus of public security). These directors, who simultaneously serve as party secretaries in these agencies, have almost total control over personnel matters. Party secretaries have a near monopoly over personnel appointments and are thus well positioned to monetize such power through *maiguan.* The large number of local officials involved in *maiguan maiguan* is almost certainly the result of the decentralization of personnel appointments to the subnational level.[5] There are more public offices at the local level than at the provincial and national levels. The pool of potential buyers is thus larger at the county and subcounty levels. As a result, they account for most

Table 3.1.   Key characteristics of the fifty sample cases of *maiguan maiguan*

	Number of positions sold	Duration of corruption (years)	Promotion during the period (%)	Total corruption income (million yuan)	Bribes from private businesses (%)	Sentence[a]
Mean	41	7.7	84	6.45	86	13
Median	27	7		3.81		13
Standard deviation	45	3.4		10.44		3

a. Years; term sentences only.

of the sample cases. Provincial- or ministerial-level officials also engage in this practice, however. A close reading of the alleged crimes committed by "fallen tigers"—officials with ranks of vice provincial governor or vice minister and above—shows that many of them have bought and sold offices. This practice is also widespread inside the Chinese military.[6]

Another notable feature of *maiguan maiguan* is that nearly all sellers of office also engage in other types of corruption. Local party chiefs operate multiple, albeit illicit, lines of business. They accept bribes from those willing to pay for promotions, contracts, and purchase of undervalued state-owned assets. In our sample, 86 percent of the officials punished for *maiguan* also accepted commercial bribery (Table 3.1). This finding does not diminish the importance of selling offices. Although the monetary income from selling offices is relatively small, it nevertheless remains considerable, particularly for officials in poorer regions. This activity also generates significant intangible benefits, such as placing loyal lieutenants in key positions that can facilitate the perpetrator's collusion with businessmen, as we will see in Chapter 5.

How the Market Values Power

Data from our sample cases also help shed some light on how the market for power values it and rewards its holders with bribes. Although the figures in Table A.1 do not show the price of individual positions, we can detect a broad trend of rising amounts of corruption income gained by perpetrators of *maiguan*. Of the fifty cases, the perpetrators in ten cases were caught before 2001 and those in thirty-six cases were caught between 2002 and 2013. Of the ten cases caught before 2001, the total corruption income for five perpetrators is less than 1 million yuan each. The average amount per perpetrator caught before 2001 is 2.45 million yuan (the median is 1.2 million yuan). The average is distorted by the outsized haul of 10.4 million yuan by one county party secretary (who received the only death sentence in our sample). If we remove this outlier from the sample, the average amount of total corruption income for each perpetrator in the pre-2001 period would be 1.8 million yuan (and the median amount would be 1 million yuan). By comparison, only five of the thirty-six perpetrators caught in the post-2001 period gained less than 1 million yuan in total corruption income. The average amount for each perpetrator in this period is 8 million yuan (the median is 5.3 million yuan). Again, the 70 million yuan in corruption income attributed to one prefecture party chief, Luo Yinguo, distorts the average. Even if we remove this outlier, the average amount per perpetrator would still be an impressive 6.23 million yuan (and the median would be 5.1 million yuan), 3.5 times that of the average amount per perpetrator in the pre-2001 period, and the median amount would be five times larger.

Although we do not have sufficient evidence showing that the prices for offices have risen as sharply since the 1990s, there are reasonable grounds to believe this is the case. Assuming the share of income from selling offices remained constant, the increase in total corruption income would imply a corresponding rise in the price of offices. Additionally, the price of an office reflects its potential to generate bribery income. If a position is seen as lucrative, its price will be bid up. The increase in the price for an office can be seen in the cases of Zhang Guiyi and Xu Shexin, party secretaries of Wuhe County in Anhui. Xu was Zhang's immediate successor as the county's party secretary and outperformed Zhang in terms of the amount of corruption income from selling office and the price charge for each position sold (Table 3.3). The median price per position was 10,000 yuan for Yang, but rose to 14,000 yuan for Xu. Besides confirming the impression that the intensity of corruption, as measured by the amount stolen by officials, has increased in recent years, this observation can also be indicative of the appreciated value of official positions.

Conventional wisdom would lead us to believe that more senior officials collect more corruption income. While this is true in our sample, the disparity of illicit income between higher- and lower-ranked officials is not very large and may be even less significant if adjusted for the longer duration of crime for more senior officials. The data in Table 3.2 reconfirm that higher officials generate more corruption income than lower officials. Of the fifty officials in this sample, one was a township official, twenty-seven perpetrators were county-level officials, seventeen were prefecture-level officials, and five were provincial-level officials.[7] The average amount of corruption income for a county-level official is 3.9 million yuan, compared with 10.4 million yuan for a prefecture-level official and 9.1 million yuan for a provincial-level official. The median amount of corruption income for county-level officials is 2.4 million yuan, and that for prefecture-level and provincial-level officials is, respectively, 5.0

Table 3.2. Corruption income, offices sold, duration of corruption, and penalty, by rank

Corruption income according to rank (million yuan)	Mean	Median	Standard deviation
County-level officials	3.9	2.4	4.6
Prefecture-level officials	10.4	5.0	17.0
Provincial-level officials	9.1	8.2	2.5
Number of offices sold, by the rank of sellers	Mean	Median	Standard deviation
County-level officials	54	33	47
Prefecture-level officials	23	13	18
Provincial-level officials	25	13	22
Duration of corruption, by rank (years)	Mean	Median	Standard deviation
County-level officials	6.5	5	2.8
Prefecture-level officials	8.3	9	2.8
Provincial-level officials	10.6	10	3.8

Severity of punishment, by rank (number of officials)	Suspended death or life sentence (%)	Term sentence in years (mean)	Term sentence in years (median)	Standard deviation
County-level officials (27)	44	12.3	13	3
Prefecture-level officials (17)	47	13.8	14	2.9
Provincial-level officials (5)	100	n.a.	n.a.	n.a.

and 8.2 million yuan. While the very large amount of corruption income of provincial-level officials is no surprise, more noteworthy is the relatively small gap between the median amounts of total corruption income among officials at the three levels. The median corruption haul of provincial-level officials is only 64 percent higher than that of prefecture-level officials and less than four times greater than that of county-level officials. The median corruption income of prefecture-level officials is only twice that of county-level officials despite the vast disparity in their political power. If we factor in the longer median duration of crime for prefecture- and provincial-level officials (nine and ten years, respectively), the amount of corruption income gained by a county-level official, adjusted for the much shorter median duration of his crime (five years), is not only impressive on its own but also indicative of the decentralized nature of predation in contemporary China.

A county party secretary can generate considerable corruption income despite his modest status in the CCP hierarchy, mainly because he is on the front line of the party-state and has abundant opportunities to extract bribes from his subordinates and private businessmen.[8] A sufficiently greedy and reckless county party boss, if given the opportunity, can loot greater wealth than his superiors—five of the top ten corruption income earners in Table A.1 were county party chiefs. Additionally, the large standard deviations in corruption income for both prefecture and county officials (17 and 4.6 million yuan, respectively) imply that bribe-extracting capacities among local officials vary enormously. They are most likely determined by the value of local state-owned assets or the government contracts that these officials could help private businessmen obtain.

What is more relevant to us here, however, is the income gained from *maiguan maiguan* by county, prefecture, and provincial officials. The data in Table 3.2 show that, on average, a county party chief sells fifty-four positions, more than twice the average for a prefecture party boss (twenty-three), who sells almost the same number of positions as a provincial-level official (twenty-five). The variations in the median number of offices sold by officials at the three levels are similar. The median number of offices sold is thirty-three for a county-level official, thirteen for a prefecture-level official, and thirteen for a provincial-level official.[9] Judging by the standard deviation in the number of offices sold at the three levels, we can see that this practice has greater variation at the county level than at the prefecture or provincial levels. A county-level party chief controls appointment power over a larger number of less pricey positions and has greater capacity to honor his commitments. By comparison, more senior officials, who control fewer but more expensive offices, are more selective in accepting bribes from buyers because the personnel appointments they make are subject to greater scrutiny and competition.

However, more senior officials, such as prefecture party chiefs, can reap more income from selling offices even though they sell fewer of them than their subordinates. This finding is not surprising because a prefecture party boss controls appointments of county party chiefs and magistrates. These positions, classified as *chu*-level appointments, are more prestigious, powerful, and desirable than the *ke*-level subcounty positions a county party chief can sell.[10] They also offer higher future returns, thus commanding a premium. In addition, potential buyers of these positions, invariably county-level officials, likely have already accumulated considerable corruption income or can finance their more costly bribes with help from businessmen.

In fourteen of our fifty cases, we have detailed information on the bribes for each purchased position. Seven of these cases involved county party secretaries and the other seven prefecture party chiefs (and provincial-level officials who sold these offices when they were prefecture party secretaries). A simple analysis of their income reveals several important features of *maiguan maiguan*. As assumed, county-level party chiefs sell offices for much less than prefecture party bosses. The median price for a position sold by the seven county party bosses included here ranges from 10,000 to 30,000 yuan, compared with 19,000–340,000 yuan for the seven prefecture-level party bosses.[11] If we aggregate these fourteen cases, the median price for a position sold by a county party chief is 20,000 yuan, only 20 percent of the median price (100,000 yuan) for a position sold by a prefecture party chief (Table 3.3).[12]

The data in Table 3.3 also indicate that the market for bribed appointments and promotions is probably more developed in counties than in prefectures, as illustrated by a higher degree of price uniformity (reflected statistically in a much smaller standard deviation in prices of offices sold) in seven counties than in seven prefectures. The median price per office in the 181 county transactions was 20,000 yuan, with a standard deviation of 18,946 yuan. By comparison, the median price of the eighty-two transactions in the seven prefectures in the sample was 100,000 yuan, with a standard deviation of 219,643 yuan—more than twice the median price. In the seven county-level cases, the highest median price per office (30,000 yuan) was three times that of the lowest (10,000 yuan). In the seven prefecture-level cases, this ratio was 17 to 1 (340,000 yuan to 19,000 yuan).[13]

One plausible explanation is that potential buyers can easily acquire better pricing information through discreet inquiries in a county, a smaller geographical jurisdiction, than in a prefecture, which typically has six to ten counties. Another possible reason is

Table 3.3. Prices of offices sold by county and prefecture officials (yuan)

County-level officials

Name	Zhang Guiyi	Xu Shexin	Zhang Zhi'an	Zhang Gaiping	Liang Bizhi	Li Gang	Wang Guohua	Total
Number of positions sold	11	58	15	26	13	33	21	181
Mean price	12,000	17,814	17,867	25,730	26,125	29,121	33,143	23,177
Median price	10,000	14,000	16,000	20,000	20,000	20,000	30,000	20,000
Standard deviation	6,588	19,024	9,303	13,916	19,397	24,548	16,051	18,946

Prefecture-level officials

Name	He Minxu[a]	Wang Guohua	Tian Zhong	Chen Shaoyong[a]	Ma De	Liu Zhuozhi[a]	Luo Yinguo	Total
Number of positions sold	10	13	12	9	12	11	15	82
Mean price	34,100	41,923	65,000	126,111	175,000	307,273	438,000	190,134
Median price	19,000	30,000	73,333	100,000	228,333	240,000	340,000	100,000
Standard deviation	31,402	27,729	32,998	69,682	145,993	209,623	307,390	219,643

a. Selling of offices occurred during tenures as prefecture party chiefs.

that those seeking subcounty-level positions may not be able to offer bigger bribes because they have not accumulated enough corruption income to fund their bids, while those seeking promotions to county-level positions likely have already amassed enough corruption income to finance their bribes, thus increasing the prices (and the range) of their desired positions. The most important factor determining the disparity of prices for offices between counties and prefectures is the value of the offices being sought. On balance, subcounty offices have less power to extract bribes than subprefecture offices. This is true even when the seller is the same individual. Wang Guohua, for instance, sold offices as both a county party chief and a prefecture director of organization. While the median price per office was the same, the average price for the positions he sold as the prefecture director of organization was 8,000 yuan more than that of the positions he sold as a county party chief (Table 3.3). In all likelihood, the price of offices he sold while serving as the prefecture director of organization was discounted because, as the director of organization, Wang had influence but not the final say in personnel decisions. In other words, had Wang been the prefecture party boss, the price per position would have been much higher. Finally, the wide pricing variations paid by buyers seeking appointments from prefecture-level officials may reflect the equally wide variations in the value of the offices in a prefecture, where jurisdictions and agencies can differ significantly in their desirability for office-seekers.

Low Detection Risks and Long Durations of Corruption

Corrupt officials in China who engage in collusion with their colleagues face low detection risks (Table 3.1). Of the forty-nine officials whose duration of corruption is known, their corrupt activities lasted an average of 7.7 years before they were arrested (the median duration is seven years). More senior officials have longer durations than junior ones. Of the twenty-seven county-level officials, the average duration is 6.5 years (the median is five years). Of the seventeen prefecture party chiefs, the average duration is 8.3 years (the median is nine years). The average duration is 10.6 years for the five provincial-level officials in the sample (the median is ten years) (Table 3.2). The longer duration of prefecture and provincial officials may be the result of the greater protection they enjoy from their patrons (whom they likely have bribed to secure their own promotions).[14]

The obvious benefit of avoiding detection is, besides raising corruption income, the opportunity to move up the hierarchy in the party-state. Table 3.1 shows that 84 percent of the officials were promoted while engaging in corruption, suggesting that the CCP has a low capability of detecting corruption among local officials, and the majority of corrupt officials can expect promotions.

Of course, those caught selling offices face, at least in nominal terms, severe punishment. However, as academic research and data from the CCDI show, corrupt officials are actually punished more lightly than ordinary citizens who break the law because many, if not most, are not prosecuted.[15] The average length of a jail sentence in the sample is thirteen years. The data in Table A.1 also show that, in general, the severity of punishment is highly correlated with the amount of corruption income, which is, in turn, connected with the rank of the offender. As a result, officials with ranks at or above the prefecture level are more likely to get life or a suspended death penalty (nearly half of the prefecture-level officials and all the provincial-level officials in the sample received such sentences).[16] However, it would be wrong to conclude that the party punishes its wayward senior officials more severely. Yongshun Cai's study of the punishment of 1,122 officials disciplined by the party shows that lower-level officials are actually punished more severely than higher-level officials.[17]

Of the fifty cases, three in four of the officials with corruption income above the median amount (3.81 million yuan) drew life or suspended death sentences. Another notable finding is the rare application of the dreaded death penalty. Only one official in our sample—a lowly county party boss—was actually executed. Those who receive a suspended death sentence usually have it reduced to a life term (which is often further reduced later).[18] This is likely the result of the party's tactic of threatening officials suspected of serious corruption with severe punishment unless they cooperate by both confessing their crimes and implicating their coconspirators. According to one news report, while this policy helps investigators, it also allows many convicted corrupt officials (as many as 70 percent) to obtain reduced sentences. A separate investigation by the Guangxi provincial procuratorate reveals that, between 2001 and 2005, 57 percent of the individuals convicted of using their public offices to commit crimes received suspended sentences or no penalty at all.[19]

The Political Economy of *Maiguan Maiguan*

In cases of *maiguan maiguan,* agents of the state effectively appropriate the power of the state. In elite recruitment, bribes, instead of merit, determine who is chosen. We further speculate that the key economic incentive behind the chief perpetrator is maximization of his corruption income. Given the practical constraints on his time and his ability to fully realize the profitability of the power he possesses during a relatively short timeframe (typically a party secretary of a county or a prefect serves three years before a lateral transfer or a promotion), a rational strategy for maximizing corruption income is to discount the prices of various offices sought by subordinates. In this section, we use the data from our sample to probe the market dynamics of *maiguan maiguan*.

Motives for Sellers

· In the subnational CCP hierarchy, party secretaries enjoy an effective monopoly over personnel decisions. The only official who may have some procedural influence over these decisions is the director of the organization department. But, by and large, the party secretary controls two critical stages of the appointment process. He nominates the candidate and gives final approval to personnel decisions made by the standing committee of the party committee. These are only his formal powers. In reality, his influence vastly exceeds his formal authority. His colleagues on the standing committee seldom dare to oppose his nominations out of fear that this will antagonize the party chief and risk his veto of their own favored candidates.

Li Tiecheng, a county party chief in Jilin who received bribes from 162 individuals seeking favors between 1991 and 2000, revealed how he manipulated the process to ensure that those who had bribed him received their desired positions without violating the formal procedures. Each time a personnel decision was to be made, according to Li, the organization department would first evaluate the potential candidates and then give a short list of candidates to the deputy party secretary in charge of personnel matters. After the deputy party chief reviewed and approved this list, he would present it to Li for approval. Only with Li's approval could this list be forwarded to the standing committee for discussion and approval. Evidently, this procedure gave Li *ex ante* veto power. Li confessed that if the list did not contain the names of those who had bribed him, he would reject the list and ask the organization department to produce a new one. Therefore, without obtaining Li's support, no official had a chance of being appointed or promoted.[20] Local party chiefs also have the power to directly "nominate" candidates to the organization department for consideration once a vacancy occurs, a crucial step in delivering the desired position to the purchaser of the position. According to Zhou Yinxiao, a prefecture party chief in the sample, after a vacancy became available, the party chief or the executive deputy party secretary had the right to nominate a potential candidate. Zhou himself used this procedure to nominate those who had bribed him.[21]

However, despite his near-monopolistic control over personnel decisions, the party secretary faces practical constraints on monetizing his power to the maximum extent. One of the insights gained from our sample is that for party secretaries, their most lucrative customers are private entrepreneurs, not subordinates with limited ability to pay. Officials who have not already accumulated sufficient corruption income or who do not have the capacity to embezzle large amounts of public funds cannot finance their purchases. By contrast, profitability from collusion with private entrepreneurs, who can afford much more risk capital, greatly exceeds that from selling offices to subordinates. In the fifty cases, forty-three of the sellers of offices simultaneously engaged in collusion with private businessmen and derived the bulk of their corruption income from bribes and kickbacks from private businessmen.

One such official was Ma De, the party chief of Suihua City in Heilongjiang and a notorious perpetrator of *maiguan maiguan* (press reports claimed that Ma sold official appointments and promotions to more than 260 individuals by the time he was caught in 2002).[22] When he was tried, Ma was accused of accepting bribes from seventeen individuals (including twelve officials) and pocketing 6 million yuan. One-third of this amount—2 million yuan—was a bribe paid by a private businessman whom Ma helped to obtain the contract to build Suihua's television broadcasting complex. According to his sentencing document, Ma received 2.73 million yuan from twelve officials. This means that more than half of Ma's total corruption income came from commercial bribes.[23] The case of Chen Zhaofeng, a county party chief in Anhui who was convicted in 2006 of crimes including the selling of official appointments and promotions to 110 individuals, also shows that this line of business does not generate as much corruption income as does the taking of bribes from private businessmen. Altogether his bribes from 110 subordinates amounted to 1.5 million yuan, less than 20 percent of his total corruption income of 8.3 million yuan.[24] Zhang Zhi'an, a party chief in a poverty-stricken county in Anhui, sold offices to fourteen subordinates and accepted commercial bribes during 1994–2007. Of his total corruption income of 3.6 million yuan, 2.94 million came from seven businessmen, one of whom gave him 1.1 million yuan.[25]

It is no surprise that the overwhelming majority of party secretaries whose main crime was pocketing large sums of money for selling offices actually gained the lion's share of their corruption income from colluding with private businessmen. Compared with government officials, private businessmen have both the money to fund their bribes and the ability to reap huge returns from government contracts and to obtain deeply discounted (or free) state-owned assets. However, when a party secretary engages in *maiguan maiguan*, monetary income is not his sole consideration. In fact, this activity is complementary to his principal business of taking bribes from private entrepreneurs. The most obvious additional benefit of selling offices to subordinates for a party secretary is that he has a network of willing accomplices strategically placed in key bureaucracies who will do his bidding, thus greatly facilitating his collusion with private businessmen. For example, among the twenty-three subordinates who bribed Li Guowei, director of the Fuzhou Transportation Bureau in Jiangxi, during 1999–2004, four used their positions to assist Li in awarding contracts to private businessmen who had bribed him.[26] In the next two chapters, we will see further evidence of this dynamic of vertical collusion at work.

Motives for Buyers

Subordinate officials are motivated by a desire for pecuniary gain, the competitive pressures inside the party-state to get ahead, and fears of job insecurity. The potential returns from being appointed to a more senior government position, particularly one with real executive authority over commercial transactions sought by private businessmen, have risen dramatically since the 1990s. Part of this rise can be attributed to the general increase in wealth due to the economic growth. But the bulk of the increase in potential returns is derived from the state's control of valuable assets and the awarding of infrastructure contracts. The real market value of these assets (land, mineral resources, and SOE property) is likely many times their nominal value. This disparity encourages private businessmen to try by any means possible to purchase these assets at the nominal price and then to reap windfall profits. The same logic applies to getting government contracts. These incentives drive private businessmen to offer attractive bribes to government officials who have influence over the disposal of these assets or over approval of government contracts. This means that the market price for official positions will rise accordingly.

While the dominant motive of buyers is economic, another likely driver is competition for status inside a hierarchy in which status comes with nonpecuniary benefits, such as respect and authority. In organizations where status can be obtained through bribery, the losers are those who do not bribe. They will not only be denied positions that carry more executive responsibility or have more potential for corruption income; they will also likely get stuck in subordinate positions supervised by those who have bribed their way up. Status-conscious officials are thus motivated to purchase official appointments and promotions simply to avoid an undesirable outcome.

The third reason is job insecurity. The practice of *maiguan maiguan* increases job insecurity for all officials because those in lucrative or high-status positions now must face bidding for these positions from their colleagues. If they do not pay off the party secretary, they risk being reassigned or demoted when someone else is willing to pay an attractive sum to the party secretary. When he was the party chief of Ningde City in Fujian during 2002–2005, Chen Shaoyong reappointed the director of the city's bureau of land resources, a lucrative position, in return for a bribe of 100,000 yuan.[27] Yu Fanglin, a prefecture party chief in Guangxi, received 105,000 yuan from the head of Qinzhou City's construction bureau in six installments during 1997–1998 in return of keeping the briber in his position. Paying bribes to increase one's job security is a necessity because a potential competitor may offer a bribe to the party secretary to have him removed. One of Yu's bribers, a director of the city's finance bureau, gave Yu 20,000 yuan in 1997, with a simple demand: to fire one of his deputies with whom he did not get along. And Yu happily obliged.[28] One of the local officials who bribed Ma De, the party chief of Suihua, testified at Ma's trial that in 2000 he gave Ma 350,000 yuan after he feared that Ma would end his political career and he assumed that the bribe had saved his job.[29]

Risk Management

To be sure, pocketing bribes in exchange for official appointments and promotions is a risky activity because the agents, in this case the local party secretaries, are effectively stealing from the principal, the CCP, which nominally owns the right to make such appointments and promotions and prefers to exercise the right itself to retain the loyalty of its appointees. However, the risks of detection can be managed. The chief perpetrator of this illicit trade—the local party chief—typically takes care to follow the formal procedures and leaves no solid evidence that he violated the party's organizational rules. According to a senior prosecutor of the Supreme People's Procuratorate, convicting sellers of government offices routinely runs into the difficulty of connecting bribes with appointments or promotions because personnel decisions are always made collectively (typically by the standing committee of the party organization department) and hard evidence of influence by a party chief is difficult to uncover.[30]

The influence of the party chief can be applied subtly and legitimately at the most critical stages of the formal procedure of personnel appointment in the party. When an opening occurs, numerous officials, including the party chief, can recommend candidates. The organization department then conducts a routine vetting process, after which the deputy party chief in charge of personnel matters and two or three officials from the organization department meet to determine a finalist, whose file is then forwarded to the party chief for approval. If the party chief approves the finalist, the party chief convenes a "party secretary administrative meeting" to formally endorse the finalist. Then the standing committee of the party organization department meets officially to appoint the finalist. As we can see, the party chief controls both the nomination and the approval of the candidates. When a party secretary nominates a candidate, officials in the organization department obviously get the message and have little choice but to comply with the wishes of the party boss. Once this hurdle is over, all the procedures that follow are purely *pro forma*. Zhou Yinxiao, who served as party chief of Fushun City in Liaoning during 2000–2004, adroitly manipulated this process to appoint subordinates who had bribed him. He approached the executive deputy director of the organization department and nominated his favored candidates, who later sailed through the formal appointment process—in full compliance with the party's personnel procedures.[31]

In addition, those who have bribed for posts obviously have a strong interest in keeping their transactions secret. The party secretaries who accept or demand bribes in exchange for these appointments and promotions will also take care to manipulate the procedures of personnel appointment and promotion so that the entire process appears to be compliant with the party's rules. Of course, losers in this market (subordinates who fail to be appointed or promoted due to their inability or reluctance to pay bribes) might choose to denounce such illicit activities to the party's disciplinary committees. While such denunciations may occasionally lead to investigations, most of the time they do not. The reasons are easy to understand. Since *maiguan maiguan* pervades the entire system, it is highly likely that the perpetrators have already bribed their superiors for their own appointments and promotions. When their superiors, now occupying higher positions in the CCP hierarchy, learn of such denunciations, they have a self-interest in quashing an investigation because they know that it could uncover their own misdeeds. Because discipline inspection committees must gain the approval of the party secretaries at the same level to launch an investigation of alleged wrongdoings by officials at a lower-level jurisdiction, the patrons of the alleged offenders are well positioned to protect their clients—and themselves.

Another factor that favors the perpetrators is the sheer volume of such reports and the relatively small staff of the party's in-house anticorruption agency, the CDIs. Hunan's CDIs at all levels, for example, received 387,800 letters and visits during 1996–2001, but were only able to verify 76,571 leads and investigate 58,345 cases, roughly 15 percent of the total. In Zhejiang, the party's discipline inspection committees at all levels received 50,828 tips through letters and visits in 2013, but only 8,915 cases (17.5 percent) were investigated.[32] They are usually too overwhelmed by denunciations, nearly all of them anonymous, to pursue the tips brought to their attention. According to an interview given in November 2011 by the head of the Guangdong CDI (who himself was arrested in 2014 for corruption), less than 5 percent of all tips were from individuals who provided their identities.[33] In the cutthroat political environment inside the CCP hierarchy, separating noise from signals is an almost impossible task.

An even more striking indication of why the risks of detection for engaging in *maiguan maiguan* are unusually low is that most of the officials engaging in these activities, at least in our sample, were uncovered accidentally. They were discovered to have sold official appointments and promotions while being investigated for other corrupt activities. One such example is Li Tiecheng, who had sold more than one hundred official positions without detection but was caught in 2000 after the authorities arrested a private businessman for fraud. The private businessman confessed that he had bribed Li for favors, thus triggering an official investigation that quickly uncovered Li's trade in *maiguan maiguan*.[34] Another case in point is Ma De, the party boss of Suihua City and a notorious seller of offices. Ma's crime of *maiguan maiguan* was accidentally uncovered when a private businessman was investigated for bribing a bank official in 2001. The authorities discovered that the private businessman had also bribed Ma to help him obtain a loan.[35] A third example is Chen Zhaofeng, a county party boss in Anhui who sold offices to 110 subordinates. He was accidentally uncovered in 2002 when the provincial discipline inspection committee acted on a tip that Chen had violated reimbursement rules and had received extra payment—a minor infraction—and confronted Chen to ask him to explain his actions.[36]

The case of Zhang Zhi'an is our final example. Zhang, who succeeded Zhang Huaqi, a county party secretary in Anhui who was imprisoned in 2004 for receiving bribes from ninety officials in return for appointments and promotions, engaged in the same trade. But his crime of *maiguan* was not exposed until he was discovered to be involved in one of the most infamous cover-ups in contemporary China. Zhang's county government built a huge office complex that resembled the U.S. Capitol in 2007. One local resident went to the higher-level authorities to report that Zhang's pet project had used up too much farmland. This resident was detained by Zhang's police department and mysteriously died in custody, an incident investigated by the *Chinese Youth Daily,* a leading national newspaper. The public outrage caused by the story, in turn, precipitated a formal investigation that led to the discovery of Zhang's other misdeeds.[37]

The acts of selling or buying offices can also be exposed as a result of confessions by officials detained for corruption unrelated to personnel matters. In order to gain leniency, such officials routinely confess selling or buying offices, thus revealing their partners in this collusive enterprise. This is how Han Guizhi, head of Heilongjiang's CCP organization department, was brought down in 2004. Ma De, who paid 800,000 yuan to Han to secure a promotion to become the party chief of Suihua City, confessed after he was detained in

2002. This, in turn, led to Han's arrest and the discovery that Han had also taken bribes from a large number of officials (including the president of the provincial high court and the provincial chief prosecutor).[38]

Market-Making and Pricing

In theory, the market for offices is relatively illiquid because the Chinese state and the CCP have regulations to limit abuse by local officials in personnel matters. For example, the party's rules on the length of tenure specify fixed terms of appointment, thus limiting the volume of trade. However, the liquidity of the market for these positions can be improved by party chiefs, who enjoy considerable discretion in personnel appointments inside the party, particularly at the county level and below. The market for prefecture-level officials and above has lower liquidity not merely because of the much smaller number of positions available but also because appointments to these positions are subject to tighter control. Prefecture-level officials are appointed by provincial party committees while provincial-level appointments and promotions are controlled by the Central Committee (technically through its Organization Department). In fact, inside the CCP hierarchy, a county party secretary is granted the most discretionary power in personnel matters despite his relatively junior status. The key to increasing liquidity in the market for official appointments and promotions is to artificially raise "turnover," equivalent to the trading volume in the stock market. A county party secretary typically creates a market for office by announcing large-scale personnel reshuffling, often several times during his tenure, under the pretense of picking the most qualified officials through a competitive process. Such reshuffling increases liquidity in the market for office. Among the cases examined in this study, county party secretaries who sold the largest number of appointments and promotions re-sorted to such artificial market-making. One party secretary partic-ularly successful in such market-making was Li Tiecheng, who sold more than one hundred appointments and promotions. During his six-year tenure as the party chief of a poor county in Jilin (1994–2000), Li made 840 personnel changes.[39] Zhang Huaqi, who was accused of selling ninety appointments and promotions, was another successful market-maker. As soon as he became the party chief of a poor county in Anhui in 1997, he convened the CCP standing committee of the county five times within a five-month period to reshuffle the county's officials. As a result, more than one hundred officials in the county's thirty-one townships and various agencies were removed, thus cre-ating desirable vacancies and demands from those seeking these positions.[40]

Even after the creation of this illicit market for offices, pricing is not always easy. Despite assertions in the Chinese press that party secre-taries (sellers) set explicit prices (amounts of bribes) for certain posi-tions, there is little hard evidence to support such allegations. One simple reason is obviously the risks of detection if a party secretary tries to maximize the income from selling a particularly desirable po-sition by setting an explicit price and even advertising it through word of mouth. The size of the market is also limited because poten-tial customers, however numerous, still constitute a relatively small minority of the local CCP members.

Yet, as we can see from our earlier analysis of the income gained by seven county party chiefs, the market for official appointments and promotions actually functions with unexpected efficiency. The standard deviation in prices paid for subcounty positions in seven cases was slightly less than the median price of 20,000 yuan, sug-gesting that the buyers did not overpay excessively and the sellers did not accept bribes that were too low. In all likelihood, the relative efficiency of the market for offices in a typical Chinese county is achieved through several channels. One possible advantage for purchasers in a county is that the small geographical size of the market allows the participants to acquire information about the approximate amount of money a party boss would deem as acceptable and about the value of the positions being sought. In a larger jurisdiction, such as a prefecture, obtaining such information is more difficult since the purchasers live in different counties. The relative inefficiency of the market for appointments and promotions in a prefecture is reflected in the greater differences in the median prices across the seven jurisdictions included in the sample (the standard deviation is twice the median price in all seven cases).

The relative efficiency of the market for offices in counties can also be due to the lower transaction costs in this market compared to those in the markets in prefectures and provinces. A county party chief is far more accessible than a prefecture party chief. In addition, due to the CCP's policy of "avoidance," an imperial legacy, the party appoints party chiefs to jurisdictions outside their hometowns. As a result, a prefecture party chief is more likely from another prefecture, while a county party boss is more likely from a different county. However, since a county party chief is from a different county in the *same* prefecture, access can be more easily arranged through friends, colleagues, and contacts that form the party chief's network. By contrast, a prefecture party boss from a different prefecture will be much more difficult to approach because his network is based in a different prefecture, a considerably bigger jurisdiction and, geographically, farther away. The same logic makes access to provincial- and national-level leaders even more difficult.

Another factor that helps improve the efficiency of this market is the culture of gift-giving. If we assume that the purchaser does not know the price he should pay for a particular position, he can take advantage of the gift-giving culture to discover the market-clearing price without overpaying. For instance, 83 percent of the 1.36 million yuan in bribes taken in by Xu Bo, the party chief of Yingshang County in Anhui convicted of selling offices and accepting commercial bribes in 2005, was given to him during holidays.[41] In our sample cases, the Chinese Spring Festival appears to be a favorite occasion for potential buyers to approach the seller and make partial payments. Other favored occasions are the Moon Festival and during hospital stays of the party chiefs.[42] According to Chinese custom, these occasions provide the perfect cover for such transactions since gift-giving allows an official seeking a desired position to offer a relatively small gift to the party chief. On these occasions, such gifts are not deemed inappropriate. The objective of offering such gifts is several-fold. Due to China's gift culture (in which the rejection of gifts is viewed as hurting the gift-giver's face), bribers reduce the risks that the party chief will reject, on the spot, their down payments, which are decent but not excessive amounts of money. This strategy also allows them greater flexibility and minimizes the risks of overpayment. If the party secretary agrees to the deal, usually through coded language, and delivers the promised appointments or promotions, the buyer typically follows up with another gift to express his gratitude. Implicitly, this payment is the final installment. If the party secretary does not deliver the promised appointment or promotion, the buyer will continue making partial payments, disguised as holiday gifts, as additional inducements. This exercise is repeated until the deal is closed.

There is evidence supporting this analysis in the cases included in our study: The number of times bribes are paid to a party secretary usually exceeds the number of individuals involved in these cases.

For example, Zhang Gaiping, a county party secretary in Shaanxi and the only female official included in our study, took bribes from twenty-eight subordinates in return for appointments and promotions during 2001–2005. Thirteen of them paid their bribes in two installments, two paid in three installments, and thirteen paid in one installment.[43] Wu Miao, director of the CCP organization department in a Hainan County, took bribes from nine subordinates during 2004–2009. Three of them made multiple payments; six made only one payment each.[44] Those who bribed Chen Shaoyong, a prefecture party chief in Fujian (2002–2005), also used installment payments to build their ties and, not coincidentally, avoid overpayment. According to the charges filed by the prosecution, nine of the fifteen subordinates who bribed him for office paid him multiple times (the average was five times).[45] There are two possible explanations for paying a party chief of Chen's status multiple bribes to secure a desired appointment. The first is that it takes more time and effort to gain access to a more senior official, thus requiring more gifts. The other explanation is the lengthy process of price-discovery in the market for an office at the prefecture level. This necessitates multiple payments until the market-clearing price is reached.

A more intriguing question is whether the prices paid for appointments and promotions actually reflect the value of these positions in terms of generating potential income. We do not have sufficient data to give a definitive answer. But based on the sample cases here, it seems that they do. Li Gang, a county party boss in Heilongjiang caught in 2002, gave positions with a greater potential for generating corruption income to those who had paid more. The highest amount received by Li was 110,000 yuan (more than five times the median price for a position in a county). Li appointed the buyer the head of the county's finance bureau, a much sought-after position because it allocates government funds. The person who paid the third-largest amount—80,000 yuan—was made the general manager of a county-owned chemical factory, a position that would allow him to receive bribes and kickbacks from those seeking business with the SOE. By comparison, the vice chairwoman of the county's women's association paid Li only 10,000 yuan for her position.[46]

The amount of bribes collected by Zhang Gaiping also reflected the relationship between the price of a position being traded and its potential for generating corruption income. One deputy secretary of the district's discipline inspection committee paid an out-sized 380,000-yuan bribe to get a position as the district's education bureau chief in 2004. Such a position can generate huge returns because education bureau chiefs have enormous power in deciding contracts for supplies, textbooks, construction, maintenance, and in appointing school principals. The two individuals who each paid 50,000 yuan, the second-largest amount in Zhang's case, were appointed, respectively, assistant county magistrate and deputy director of an office in charge of forced relocations for the construction of a superhighway. The first position would give the briber a significant advantage in terms of becoming a deputy county magistrate, a crucial step toward future promotions. The second position also had rich potential for extracting bribes from contractors requiring government assistance to evict farmers and residents. The person who paid the third-largest amount—48,000 yuan—was made the district's finance bureau chief. In contrast, those who paid Zhang less received positions unlikely to generate large returns. The person who paid her only 5,000 yuan, one-quarter of the median price, was appointed head of the district's quarantine station. Another individual who paid her 10,000 yuan was given the position of director of a neighborhood office.[47]

Whatever the prices paid by those seeking positions in local governments, their potential returns are usually high. This is particularly true of a purchaser who is able to secure a position with high potential for corruption income. In the case of Li Gang, he paid 500,000 yuan for his two positions, first as the county magistrate in 1998 and then as the county party secretary in 2000. From these initial investments, Li generated 2.2 million yuan in total corruption income, more than four times his bribes.[48] In Maoming, a Guangdong city where *maiguan maiguan* was endemic under Luo Yinguo and his predecessor, Zhou Zhenhong, during 2002–2011, a local official, Zhu Yuying, paid Zhou a total of 340,000 yuan for two promotions between 2003 and 2008. The total corruption income Zhu received while in his two purchased positions was over 13 million yuan, representing a thirty-eight-fold return on his investment.[49] In 2007 Yang Qiang, a local police chief, paid 300,000 Hong Kong dollars to Ni Junxiong, the Maoming police chief, for a promotion. When he was caught in 2011, Yang's total corruption income had reached 13.3 million yuan, including 3.45 million in bribes he took from junior officers seeking promotions.[50]

The last puzzle about pricing in *maiguan maiguan* is whether the buyer should explicitly bid for a position at the outset of the process or should refrain from identifying the position he is seeking even as he starts making installment payments. Purchasers have two options. The first is to give the party chief a large bribe and ask for a specific appointment directly and explicitly. The second is to pay the party chief a respectable, but not overly large, bribe (disguised as a holiday gift) first and then ask for a specific position later. Each approach has advantages and disadvantages. The first option entails a higher risk of rejection and overpayment, but it can deliver faster results and prevent the loss of the desired position to other bidders. The second option lowers the risk of outright rejection and overpayment, but it requires patience and raises the risk of losing the desired position to other bidders. In our sample, the purchasers used both approaches, perhaps indicating that another variable—how well the purchaser knows the seller—may be at play. Logically, buyers who know the seller well enough prefer the second option to minimize overpayment, while those who know the seller less well may want to make an offer so attractive that the seller will accept it on the spot. Therefore, it is reasonable to argue that the market for office has two tiers. In the first tier, those who know the sellers well can leverage their personal friendship and gain a steep discount, while second-tier buyers who do not know the seller well enough must pay fully or overpay for their purchases.

Income Maximizing Strategy and Financing

Party chiefs have two strategies to maximize income from the selling of offices. One is to sell a large number of offices for relatively small amounts per position. Our analysis shows that county party secretaries, particularly in poor regions where their underlings have fewer resources to fund their purchases, favor this low-price, high-volume strategy. Obviously, this strategy carries greater risks of detection due to the larger number of involved transactions. The other strategy is to sell a small number of highly desirable positions to a few officials at premium prices. Officials holding ranks at the prefecture level or higher, such as those in our sample, follow this strategy. Evidently, the positions they can sell are more important and have greater potential to generate higher returns, thus justifying premium pricing. The purchasers of these positions are also more highly placed officials (some of them are county-level party secretaries who are sellers of offices in their own jurisdictions). They have the ability to pay higher prices. An added advantage of this strategy is a reduction in detection risks because fewer deals are involved.

What this analysis shows is that this particular form of collusion among elites is highly destructive and predatory. Even though the income from this practice contributes a relatively small share to the total corruption income of the sellers, such collusion produces a self-reinforcing dynamic because purchasers eager to recover or seek gains from their investments (purchased offices) are incentivized to engage in corrupt acts themselves. Inevitably, the prices of these positions tend to rise quickly because the attractive returns gained by those who have purchased their offices will encourage more purchasers to enter the market and offer more money to the sellers. Should they be successful, they will attempt to recover their costs by engaging in even more egregious acts of corruption. This is one of the underlying dynamics driving corruption in China.

The last puzzle about the political economy of *maiguan maiguan* is the financing of these transactions. Local officials in China are normally paid low salaries and would have difficulty financing their bids, especially for those desirable and more costly positions. Our case studies reveal that most such transactions are not funded by the personal savings of the purchasers. Instead, the funds come from three sources.

The primary source is embezzled public funds. Typically, lower-level officials who bribe their superiors for an office use fake receipts for business expenses to get reimbursed. Of the more than one hundred individuals who bribed Zhang Huaqi, a county party chief in Anhui arrested in 2003, 700,000 yuan was actually reimbursed by thirty-three different "units" as entertainment expenses (fake receipts were used to obtain reimbursement of 90,000 yuan).[51] Many officials who bribed Yang Jianguo, a county party chief in Anhui sentenced to life in 2006, also used fake receipts to be reimbursed. Most of the funds used by officials who bribed Zheng Yuansheng, a county party chief in Guangxi and an earlier practitioner of the trade during his tenure (2001–2005), were misappropriated public funds.[52] Of the thirty-three officials who bribed Xie Lianzhang, a county party chief in Yanling in Henan during the period of 2001–2013, twenty-six used fake receipts to reimburse themselves the full amounts of the bribes.[53] When Kong Qingguo, a township party chief who bribed Liu Zhenjian, the party boss of Heze, Shandong, for a promotion in 2009, he used stolen public funds as well, including 60,000 yuan in fines collected from the enforcement of the family-planning policy.[54]

The second source is savings from corruption income. Officials who purchase public offices are more likely to be corrupt and to have accumulated savings from their prior corrupt activities. Such savings give them a financial edge and enable them to fund their purchases of the desired offices. Li Gang, a county party boss in Heilongjiang, is a typical example. He financed his initial purchase of the position of county magistrate with 100,000 yuan in 1998. This position enabled him to collect bribes, which helped finance his most expensive investment—300,000 yuan—paid to Ma De, the prefecture party boss, for promotion to the position of county party secretary in 2000.[55]

The third source of funding is money raised from private sources, most often businessmen. Aspiring officials will approach a private business and ask for a "loan" to finance their purchases. One such individual, who bought his position as a county magistrate in Heilongjiang from Ma De for 500,000 yuan in 2001, financed his purchase partly with a "loan" of 200,000 yuan from a private businessman (the bulk of the balance was borrowed from other private businessmen). The person who overpaid for the position of the director of the education bureau in Shangzhou District in Shaanxi in 2004 funded his purchase (380,000 yuan) with 330,000 yuan in loans from five individuals (one of whom illegally loaned him public funds).[56] For private businessmen, extending credit to officials seeking higher offices makes good sense because these officials are likely to repay the "loans" with much more lucrative favors once they get their desired positions. In the mega scandal in Maoming in Guangdong, a wealthy businessman bribed two successive city party chiefs during 2002–2011 to promote three local officials, including a police chief, thus effectively financing their bribes. Two other businessmen each gave 100,000 Hong Kong dollars to Yang Guangliang, the executive deputy mayor, to help make him a more competitive candidate for mayor in 2007.[57]

Competition and Commitment

The sample cases provide some tantalizing clues about the degree of competition in the market for offices in local jurisdictions and the commitments by the sellers to fulfill their promise of delivering the desired appointments to the buyers. Specific reference to competition for the same office occurred in only two of the fifty cases identified for this study. In both cases, the buyer paying the largest bribe received the appointment. Liu Xiutian, the party boss of Pingshan County in Hebei, faced such a problem in 2000. Several individuals coveted the position of director of the bureau of water management. Liu appointed the person who gave him the biggest bribe.[58] Zhang Gaiping, a local party chief in Shaanxi, reportedly also refunded five or six seekers of the position of director of her district's education bureau after she awarded the spot to the highest bidder in 2004.[59]

A related question about this market is the seller's commitment to fulfilling his part of the bargain. The sample cases in this chapter do not contain specific or detailed examples in which the seller pocketed the bribe and failed to deliver the desired appointment. In one case, a deputy director of the county's justice bureau approached Zhang Guiyi, a county party chief in Anhui, to express his desire to be made the head of the education bureau and he paid Zhang a total of 32,000 yuan in 2003. But Zhang was unable to appoint the person and subsequently gave him a partial refund of 20,000 yuan.[60]

It is plausible to argue that the lack of reference to instances in which the seller fails to deliver after taking the bribe is the result of the strong incentive on the part of the seller to maintain his credibility in a niche market. If a seller consistently cheats his customers in the market for offices, he runs the risk of losing them altogether because his victims will spread the information and warn away potential bribers. To be sure, competition for the most desirable positions in these markets is fierce, but not necessarily unmanageable, as long as the seller follows the principle of awarding the highest bidders their desired positions. As for the losers, they do not necessarily waste their investments. The party chiefs may offer them other positions that may not be as desirable as the ones they originally sought but will nevertheless represent a promotion.

The analysis of the fifty sample cases of *maiguan maiguan* illustrates the micro-level dynamics of late-stage regime decay in contemporary China. Despite its outward resilience, the CCP's organizational integrity has fallen prey to powerful forces unleashed by the combination of the overconcentration of the power of local party chiefs, the inherent difficulties in detecting collusion among local elites, and the irresistible profitability of corruption in an environment where party officials are routinely tempted with huge bribes from private businessmen. To be sure, mainly out of concern about losing its own monopoly over personnel appointments, the CCP's top leadership has repeatedly cracked down on *maiguan maiguan,* but without success. In light of the underlying political economy of *maiguan maiguan,* such failure is predictable. In this illicit market, sellers know how to create demand, increase liquidity, and determine prices, while buyers have learned how to bid and finance their bids. Because of the low detection risks, these transactions have high reward–risk ratios. Those who successfully purchase their desired appointments or promotions can expect quick and handsome returns.

Even more worrisome for the CCP's central authorities is the destruction of norms caused by *maiguan maiguan.* Once the taboo against awarding official positions was broken by small gifts, as in the early 1990s, the normative defense against such collusion became no match for the dynamics of competitive bidding or a political "arms race," with seekers of government positions escalating their bidding to secure their desired appointments. Gradually, this market will follow the perverse but familiar logic of "bad money driving out good money." Honest officials refusing to pay bribes will be denied the advantages gained by their less upright colleagues. The less scrupulous but more ambitious climbers of the CCP hierarchy have systematic advantages in the race to the top. They are likely to have accumulated a war chest through prior corruption to make an attractive opening bid to local party chiefs. They can further supplement such purchases with embezzled public funds. For really high-priced deals, they can obtain financing from helpful private businessmen. Over time, in jurisdictions where public offices are traded mostly on this illicit market, only the most corrupt officials can get ahead. Obviously, in these jurisdictions corruption initially generated from *maiguan maiguan* will spawn corruption in commercial activities, which will deliver much greater profitability and provide the economic returns sought by the purchasers of government office.

In the more extreme cases, the self-reinforcing dynamics of *mai-guan maiguan* help create local mafia states—jurisdictions where most senior officials are corrupt and, once they are removed, they are succeeded by officials who soon succumb to corruption as well. In Chapter 7 we will provide several representative cases in this category. These cases should further confirm our suspicion that, to the extent that collusion among political elites destroys the institutional integrity of a Leninist regime, the decay of the CCP may have reached an advanced stage.

4

Cronyism in Action:
Collusion between Officials and Businessmen

> Our officials have turned the areas they oversee into private
> domains. . . . *Guanxi* networks of all kinds have grown ever
> tighter and denser.
>
> —Xi Jinping, January 14, 2014

CHINESE POLITICAL ELITES engaged in collusion with private businessmen would have no difficulty understanding Willie Hutton, who reportedly said that he robbed banks because that was where the money was. By forming dense networks of connections (*guanxi*) with private businessmen, officials can generate lucrative profits by, as Xi points out, turning the public authority entrusted to them into instruments to seek private gains. The economics of collusion between political elites and private businessmen in a one-party regime is straightforward. The political power controlled by the officials in a one-party state can be converted into immense wealth quickly. However, this conversion is difficult to execute without colluding partners in the private sector. Most Chinese officials who have the ability to seize state-owned assets have also incurred considerable sunken costs—their lifelong investments in their political careers in the party. Abandoning a rewarding position inside the regime is unattractive. That is why family members of these officials, but not the officials themselves, are in the private sector. Chinese political elites have another disadvantage in converting monopolistic political power into economic wealth themselves: their lack of the entrepreneurial skills needed to realize the full market value of the state-owned assets under their control. Even for those who may have such skills, openly giving up a successful and promising political career carries enormous risks. From their own experience they will understand that private wealth unconnected with political power is inherently insecure under a predatory regime. More importantly, by exiting, they may also provoke the wrath of the party for displaying disloyalty. That is perhaps why only relatively few officials have opted for *xiahai*, or jumping into the sea of commerce. A keyword search for "mayor jumping into the sea" in the China Knowledge Resource Integrated Database (cnki.net) yields twenty references for the period 1994–2015. A search for "county or city party secretary jumping into the sea" returns only one reference. A close examination of these references shows that in the twenty-one-year period, a grand total of ten officials, seven prefecture-level and three county-level, have quit their government positions to become senior executives in private companies or to lead buyouts of bankrupt SOEs (in two cases).[1]

Therefore, the optimal solution for officials eager to cash in on their political power is to set up their immediate family members in business or to find partners in the private sector. This strategy allows these officials to remain inside the regime and at the same time amass wealth through the use of their power. For private businessmen, this partnership is also attractive because it can unlock the enormous value embedded in the state-owned assets under the control of these officials. Of course, collusion with Chinese officials may lead to the loss of both fortune and freedom if their criminal activities are discovered. But on balance these risks are worth taking because, for private entrepreneurs, the near certainty of windfall profits from collusion far outweighs the downside of detection.

Such compelling logic has made the marriage between power and money the defining characteristic of crony capitalism in China. In practice, this union manifests itself in the collusion between government officials who control the allocation and disposal of valuable state-owned assets and economic resources and private businessmen trying to seize these assets. Although aggregate official data on corruption do not provide much information on collusion between officials and private businessmen, it is reasonable to hypothesize that these activities make up a very large share of all uncovered corruption cases because collusive corruption accounts for roughly 40 percent of corruption cases in some localities and also because commercial bribery, classified as one of the "crimes committed through the use of one's office" (*zhiwu fanzui*) when the recipient is a public official, accounts for a large share of corruption cases. The work report of China's chief prosecutor in 2013 revealed that during the five-year period of 2008–2012, the Chinese procuratorate filed 165,787 cases of *zhiwu fanzui* involving 218,639 individuals, including 13,173 officials holding the rank of county or *chu* (department) and above (950, and thirty of them were, respectively, bureau- or prefecture-level officials or provincial or ministerial officials).[2] Based on annual data provided by the Chinese Supreme Procuratorate, close to 60 percent of the cases in the category of *zhiwu fanzui* are "major" embezzlement and bribery cases involving more than 50,000 yuan. For instance, in 2011, the Chinese government prosecuted 32,567 cases classified as "crimes committed through the use of one's office." Commercial bribery cases in "natural resources exploitation, trade in property rights, and government procurement" accounted for 10,542 cases. Of the 32,567 cases of "crimes committed through the use of one's office," 18,464 (57 percent) were labeled "major cases of embezzlement and bribery."[3]

Independent academic research also confirms that a very large portion of corruption cases falls into the category of commercial transactions that involve interactions between officials and private businessmen. According to one study that examined 2,802 corruption cases reported from 2000 to 2009 in *Jiancha Ribao* (Prosecutorial Daily), a publication of the Supreme People's Procuratorate, 1,583 (56 percent) of them fell into four areas: government procurement and construction contracts (731); land, real estate, and urban planning (307); finance, investment, loans, allocations, and payment of funds (298); administration of commerce, enterprise management, and restructuring of enterprise ownership (247).[4] Another study of 142 party chiefs, mayors, heads of municipal people's congresses, and chairmen of municipal people's political consultative conferences who were prosecuted for corruption between 1983 and 2012 shows that 115 of them were involved in illegal activities in sectors such as approvals of land transfers, real estate development, loans for enterprises, tax reductions, stock market listings, restructuring of SOEs, construction contracts, and approvals of mining rights.[5] Research on corruption in the real estate sector in China also indicates that the immense profitability generated by rent-seeking, unclear property rights, and segmented regulatory authority in this sector attracts collusion between officials and developers.[6]

Key Findings

A summary of the key characteristics of the fifty cases (Table A.2 in the Appendix) provides useful clues about the collusion between officials and private businessmen. In terms of the seniority of the officials involved, seven chief perpetrators were provincial-level officials, twenty-five occupied prefecture-level positions, fourteen were county-level officials, and four held subcounty positions. Compared with the cases of *maiguan maiguan* we saw earlier, the chief perpetrators included in the sample cases in this chapter are more senior (60 percent of the officials in this sample held prefecture- or provincial-level positions, compared with 40 percent of the officials in Chapter 3). The nature of the main corrupt activities—commercial bribery—and the higher ranks of the chief perpetrators likely account for the larger amounts of total corruption income generated by officials who collude with businessmen than officials who sell government offices (even though income from *maiguan* made up less than one-half of their total corruption income in most cases). As for geographic representation, the chief perpetrators were from twenty-one provinces, an indicator that collusion between officials and businessmen is a national phenomenon.

In terms of total corruption income, the median total corruption income gained by the chief perpetrators in these cases is 9.5 million yuan, almost 50 percent higher than that reaped by the chief perpetrators in collusion among SOE executives (Table A.3). The mean corruption income of officials selling offices is 3.8 million yuan, about 40 percent of the corruption income gained by those colluding with businessmen. The median number of officials involved or implicated in the fifty cases here is eleven, the same as for the cases of colluding SOE executives but much lower than the median number of positions sold (twenty-seven) by officials in the fifty cases in Chapter 3. The smaller number of individuals involved or implicated in collusion with businessmen again likely reflects the higher status and greater power held by the chief perpetrators represented here. More senior officials can simply order their subordinates to grant favors to private businessmen, instead of directly recruiting them into the collusive ring.

One striking aspect of the data provided in Table A.2 is the long duration of the corruption and the high probability of promotion for the chief perpetrators even when they are engaged in corrupt activities. The median duration of corruption (between the onset of corrupt activities and arrest) in these cases is eight years, one year more than that in cases of selling offices and collusion among SOE executives (seven years). Among the fifty chief perpetrators who colluded with private businessmen, forty-two received promotions while committing their crimes. The relatively long duration of corruption and the high probability of promotion (84 percent) indicate that the detection risk is low. Also notable is the fact that officials who collude with private businessmen, as we theorize, engage in multiline businesses that include *maiguan maiguan* as a sideline and, more crucially, as a means of building a collusive network. Of the fifty chief perpetrators, thirty-four (or 68 percent) were explicitly charged with *maiguan maiguan*. Based on the sectors in which collusion between officials and private businessmen occurs, our sample confirms our hypothesis that contested property rights and multiagency approvals necessitate collusion, both within the bureaucracy and between the bureaucracy and private businessmen. In the fifty cases, collusion is concentrated in four sectors: real estate and land transactions (in thirty-four cases); infrastructure and construction (twenty-eight); mining (thirteen); and SOE restructuring (ten).[7] These four sectors are generally considered the most corruption-prone because of the enormous profits that can be realized through collusion. In the case of land, real estate transactions, mining rights, and SOE restructuring, the profitability comes chiefly from the severe undervaluation of the underlying assets. In infrastructure and construction, rents are embedded in the large size of the contracts, cost inflation, and substandard quality.

In terms of the last positions they occupied before they were arrested, a large number (eighteen) were county- and prefecture-level party secretaries, the most powerful politicians in these jurisdictions, and eight were mayors and executive deputy mayors, officials directly in charge of local economic affairs.[8] Local party chiefs are well positioned to capitalize on their near-dictatorial power, as explained by our model of vertical collusion. Since they wield virtually unchallenged clout in the appointment of key officials in local administrative agencies (in many cases they give these appointments to those who bribe them, thus gaining their loyalty), they can easily ask these officials to help private businessmen who have bribed them. The only official who has direct administrative responsibility in local.government is the mayor or county magistrate. Although they have the ability to collude with lower-level officials in local administrative agencies, they are less able to compel compliance from their subordinates because they do not control personnel appointments. This is the principal reason why the majority of chief perpetrators in our study of collusion among officials and between officials and private businessmen are party chiefs in counties and prefectures.

The data in Table A.2 also confirm the overall positive correlation between seniority inside the CCP and total corruption income: Officials with higher ranks gain greater corruption income than those with lower ranks.[9] Of the twenty-five individuals whose total corruption income was above the median (9.5 million yuan), six were provincial-level officials, fourteen were prefecture-level officials, and five were county-level officials.[10] Two factors account for this disparity. More senior officials have longer durations of corruption during which they can generate more illicit income. In addition, they wield more power, allowing them to trade bigger favors for larger bribes. However, lower-level officials who can determine the disposal of valuable state-owned assets, such as land, mines, and SOEs, also have considerable capacity to raise their corruption income. Of the five county-level officials who gained above-median total corruption income, four received outsized bribes for giving state-owned assets and infrastructure contracts to private businessmen. But officials who have gained less total corruption income may have one consolation prize: lighter punishment. As usual, the severity of punishment for officials caught for corruption involving private businessmen depends mostly on the total amount of corruption income. Of the twenty-five chief perpetrators whose corruption income was at or below the median of 9.5 million yuan, only six (24 percent) received life, suspended death, or death sentences. By contrast, of the twenty-five officials with above-median corruption income, we know the sentences for twenty-two. Eighteen of them were given life, suspended death, or death sentences. What is noteworthy about the punishment of corrupt officials is that only a small number of them were actually executed because suspended death sentences are always commuted to life sentences. In our sample, only four officials, all of whom committed particularly egregious crimes, even by the standards of the CCP, received the death penalty.

Patterns of Collusion

As we noted earlier, while many corruption cases are explicitly identified as *wo'an* or *chuan'an,* the exact mechanisms of collusion remain a mystery. In this section, we probe the mechanisms of collusion between local officials and private businessmen. Revealing details of the fifty sample cases allow us to reconstruct three patterns of collusion.

Vertical Collusion

Whether explicit and direct collusion is required depends largely on the success with which a private businessman buys off the most powerful official in his jurisdiction, the party chief in nearly all cases. If he does, the party chief can usually use his enormous—and often coercive—power to help the businessman obtain his objectives. In such cases, the private businessman in question does not need to separately bribe and coordinate veto-wielding bureaucrats in various government agencies because the party chief performs, on his behalf, the critical coordination function. A businessman tends to pay the local party chief considerably larger bribes than he pays to lower-level officials in the functional bureaucracies because he is also buying his role in coordination. In effect, he is paying a lump sum for a bundle of services performed by the local party chief, with a high degree of confidence that the latter will deliver. From the perspective of the businessman, buying off the local party chief, even for a high premium, may be the optimal strategy.

For local party chiefs, intervening on behalf of businessmen is not risk-free. Procedurally, officials are not supposed to interfere in administrative decisions made by lower-level agencies or on issues outside their assigned portfolios, which, for local party bosses, do not include economic matters. However, party chiefs can sometimes justify such interference either as support for a project that can boost local economic growth or as "recommendations" or "advice" even though the real intent often arouses suspicion among cynical subordinates, and the consequences of noncompliance are mutually understood. In such cases, subordinate officials who comply typically suspect that their superiors must have accepted bribes from the private businessmen involved. Yet they violate rules or procedures to carry out their superiors' orders due to the superiors' explicit or implicit coercion.

A typical example in our sample is Xie Lianzhang, who served as a county party chief in Yanling, Henan; he received 1.86 million yuan from eighteen businessmen between 2001 and 2006. Xie would call subordinates and order them to give these businessmen land leases, bank loans, and zoning approvals.[11] Li Dalun, the domineering party chief of Chenzhou in Hunan during 1999–2006, also helped many businessmen obtain desirable mining, real estate, and construction deals in this way. As alleged by his sentencing document, Li would, at the behest of businessmen seeking favors, call or meet in person with the heads of the city's departments (some of whom had purchased their offices from Li or were engaged in their own corrupt activities). He always got his way.[12] Wang Huaizhong, who committed most of his crimes while he was the party chief of Fuyang in Anhui from 1995 to 1999, took such coercive tactics to a higher level. Wang routinely gave direct orders to the heads of the city's various bureaus to help private businessmen who had bribed him. He also applied a far more efficient tactic to achieve a coordinated outcome. When a favor to a businessman involved receiving approval from several agencies, he would convene a *xietiaohui,* or a coordination meeting that the directors of all the relevant agencies were required to attend. Invariably, Wang was able to impose his will on his subordinates at these meetings.[13] Liu Jiakun, a party chief in a county in Fuyang during 2007–2012, deployed the same tactic to help his businessmen friends gain land and contracts in his county, as detailed in his sentencing document.[14]

Though senior local officials, CCP chiefs in particular, may abuse their power to force subordinates to help their cronies in the private sector, this tactic can be risky and requires constant follow-up to ensure compliance. A better solution is to have loyal and willing accomplices occupying key bureaucratic positions who will eagerly and reliably carry out their orders. In other words, their collusion with businessmen will be less risky and labor intensive if they have a network of allies. The spread of *maiguan maiguan* has greatly helped senior local officials construct such networks because junior officials who have bribed them for their posts are not only more loyal and reliable, but also more likely to be greedy and corrupt. They can count on their help in delivering on their promises to private businessmen. Significantly, of the fifty chief perpetrators in this sample, thirty-four (68 percent) engaged in selling offices, thus providing a crucial piece of evidence that the networks built through *maiguan maiguan* facilitate the collusion between officials and businessmen.

One such example in our sample is Tan Dengyao, the mayor of Dongfang in Hainan. In 2009, a private businessman trying to sell the land he had purchased at a low price back to the city for a huge profit approached Tan for help (and later gave him a bribe of 2.5 million yuan). Tan then asked the head of the city's transportation bureau, who had bribed him before, to assist the businessman. The transportation chief obliged. In addition, another accomplice in this deal, the head of the city's development corporation, who was responsible for selecting the lot to be purchased for the city's land reserve, had also bribed the mayor for his own promotion. The head of the city's finance bureau, which made the payment to the businessman for the purchase of the land, had similarly bribed the mayor to get his job.[15] Liu Zhuozhi, a former deputy governor of Inner Mongolia, took 420,000 yuan and $30,000 from Niu Zhimei, a local official, in return for appointing him the party chief of a county-level city in 2004. In subsequent years, Liu repeatedly asked Niu to help a businessman who had given Liu 460,000 yuan and $20,000 in

bribes.[16] Quan Junliang, who as a county party chief helped a businessman purchase a state-owned iron ore mine at 500 million yuan
below its fair market value in 2010, was assisted in his criminal act by
the director of the county bureau of land resources, who had bribed
Quan with 33,000 yuan in cash to obtain his position.[17] Yang Yueguo,
the party chief of Ruili in Yunnan, specialized in assisting real estate
developers gain highly desired land plots. He also had an indispensable accomplice, the director of the city's bureau of land resources,
who had paid him 400,000 yuan for the position (the director himself took 2.28 million yuan in bribes from real estate developers between 2009 and 2013).[18] In Maoming in Guangdong, the party chief,
Zhou Zhenhong, took bribes from officials whom he appointed to
many of the city's most important positions, such as the executive
vice mayor, two vice mayors, propaganda chief, and police chief (all
of them were arrested for corruption). This corruption network almost certainly enabled Zhou to help many of his business friends in
a wide range of shady deals during his tenure (2001–2007).[19]

Outsider–Insider Collusion

In outsider–insider collusion, private entrepreneurs seeking undervalued assets nominally owned by the state or large contracts act as
indispensable coordinators in collusion among officials in multiple
government agencies. Without the coordination provided by private
entrepreneurs, collusion among officials would be significantly
more difficult. In the case of collusion with guidance from a private
businessman, the latter separately approaches officials in the agencies
that have approval authority over his desired transactions and reas-
sures them, explicitly or implicitly, that he has bribed or gained a
promise of assistance from other key officials. Such knowledge and
reassurance make it more likely that an official who has the power to

approve one aspect of the desired transaction will accept the bribes offered. If his colleagues in other agencies are also on the take, he will have fewer concerns about detection and more confidence that the transaction desired by the businessman will be approved.

One such example is the private businessman who tried to acquire a power station owned by a local government in Sichuan during 2002–2004. He delivered 100,000 yuan in an envelope to the county magistrate and reassured him that the county party chief "had been taken care of."[20] Zhu Siyi, a coal tycoon in Guangdong, used the same tactic. Between 2002 and 2008, he personally bribed all the key executives, including the chairman of the board of a state-owned steel mill, to ensure that the mill would purchase the coal produced by his company.[21] In a scandal in Nanchong City in Sichuan, a real estate developer first offered equity stakes worth 4 million yuan in 1999 to the city's head of administration of industry and commerce if he could deliver the development rights for a large real estate project to the developer. Then he bribed the local official in charge of the real estate project, the party chief of the district where the project was located, and the two managers of a cinema that sat on the land on which the project was to be built. To ensure that the designated project, which violated the city's building codes, would receive approval, the developer bribed the head of the city's construction bureau as well as the head of the urban planning bureau.[22]

Wang Chuncheng, a coal baron from Liaoning, wanted to build a 496-kilometer railway that could connect his mega coal mines in Inner Mongolia to the coal-fired power plants in Liaoning. In 2005, to obtain approval for the difficult and costly project, he paid 600,000 yuan to a deputy party chief of the prefecture where his mine was located, and $180,000 to a deputy governor of Inner Mongolia (in seven installments during 2006–2010). Support from the two officials helped Wang's project receive approval from the National Development and Reform Commission in 2007.[23] In Nandan County in Guangxi, private mine operators paid millions of yuan to the local party chief, county magistrate, two deputy party secretaries, a deputy county magistrate, and other local officials to allow them to operate illegally and to encroach on state-owned mineral resources. When a mining disaster killed eighty-one miners in 2001, the local party chief, Wan Ruizhong, who himself had received 3.21 million yuan in bribes, colluded with some of these officials and agreed to cover up the accident. Wan's role in the cover-up, rather than his greed, most likely earned him a rare death penalty for disgraced officials.[24]

Collusion among Insiders

Direct and explicit collusion among officials who act to benefit businessmen is a common occurrence in our sample. This pattern of collusion among insiders takes place when participants have more or less equal political status or executive power or when the disparity between their status and power is relatively modest. If the lead culprit is a senior official who has dependable loyalists or personal friends positioned in key government agencies, collusion is easier and simpler. Whenever the chief culprit approaches such subordinate officials for their help to facilitate his illegal activities, these individuals usually view compliance with their superior's wishes as an opportunity to curry favor with him or to deepen their friendship. Under these circumstances, subordinate officials are, for the most part, willing accomplices.

One such example is the mega scandal that implicated nearly all the senior officials in the city of Chenzhou in Hunan in 2006. A private developer approached a deputy mayor, Lei Liyuan, and suggested that they recruit the head of the city's housing fund into a scheme to use the city's housing reserve fund to finance a real estate project. Lei, whose portfolio gave him oversight of the housing fund, then called the official into his office and, along with the developer, devised a plan that illegally lent the money to the private developer for his project.[25] Another example that illustrates such collusion is a case in the city of Shaoxing, a prefecture-level city in Zhejiang. The mayor and his protégé, a vice mayor, together forced through a municipal government decision in 2000 that allowed a local developer to acquire a plot of land at a reduced price even though his competition offered 32 million yuan more. The vice mayor took 3.25 million yuan in bribes from the developer.[26] In 1998, the executive deputy mayor of Shenyang, Ma Xiangdong, conspired with the director of the municipal finance bureau and the director of the municipal construction committee to embezzle $120,000 in city funds, which they shared equally. In the previous year, Ma and the head of the municipal construction committee had also extracted a $500,000 bribe from a real estate developer whom they exempted from a 12 million yuan city levy. The bribe funded the duo's gambling binges in Macau.[27]

The scandal in Pinghu City in Zhejiang started when the owner of one of the city's largest private companies learned of a large land reclamation project the city was about to launch in 2004. Eager to get part of the project, the chairman and the general manager of the firm had dinner with two key officials in charge of the project, the head of the city's water resources bureau and the vice mayor of the city, who was the head of the special agency set up to oversee the project. At the dinner they drew up a plan to make the company a subcontractor for the project. In return, the company would give the two officials 8 percent of the profits (10 million yuan) from the deal. In a separate real estate development, the two businessmen also conspired with the two officials to get a piece of land at a price that was about 15 percent below the minimum reserve price initially set by the city. The reward for the two officials was 6 million yuan, which represented 20 percent of the profits of the project.[28]

The example below shows that, on occasion, officials involved in collusion with private businessmen try to set up rules to reduce conflict among officials who have received competing bribes from rival businessmen. In this particular case, which sent three deputy directors of the Hunan Transportation Department and seventeen of their colleagues to jail in 2014, officials who had taken bribes from some businessmen could not deliver the promised highway construction contracts because other businessmen had bribed other, more senior officials. As a result, one deputy director of the department drew up a rule for his subordinates: His superiors' directives to help businessmen to receive contracts overrode his own; when a project manager received competing directives from his superiors, it was his job to coordinate and settle the problem; at least one-quarter to one-third of the length of a major project must be granted to bids that received no help from officials.[29] Such collusion designed to help favored businessmen gain contracts is also found in townships. Xiang Hongzu, a township party chief imprisoned in 2013 for corruption, routinely called his colleagues into his office to strategize how to give their town's infrastructure contracts to bidders who had bribed him.[30]

Given the culture of corruption that pervades the Chinese regime, implicit horizontal collusion can occur as a result of knowledge or awareness of corruption committed by one's colleagues. In this environment, officials in various government agencies who accept bribes from private businessmen usually suspect that the same private businessmen must also have bribed their colleagues in other departments in order to ensure completion of their desired transactions. In some instances, they are most likely to be aware of the close ties between the businessmen who have bribed them and their superiors or colleagues in other government departments. In other cases, the bribe-giver may provide oblique hints about assured cooperation from officials in other departments in order to alleviate concerns that may prevent his targets from agreeing to participate in the scheme. In other words, officials whose favors are being sought by private businessmen do not need to be informed explicitly about the collusion of others. Their direct knowledge, supposition, or suspicion about possible cooperation by other officials may give them the reassurance and confidence needed to take the offered bribes and give the favors sought by the businessmen. In these cases, knowledge and suspicion of other officials' corrupt acts arguably facilitate collusion. If the lead culprit's hunch is proved right and the targeted official accepts the bribe offered by the private businessman, an act of implicit collusion occurs.

In 2002, Tian Yufei, a county party chief in Sichuan, instructed the private businessman who had bribed him to also bribe the county magistrate, who was in charge of restructuring the SOEs in the county, because the magistrate was "greedy and several hundred thousand yuan should be enough" to take care of him.[31] In the illegal land transactions in Dongfang City in Hainan during 2007–2008, the city's deputy party chief, who was not directly involved in the transactions, became aware of the collusion among the officials who helped the private businessman to turn a windfall profit. He subsequently approached the official who helped the businessman and asked him to deliver a "request" to the businessman for a "loan" of 1 million yuan.[32] Mao Shaolie, a deputy mayor in Guangxi included in our cases, also knew of the corrupt acts of at least one of his colleagues. After Mao was arrested in 2012, he told investigators that his colleague, another deputy mayor, had accepted a bribe of 1.26 million yuan and had committed other crimes.[33] Yu Zhijun, a coconspirator in a land scandal in Qingdao that generated more than 19 million yuan in bribes between 2001 and 2003, also provided information on crimes committed by others to investigators after his arrest in 2003. Ma De, the infamous Suihua party chief who sold numerous offices and also pocketed commercial bribes, provided information about the corruption of his former colleague, mayor Wang Shenyi, immediately after his arrest in 2002.[34]

Crony Networks and Windfall Profits

Our sample cases provide some clues into the construction and maintenance of networks of corrupt officials and private businessmen. The first steps typically involve invitations to dinners at high-end restaurants, visits to foot-massage salons, and the presentation of small gifts and tokens of appreciation by private businessmen to officials they hope to befriend. A perfect example in our cases is Zhu Siyi, a coal tycoon in Guangdong who bribed a very large number of local officials. After his arrest in 2008, he described his proven system of currying favor with officials. The first step was "opening the door." Typically, he would give a prefecture-level official a small cash gift of 10,000–20,000 yuan just to see if he would take it. If he did, then Zhu would "deepen the friendship" by offering him a 20,000–30,000 yuan cash gift. If the official took it again, Zhu would proceed to the final step—"solidifying the relationship"—with 50,000 yuan in cash gifts during holidays (multiple times a year). By this stage, Zhu said he was sure that the prefecture-level official could be counted on for favors in the future.[35] During the Spring Festival in 2003, a businessman owning a construction company approached Peng Jinyu, a county CCP chief in Guangxi implicated in the corruption of his predecessor, with a gift of two smoked chickens and a package of dry goods. Peng took the gifts because they were part of the local custom and they did not seem excessively valuable. But when he unpacked the gift, he found an envelope containing 10,000 yuan in cash, which he pocketed after rationalizing it as a token of appreciation for a minor favor he had done for the businessman earlier. Their relationship began to flourish and, a year later, the businessman gave 100,000 yuan toward the purchase of a car for Peng's wife. This was followed by another gift of 100,000 yuan for an expensive set of furniture for Peng.[36]

Besides officials and their business cronies, the crony networks also have other key members—family members and mistresses of the officials. Evidence from our cases confirms the supporting role played by these members in collusive corruption. Typically, spouses accept or demand bribes on behalf of their husbands (in Chinese culture, even greedy officials need, from time to time, to maintain some respectful distance from the bribe-givers). Spouses are also the nominal owners of bank and brokerage accounts, real estate, and equity stakes in companies. In our sample, the spouses of Hong Jinzhou (the mayor of Kaili in Guizhou), Liu Zhuozhi (a deputy governor of Inner Mongolia), Wang Suyi (another provincial official in Inner Mongolia), Zhu Weiping (a district party chief in Jiangsu), and many others were intimately involved in the corrupt activities of their husbands.[37] A large number of corrupt officials also maintain mistresses, who often perform the same functions as their legal spouses. Zhao Xiali, the mistress of Liu Jiakun, a county party chief in Anhui, was the conduit through which several businessmen bribed her lover to gain land and contracts. Mao Shaolie, a deputy mayor in Guangxi, hid part of his corruption proceeds in his mistress's home. Yang Guangliang, the executive deputy mayor of Maoming City in

Guangdong, used his mistress as a front for trading stocks and buying real estate.[38] Kuang Li'er, a mistress of Zeng Jinchun, Chenzhou's notorious CCP secretary of discipline inspection, was the custodian of 16 million yuan of Zeng's loot.[39]

Most of the officials (typically age 60 and under) in the sample have children or close relatives who may be too young to go into business on their own. We find only two such cases. Shu Nanming, a local director of land resources in Jiangxi implicated in the case of Ye Jinyin (head of a land resources bureau and convicted of bribery in 2013), had a nephew who formed a land value assessment firm with the brother-in-law of a deputy director of his bureau that apparently used their contacts inside the bureau to get business.[40] The party chief of Ji'nan, Wang Min (who was detained in 2014), had a son-in-law in the real estate development business.[41] Children of more senior officials, especially those of provincial party chiefs and Politburo members (who are usually age 60 or over) are more likely to own private businesses that benefit significantly from their parents' power. The example of Zhou Bin, the forty-two-year-old son of Zhou Yongkang, the former member of the Standing Committee of the Politburo purged in late 2014, indicates that children of the most senior Chinese leaders have fully grown into their roles as red crony capitalists. Another case is Wen Yunsun, the son of former prime minister Wen Jiabao, who had amassed a huge fortune as a private equity investor. Liu Lefei, the elder son of Politburo Standing Committee member Liu Yunshan, is also a successful private equity investor.[42]

The siblings of the officials are more active members of these crony networks. The brother of Chen Liangyu, the former Shanghai party chief and Politburo member involved in the Shanghai Social Security Fund scandal, used his connections to purchase use rights to a plot of land in Shanghai and quickly flipped them into a profit of

118 million yuan in 2003. The siblings of Zhou Yongkang (and their spouses) also acquired significant private fortunes due to Zhou's position and power.[43] In our sample, Zhou Zhengkun, the former mayor of Chenzhou implicated in Li Dalun's corruption case, had two brothers in private business who were arrested before Zhou's downfall in 2007.[44] A younger brother of Hu Xing, a deputy mayor of Kunming (2001–2004), formed a real estate company at the direction of Hu. Hu manipulated the bidding process and helped his brother acquire the land to develop three projects, netting 153 million yuan in total profits.[45] The brother and sister of Feng Weilin, director of the Hunan Highway Bureau arrested in 2011, became middlemen peddling their family ties to Feng to contractors.[46] The sister of Kuang Guanghua, a county party boss in Jiangxi, operated rare-earth mines in his county and engaged in illegal mining and bribery during 2011–2013.[47]

The sample cases also confirm that participants, especially private businessmen, can reap enormous illicit profits. The sectors promising the highest returns are real estate, mining, and SOE restructuring. In the land scandal in Dongfang city in Hainan, the private businessman at the center of the case, Zhang Yan'an, completed two land transactions in 2008–2009. In the first transaction, his bribe of 1 million yuan yielded a net profit of 21.9 million yuan. He realized the same rate of return in his second land transaction. He paid 8 million yuan for a parcel of land and gave 8.47 million yuan in bribes to several officials. After deducting these expenses, he earned a profit of 38.94 million yuan with a business partner.[48] In the corruption case in Shaoxing in Zhejiang, a developer paid a vice mayor 3.5 million yuan in 2000 and the vice mayor helped him get a plot of land for 32 million yuan less than the rival bid, effectively yielding a return of nine times his investment (the amount of the bribe).[49] In 2005, Liu Zhuozhi, then a prefecture party chief in Inner Mongolia, helped a private firm acquire land at 2,000 yuan per *mu* (about one-third of an acre). In 2010, the private company resold the land at 230,000 yuan per *mu*.[50]

Purchasing undervalued natural resource assets owned by the state and then quickly selling them for a huge profit is another preferred route to wealth among well-connected businessmen. The party chief of Lingyuan City in Liaoning ordered a township under his jurisdiction to sell its rich iron ore mine to a Fujian businessman for 20 million yuan at the end of 2005. Two years later, the Fujian businessman sold an 83 percent share in the mine for 172 million yuan, netting more than 150 million yuan in profit.[51] Jie Lichang, owner of a large private mining company in Anhui, gave Quan Junliang, a county party chief, 730,000 yuan in cash and real estate worth 2.04 million yuan between 2005 and 2011. In 2010, Jie, together with a large SOE as his partner, wanted to purchase a state-owned iron ore mine in Quan's jurisdiction. Jie insisted that the price should be under 150 million yuan. Quan duly obliged by ordering the county government to set the price at 289 million yuan and to give Jie and his joint venture partner tax and other subsidies totaling 139 million yuan. The fair market price of the mine was 815 million yuan. Since Jie owned 49 percent of the joint venture, he effectively gained 260 million yuan in unrealized profits.[52]

Outsized, though less spectacular, returns can also be realized in transactions involving undervalued SOE assets. In the privatization of Jianwei Power Station in Sichuan in 2002, the business tycoon who was acquiring the station paid 40 million yuan for the station and spent 28 million yuan on bribes. The market value of the power station was likely significantly higher because it was one of Sichuan's 500 largest companies. What is known is that his purchase price was lower than the two other bids, one offering 80 million yuan and the other 100 million yuan. In a genuine auction, the highest bidder would have won. In effect, the business tycoon underpaid by 32 million yuan even after factoring in his huge bribes.[53]

The most lucrative deal in absolute terms in our sample was struck by Zhang Rongkun, a toll-road operator at the center of the Shanghai Social Security Fund scandal that ended the political career of the city's party chief and Politburo member Chen Liangyu in 2006. With very little of his own capital, Zhang Rongkun spent 12 million yuan in total bribes in order to raise the funds from banks and the Shanghai Municipal Social Security Fund. In a deal completely financed by debt in 2002, he paid 1.01 billion yuan (in addition to assuming the outstanding debt) for the Shanghai Toll Roads and Bridges Corp. (an SOE), which had a net asset value of 1.33 billion yuan. Zhang's implicit discount was 330 million yuan.[54]

The Unraveling of the Crony Networks

Chief perpetrators in our sample cases could expect to engage in corrupt activities for an average of nine years (the median is eight years) before detection. Though the risk of detection in collusive corruption is mitigated by the interests shared by all the perpetrators in concealing their crimes, it cannot be entirely eliminated. Based on official data, of the 151,350 corruption cases involving embezzlement and bribery (the two most common crimes committed by officials) prosecuted by the government between January 2008 and August 2012, 32.1 percent were based on tips provided by "the masses," 35.4 percent on investigations conducted by the prosecutors, 9.5 percent on cases transferred by the CCP committees for discipline inspection (CDIs), and the remaining 23 percent on cases transferred from other law enforcement agencies and voluntary surrenders by the suspects.[55] What is noteworthy about these numbers is that detection risks arise chiefly from tips and investigations conducted by the prosecutors, since they account for two-thirds of the cases prosecuted. What is unclear is how the cases transferred from the CDIs are counted. Since the CDIs have small staffs and normally do not initiate investigations without receiving reliable leads, it is reasonable to infer that most, if not all, of their investigations are based on tips provided by "the masses." The Chinese procuratorate also has a relatively small staff and lacks the capacity to initiate investigations without credible leads.[56] Yet slightly over one-third of the cases it prosecutes are based on "self-initiated investigations." It is likely that the leads for these investigations are mostly derived from tips initially provided by "the masses." This hypothesis is based on the fact that, because a large share of corruption cases in contemporary China involve collusive corruption, one tip can generate leads for multiple investigations. The problem, however, is the definition of "the masses." It is highly unlikely that this term refers to ordinary citizens, who normally have little contact with Chinese officials. If anything, "the masses" likely refer to officials or civil servants who are not part of the crony networks but who have credible information about the misconduct of their colleagues.

A fatal weakness of corruption networks is their overreliance on the political security of their chief political patron, typically a powerful party boss. When such a leader falls from grace, usually as a result of an internal power struggle, his loyalists, as described by the colorful Chinese saying "monkeys scatter when their tree falls," are usually scooped up in a purge. This happened to the networks of Zhou Yongkang, Ling Jihua, Su Rong, and many others.[57] However, for most local networks of collusion, their unraveling begins differently. Usually Chinese authorities respond to credible tips provided by someone who is not part of the crony network but has detailed knowledge about the acts of corruption committed by the officials and their associates. If the tipster blows the whistle and his information results in an investigation, the probe of the denounced official is likely to uncover his collaborators as well. Although the CDIs and the procuratorate likely discard the majority of the tips from "the masses," the tips that are acted upon can generate fruitful investigations. In these cases, investigators are able to break the first suspected official and make him reveal the identities and actions of his coconspirators in exchange for leniency.

The unraveling of the corruption network in Pinghu City in Zhejiang started when prosecutors questioned a low-level official in 2009, reportedly because of a tip from "the masses." The official quickly provided information on the crimes committed by the city's deputy mayor and director of the water resources bureau of the city, leading to their arrests soon afterward.[58] The infamous "White House" scandal in Loudi in Hunan was exposed in 2007 after one detained official told the prosecutors that his close friend and superior was also involved. The Loudi city government had spent 500 million yuan to construct a municipal administrative complex in which seven buildings had domes similar to that of the U.S. Capitol.[59] Another similar instance is the Shaoxing case. In November 2006, a deputy party chief and a deputy mayor of Shangyu, a city that is part of Shaoxing, were detained for corruption. One of them cooperated and gave investigators damaging information on Shangyu's long-serving party chief. During the investigation of the party chief, prosecutors summoned a real estate developer who had given the party chief 110,000 yuan in bribes. When interrogated, the businessman confessed that he had also bribed another local official.[60] Cooperation by officials first detained by investigators can help expose not only their partners in corruption but also their corrupt activities the investigators often do not know about. Court documents contain many references to "honest confessions of criminal acts that were committed but not known to the investigators" as factors meriting reduced sentences.

In some instances, the initial investigation is triggered by pure accident. Chinese media often report the accidental discovery of large piles of cash in the homes of corrupt officials (such as in a burglary). In some instances, a major "public incident" such as mass rioting that attracted the attention of top leaders can initiate an anticorruption probe. Typically, in the aftermath of the riot, higher authorities want to punish the local officials to appease public anger. Charging them with corruption is a popular tactic. In our sample, Hanyuan's corruption case was uncovered after a mass riot in 2004 sparked by angry farmers threatened with displacement by a hydroelectric power project.[61] The collusion between private mine owners and local officials in Nandan in Guangxi came to light only after a deadly mining disaster in 2001 and an egregious cover-up attempt attracted media attention and investigation by a special team dispatched from Beijing.[62]

Frequently, incriminating information is provided by businessmen who have been victimized by corruption. In Lanzhou, a former mayor of the city was denounced to the anticorruption authorities by a private businessman whose real estate development project was blocked in 1998 by the mayor, who demanded that his wife be given a 51 percent share in the project, a request the businessman turned down.[63] In the case of Chenzhou in Hunan, four businessmen victimized by Zeng Jinchun, the head of the municipal CDI, banded together in 2004 to report his wrongdoings to the higher authorities.[64] In Shaoxing, Zhejiang, a real estate developer falsely convicted of tax evasion and sent to jail by the city's party chief (who was angered by the businessman's rival bid in 2000 for a plot of land already promised to another developer who had bribed the party chief), mailed incriminating materials to the CCDI under his real name.[65] Denunciations by jilted or unhappy mistresses pose yet another risk for corrupt officials. Chinese media frequently report such instances. In our sample, only one official, Shan Zengde, who had served as an executive deputy mayor of a large city in Shandong, was brought down by his unforgiving mistress, who in 2012 posted on the Internet a handwritten note by Shan promising to divorce his wife and marry her (which he did not do).[66]

Political rivals of officials colluding with private businessmen also provide useful information to investigators that can result in the discovery of crimes committed by these officials. In most cases, these rivals are themselves corrupt. One such example is the detection of Xu Zongheng, the mayor of Shenzhen. He was denounced by Wang Huayuan, who as Guangdong's CCP anticorruption chief had long suspected or had materials on Xu, whom he disliked deeply. Most likely because he himself was dirty as well, Wang did not bring a case against Xu while he was in charge of Guangdong's CDI. But he gave investigators information about Xu as soon as he was arrested in 2009 for helping a criminal suspect elude arrest.[67] Another high-profile corruption case that involved rivalry between a mayor and his boss, the party chief, occurred in the city of Lanzhou. Zhang Yushun, a former mayor, went to great lengths to gather dirt on his two colleagues, the city party chief, Wang Jun, and the executive vice mayor. Zhang mailed the materials anonymously to the CCDI when it was investigating a real estate developer connected with the two rivals. Largely because the information provided by Zhang was too credible to ignore, the CCDI began to scrutinize the activities of Zhang's rivals. Ironically, the probe also uncovered Zhang's own corrupt acts, for which he received a long jail sentence.[68] Bitter rivalry among local officials that ultimately ends in "mutually assured destruction" is common. The party chief of Nanjing, Yang Weize, was denounced by the father-in-law of his foe, the mayor of Nanjing, as soon as the mayor was arrested by the CCDI in 2013. After the CCDI detained the head of the Tianjin procuratorate in 2006, he immediately provided the investigators incriminating information on the corruption of his nemesis, Tianjin's police chief Song Pingshun (who later committed suicide).[69]

However, by far the most potent tool available to investigators is to detain the spider in this web of corruption—the businessman who has bribed most of the officials—and force him to reveal his coconspirators. In our sample, incriminating information extracted from private businessmen constituted the most reliable leads that resulted in the discovery of official misconduct. In this process, the unraveling begins when the private businessman is arrested for reasons that are often unrelated to the officials with whom he has colluded. Once he is in custody, he has an incentive to seek leniency by exposing the officials he has bribed. In the Shaoxing case, a real estate developer was arrested for bribing officials in 2007; he then told investigators that he had also bribed six other officials, who were soon detained.[70] In some cases, businessmen who have bribed multiple officials also keep a detailed record of the amounts and the recipients, giving investigators documentary evidence and substantial assistance in identifying the involved officials. One typical case is the land scandal in Feidong County in Anhui in 2006. The crime was uncovered when a real estate developer was questioned about commercial bribery. During the investigation, he confessed that he had bribed the head of the county land bureau, its deputy chief, a district mayor, a deputy county party chief, and many others. These leads then enabled the investigators to find even more officials who were not connected with the businessman.[71]

Cronyism and Governance

Cronyism not only produces illicit windfall profits for government officials and private businessmen, but also generates harmful spill-over effects undermining local governance, including judicial integrity, law and order, and public safety. In some cases, such effects are the direct and deliberate consequences of the actions taken by the colluding officials and businessmen. In other cases, these effects indirectly result from their illicit activities.

One common practice found in our sample is the violation of safety or environmental rules or a cover-up of such violations that directly harms public safety and undermines law enforcement. Typically, government officials who have accepted bribes from businessmen allow the tolerance of such violations or cover-ups to protect the business interests of the bribers. One example is the police chief in a prefecture in northern Guangdong. After he took 300,000 yuan from the owner of a private coal company during 2005–2008, the police chief made sure that his highway patrol officers would no longer stop the company's overloaded coal trucks. A few years later, the businessman also gave 2 million yuan to the police chief and asked him to intervene in a criminal probe.[72] Shan Zengde, a local official in Shandong, helped reduce environmental fines levied on the firms owned by a businessman who had given him 1.31 million yuan in bribes over a decade before Shan's fall in 2013.[73] In the 2006 scandal in Chenzhou City in Hunan, the municipal propaganda chief censored local media coverage of mining accidents to protect coal mine owners who had bribed his patron and boss, the municipal party chief.[74]

Officials have also helped their friends, tycoons and crime bosses alike, to evade the law or seize public property. When he found that he was the target of a criminal investigation in 2006, Huang Guangyu, founder of Gome Electronics Stores and once China's richest businessman, bribed a succession of senior law enforcement officers in 2006 who were investigating him for money laundering, insider trading, and financial fraud. His case led to the fall of Guangdong's former provincial police chief, the former head of the provincial CDI, an assistant minister of public security, a deputy director of the economic crime investigation bureau of the ministry of public security, the mayor of Shenzhen, and several others.[75] In 2008, Wang Huayuan, the former head of the Guangdong CDI implicated in the Huang case, alerted a businessman, who was engaged in money laundering and other crimes, about his pending arrest, enabling him to escape.[76] Li Qiliang, a county party chief in Guangxi, took bribes from a local mobster in return for helping him get mining permits and land during 2005–2007. His successor was bought off by the same mobster, as were the executive deputy county magistrate and the CCP secretary in charge of law enforcement.[77] The private mine operators who bribed Wan Ruizhong and his colleagues in Nandan, Guangxi, also allegedly had ties to organized crime.[78]

The sample cases yield some evidence of the dark role played by corrupt officials in forced evictions in urban and rural areas. Such evictions typically involve the use of intimidation and force by the police and even organized crime in order to drive urban residents out of their houses and farmers off of their land. Victims often resist such evictions because the real estate developers acquiring the land usually offer insufficient compensation. However, with the support of local officials, these evictions can be carried out despite public outrage and occasional riots. In such cases, local officials are suspected of taking bribes to help the businessmen carry out the evictions and seize the land. In our sample, we have official documentary evidence establishing the link between bribes paid to local officials and forced evictions. In the list of bribes collected by Wang Xianmin, a county CCP chief in Gansu, he took 150,000 yuan from a businessman to help his hydropower station evict residents and remove those who resisted eviction during 2007–2009.[79] Wang Huaizhong, former party chief of Fuyang in Anhui, personally intervened to help a real estate developer evict local residents. Wang later received a bribe of 200,000 yuan.[80] Li Dalun, the Chenzhou party boss, also received a request for help from a real estate developer in 2005 when he encountered violent resistance from villagers whose land he was trying to acquire. Li duly obliged because the businessman had given him $4,000 and a Rolex watch worth 40,000 Hong Kong dollars.[81]

Another common practice found in our sample cases is interference in commercial disputes undertaken by powerful officials that would benefit their business cronies. The head of the municipal CDI in Chenzhou, Zeng Jinchun, interfered in court proceedings at least three times, according to his indictment. In a bitter legal fight between two businessmen during 2002–2004, Zeng took bribes from both sides, but directed a vice president of the Chenzhou Intermediate Court to render a ruling favoring the defendant who had given him the bigger bribe. Zeng also ensured that those who bribed him could operate illegal mines with impunity.[82] In addition, Zeng ran a mafia-style protection racket. He sold special logos to private firms for an annual payment to avoid harassment by local authorities. Private entrepreneurs refusing to purchase such protection were arrested and detained until they paid what were, in effect, ransoms.[83] In Maoming in Guangdong, a private businessman who illegally seized control of a plot of land purchased by a group of investors bribed the city's party chief and deputy executive mayor, who instructed the local court to grant the businessman legal title to the land. One of the investors who went to the police to report the illegal seizure of his property was arrested in 2009.[84] In Guangdong, the head of the provincial CDI intervened in 2006 in a commercial dispute on behalf of a Hong Kong businessman who had bribed him.[85]

Wealthy private businessmen who have developed close ties with local officials are also eager to gain political status through bribes. Our cases indicate that the presence of private businessmen in the national and local people's congresses and the people's political consultative conferences is both significant and likely the result of bribes. Zhu Siyi, a coal tycoon in Guangdong, paid 200,000 yuan in bribes to secure a seat on the National People's Congress in 2008. He also paid 1 million yuan to the head of the provincial United Front Department for a vice chairmanship of the provincial federation of industry and commerce because this position would give him opportunities to network.[86] During 2007–2008, Zhou Zhenhong, the former party chief of Maoming and head of Guangdong's Department of United Front, took 1.8 million yuan in bribes from five real estate developers and helped them become members of the Guangdong People's Political Consultative Conference (two of them members of its standing committee).[87] The deputy governor of Inner Mongolia, Liu Zhuozhi, also took bribes and helped two local businessmen become members of the local people's political consultative conference while he was party chief of a prefecture in Inner Mongolia during 2004–2008.[88] As we shall show, even many mafia bosses have managed to buy their way into local people's congresses and political consultative conferences.

As hypothesized earlier, collusion is most likely in sectors where partially reformed and contested property rights attract rent-seeking businessmen. Collusion allows private businessmen to overcome veto threats from claimants contesting the rights to the assets they seek to acquire and from various bureaucratic agencies with authority over the disposal of these assets. For the most part, a salient feature of these sectors is the high degree of state control of the markets in which these assets are traded. As a result, businessmen succeeding in acquiring these assets can expect windfall profits by bribing officials. This process benefits both sides. What is notable is the total absence of such collusion in competitive sectors where economic reforms are more thorough and property rights are more clearly defined. There are few cases of collusion between officials and businessmen in the more marketized and highly competitive sectors such as retail, light manufacturing, and export-oriented industries.

Collusion with officials may be immensely profitable for private businessmen, but it benefits a small minority and harms a large majority. Obviously, the majority of the victims include legitimate claimants for contested property rights, such as workers, peasants, and urban residents. However, many, if not a majority, of private businessmen are also victimized by crony capitalism. Our cases show that unscrupulous private businessmen often manage to bribe powerful officials who then use the police and the judiciary to arrest and jail the competitors of their cronies. The "bad money driving out good money" dynamic prevails in the world of crony capitalism. The unavoidable outcome is the dominance of these lucrative sectors by the most well-connected private businessmen.

Because of this dynamic, the crony networks connecting officials and private businessmen have become deeply embedded in the fabric of China's politics and economy. These networks have developed their own operational rules, codes, and tactics, which in turn have become widespread among officials and businessmen and have facilitated their illicit transactions. It can be argued that a market for influence and corruption has fully matured—particularly in sectors where market forces are either weak or nonexistent. Despite its periodic crackdowns on corruption, the Chinese party-state has proven largely ineffective in eradicating these crony networks. To be sure, at the tactical level, Chinese anticorruption investigators have potent tools in uncovering and prosecuting individuals involved in collusive corruption. But these tactics are useless in eradicating the systemic causes of the collusion in China. The patron–client relationship that underpins the hierarchy of the CCP is one that forms closely knit cliques among officials based on personal ties and, in many instances, complicity in crime. As long as such relationships endure, officials engaged in corruption can count on protection from their friends and colleagues in higher places. The other reason that collusion between officials and businessmen is impossible to eradicate is the continuation of state dominance in key sectors of the economy, which creates abundant rents that attract enterprising businessmen and allows officials allocating such rents to cash in on their power.

Finally, collusion between officials and businessmen has pernicious effects on governance and leads to the concentration of power in the hands of a minority of cronies. Our sample cases show that such collusion can easily spawn lawlessness in the marketplace, compromised public safety, violations of human rights, and immunity granted to a small elite. Most worryingly, some evidence in our cases suggests that crony networks have gained dominance in the political and economic activities of prefecture-sized jurisdictions (Fuyang in Anhui, Chenzhou in Hunan, and Maoming in Guangdong) where corrupt party chiefs, mayors, police chiefs, and their business allies have turned their jurisdictions into virtual local mafia states. Additionally, it appears that private businessmen who have succeeded in making windfall profits through collaboration with local officials are not content with their financial gains. They seek formal political influence and status, such as that which can be delivered by membership on national and local legislatures and on people's political consultative conferences at various levels. At the moment, these bodies have mostly symbolic influence. However, such concentration of wealth and power bodes poorly for China's democratic future. In the event of a regime transition, businessmen who have gained illicit wealth and access to political power could well become China's new oligarchs, with real political power.

5

Stealing from the State:
Collusive Corruption in
State-Owned Enterprises

A ruling party has enormous power in allocating resources.

—Xi Jinping, May 9, 2014

EXECUTIVES of Chinese SOEs, all of them CCP members, probably need no reminder from their general secretary that they wield enormous power over economic resources. But based on press reports and official data on widespread collusion in SOEs, these executives may not use such power in ways Xi would endorse.[1] Compared with officials in other state institutions, executives in SOEs clearly have more direct control over state-owned property and more opportunities to steal. Such theft, now systematic and endemic, is another defining aspect of crony capitalism in post-Tiananmen China. To be sure, corruption in SOEs also occurred in the 1980s. However, since the early 1990s such corruption has acquired qualitatively different characteristics and now resembles looting more than petty theft. As we have seen, the combination of decentralized control of property rights and greater executive autonomy in SOEs has made the plunder of the property of the Chinese state easier to perpetrate. It is thus no surprise that the most salient characteristic of corruption in SOEs since the early 1990s is its collusive nature.[2]

Although the Chinese government does not provide much data on collusive corruption in SOEs, available evidence suggests that it is widespread. In Jiangsu, according to the provincial procuratorate, 60 percent of all *wo'an* and *chuan'an* prosecuted in 2000 occurred in SOEs. In Shanghai, 80 percent of all *wo'an* and *chuan'an* prosecuted in 2000 took place in SOEs. Zhejiang's provincial procuratorate reported that, between 2001 and 2013, 20 percent of the corruption cases in SOEs were *wo'an* or *chuan'an*.[3] One annual report that tracks crimes committed by Chinese businessmen in both SOEs and private companies that were covered by the Chinese press notes that such cases account for a large share of all publicized corruption cases in SOEs. Of the eighty-two corruption cases in SOEs reported in detail in the media in 2012, thirty-nine involved multiple individuals (roughly half of them involved more than three people). Altogether 225 people were involved in thirty-nine cases (averaging 5.5 individuals per case). Eighteen of the thirty-nine cases involved senior executives and their subordinates.[4] Of the sixty-one SOE corruption cases reported in the media in 2013 for which the number of perpetrators was known, twenty-four involved multiple perpetrators (averaging 7.6 per case).[5] Of the 245 prosecuted criminal cases against SOE executives in 2014, forty-two were explicitly identified as cases of collusion.[6] The data provided by the annual reports during the period 2011–2014 reveal four salient characteristics of corruption in SOEs.

First, these cases often involve very large sums. In 2011, the average amount per case was nearly 21 million yuan. The category of crime that involved the largest amount of money was "unauthorized use of public funds." In most cases, SOE executives use their company's funds to invest in stocks or to fund loans to other companies and then pocket the income. In 2011, the average amount involved in this category was about 85 million yuan. The average amount in embezzlement cases was 15 million yuan. The average amount in bribery cases (involving SOE executives only) was 2.5 million yuan.[7] However, the amounts reported for 2012 were much smaller. According to the 2012 report, the average amount was 430,000 yuan in bribe-taking cases and 1.9 million yuan in embezzlement cases. (The 2013 and 2014 reports did not provide similar data.)[8]

Second, in terms of occurrence, bribe-taking, embezzlement, and unauthorized use of public funds are, in that order, the three most commonly committed crimes by SOEs executives. In 2011, of the eighty-eight SOE corruption cases, bribe-taking occurred in forty-five of them, twenty-four were embezzlement cases, and eleven were cases of unauthorized use of public funds. In 2012, of the eighty-five SOE corruption cases, thirty-nine were classified as bribe-taking, twenty-four involved embezzlement, and eight were cases of unauthorized use of public funds. The share of these three crimes was roughly the same in 2013. In 2014, of the 245 cases, specific criminal complaints against SOE executives were provided in 181 of the cases. Charges of bribery, embezzlement, and misappropriation of public funds were filed in 67, 28, and 17 percent of the cases, respectively.[9]

Third, corruption is most likely to occur in financial management, contract bidding, capital-raising, and personnel management (code word for *maiguan maiguan*). In 2012, sixty-nine of the eighty-five SOE corruption cases identified the specific activities: Thirty-one cases involved financial management, thirteen contract bidding, seven raising capital, and seven *maiguan maiguan*. In 2014, specific criminal activities were identified in 227 of the 245 cases. Of these, forty-seven were in financial management, thirty-four in contract bidding, and thirty-one in *maiguan maiguan*.[10]

Fourth, corruption is more common in large SOEs. Based on the 2014 report, which identifies the size of 190 of the 245 SOEs, 176 were large SOEs and four were mega SOEs.[11] One explanation is that after the restructuring of the SOEs in the late 1990s, the state retained most of the large SOEs. The other is that large SOEs have complex operations and conduct high-value transactions that can make them attractive targets for potential bribe-givers and that allow corrupt executives to carry out and hide their criminal activities with greater ease.

While aggregate data may give us a broad picture of collusive corruption in SOEs, they are insufficient to help us understand the complex processes, relationships, and methods in this type of corruption. In the section below, we examine fifty such cases that have received extensive coverage in the Chinese media.

Key Findings

The data in Table A.3 in the Appendix capture some of the broad trends and parameters of collusive corruption in SOEs. It is clear that collusive corruption in SOEs is geographically widespread. Of the fifty cases sampled here, forty-two involved SOEs owned by municipal and provincial governments in eighteen provinces, and eight occurred inside giant national SOEs and their provincial subsidiaries. Another notable feature of collusive corruption in SOEs is that it has pervaded all sectors, including retail, manufacturing, services, utilities, banking, and natural resources. It is also evident that the amount stolen by the chief culprit was relatively small in the 1990s and early 2000s but it has risen to astronomical levels since the late 2000s. For instance, there were eleven cases in which the lead culprit was caught by 2003. Of these cases, the amount of corruption income attributed to the lead culprit exceeded 6.4 million yuan, the median in the sample, in only one case. There is also a rough correlation between the amount of money the chief culprit is charged with stealing and the total amount of money involved in the corruption case.[12] Of the twenty-four cases for which the alleged total corruption income of the lead culprit was below the 6.4 million yuan median, the total amount of money involved exceeded the median amount—28 million yuan—in only four cases. By contrast, of the twenty-four cases for which the alleged total corruption income of the lead culprit was above the 6.4 million yuan median, the total amount of money involved exceeded the median amount in fourteen cases. One explanation may be the copycat effect: Under a greedier chief culprit, his co-conspirators or other underlings have fewer inhibitions against theft. The other explanation is the cost of greed: The chief culprit is willing to take big risks to realize large sums of corruption income.

Generally speaking, participation in collusive corruption in SOEs can yield attractive returns for its perpetrators. Compared with local officials engaged in selling offices and other corrupt activities studied in Chapter 3, corrupt SOE executives in the sample report much more total corruption income. While the average amount of corruption income for local officials is 6.45 million yuan (see Table 3.1), that for SOE executives is almost 30 million yuan, nearly five times more. The median amount for local officials is 3.81 million yuan, but that for SOE executives is 6.4 million yuan, two-thirds more (Table A.3). Of course, there is greater variation in SOE executives' capacity to steal. The standard deviation in total corruption income for SOE executives is about 63.7 million yuan, ten times the median amount. By comparison, the standard deviation in corruption income for local officials caught for selling offices and other corrupt activities is 10.5 million yuan, less than three times the median. One explanation for such a disparity is that SOE executives, especially those in large firms, directly control more economic resources, such as contracts, cash, and state-owned assets, than local officials. Such control allows them to steal more or to demand bigger bribes from private entrepreneurs. In addition, SOE executives are better positioned to illicitly privatize state-owned assets than local party chiefs, enabling them to amass large ill-gotten wealth. Of the forty-eight cases for which the corruption income of the lead culprit is available, acts such as transferring state-owned assets—land, shares, real estate, and profitable businesses—to private firms owned by SOE executives or their relatives occurred in thirty-two of them.

The number of individuals implicated or arrested as a result of investigations into these cases varies widely, from as few as three to as many as eighty-one. The median number of individuals directly involved or arrested as a result of investigations is eleven. It is worth noting that not all of the individuals involved in a particular case were executives in SOEs; some were private businessmen who bribed the SOE executives or acted as coconspirators in other capacities.[13] But in each case, multiple executives participated in the alleged corrupt activities. Compared with cases of selling offices, corruption in SOEs may not need to involve a very large number of executives. While local party chiefs need to sell a large number of appointments and promotions to generate significant income, SOE executives usually only need the help of a smaller number of accomplices to carry out their crimes without diluting their income.

The average duration of crimes for the lead perpetrator in our sample is 7.4 years. The median duration is seven years, with a standard deviation of 3.4 years, roughly similar to that of local officials caught for *maiguan maiguan*. The relatively long duration of crimes, during which the lead culprit repeatedly takes bribes or embezzles public funds undetected, suggests that, like *maiguan maiguan*, collusive corruption in SOEs is difficult to detect. In addition, the lead culprits, often the chairmen or the presidents, typically receive promotions during this period, another indication of the relative inefficiency of Chinese antigraft authorities in detecting theft.

The data in Table A.3 also confirm that collusive corruption in SOEs is mainly perpetrated by senior executives, often the chairmen, presidents, or general managers. Of the fifty cases in our sample, chairmen, presidents, or general managers are the ringleaders in forty-four cases. Given the enormous concentration of power in the hands of chairmen, presidents, and general managers inside Chinese SOEs, vertical collusion is understandably the dominant pattern. SOE executives caught for egregious acts of corruption do not necessarily receive more severe punishments than local party chiefs, even though they gain much larger amounts of corruption income. Of the fifty lead culprits in our sample, twenty-two received term sentences, ten received life, eight drew suspended death sentences, and two were executed.[14] Sentences for six perpetrators were not known. Forty-five percent of the lead culprits in SOE corruption cases received severe punishment (life, suspended death sentence, or death), compared with 48 percent of the local party chiefs caught for selling offices. The term sentences meted out to SOE executives are also comparable to those given to local party chiefs. The average and median term sentences for the former is 12.5 and 13 years, respectively, compared with 13.3 and 13.5 years, respectively, for the latter. Despite their larger corruption income, SOE executives do not receive more severe punishment than local party chiefs, most probably due to the declining progressivity of punishment embedded in China's sentencing practices. What is notable from the one hundred cases analyzed here and in Chapter 3 is the rare application of the death penalty. Only one mid-level local party chief and two low-ranking SOE executives were executed. The data on punishment for officials prosecuted for corruption further confirm this observation: The party is loath to execute its own agents in all but a handful of cases, in contrast to its liberal use of such punishment in the handling of ordinary criminal cases.[15] The only plausible explanation is that the CCP has effectively granted most of its elite members a highly prized privilege: immunity from capital punishment even when they commit the most serious economic crimes.[16]

Typical Corrupt Activities inside SOEs

Analysis of the details of the selected cases of corruption inside SOEs shows that such activities consist of garden-variety acts of theft and greed, such as embezzlement, bribery, and misappropriation of public funds, as well as more pernicious forms of looting, such as channeling lucrative deals to family members and stealing valuable SOE assets through illicit privatization. What makes these activities unique is that they often require collusion among the key executives.

Bribery, including kickbacks, occurred in nearly every case in this sample. Typically, managers of other firms (both private and state-owned) that do business with SOEs offer bribes or kickbacks to SOE executives to secure contracts or maintain existing business relationships. For example, in the case of Gansu Lanzhou Tansu Group, a key producer of carbon that had 20 percent of the national market share, its chairman and president, Pan Xiguang, and five other executives collected 3.54 million yuan in bribes from their suppliers between 1999 and the mid-2000s. In return, they purchased inputs from connected businessmen at a 10–20 percent markup, while selling the company's products at an 18–26 percent discount.[17] In the scandal at Fujian Long Steel Group (uncovered in 2003), two successive presidents and a vice president accepted relatively small bribes from suppliers.[18] The two successive presidents of Hengshan Iron Corp., a Zhejiang-based metal company that later went bankrupt, took kickbacks from private businessmen during 1994–2003, while several mid-level managers in the firm received bribes from customers for selling them "waste" that could be reprocessed.[19]

Obviously, the amount of bribes can be large if the executives are in charge of giant SOEs that hand out lucrative contracts. In 2013, Lu Xiangdong, vice president of China Mobile, the nation's largest telecom firm, was convicted of accepting more than 20 million yuan in bribes from ad agencies for giving them China Mobile's ad business.[20] Wang Xiaojin, the longtime chairman and president of Gujin Group, a large spirit maker based in Anhui, received more than 10 million yuan in bribes from suppliers, ad agencies, and other parties that did business with his firm during 1991–2007. Guo Xinmin, a deputy general manager in charge of sales, was convicted of accepting 6.8 million yuan in bribes and possessing 28.8 million yuan in "unexplained large amounts of wealth." Another four senior executives in the company each pocketed over 5 million yuan in bribes.[21] A similar example is the scandal in Shaanxi Electric Power Group, which received 7.7 billion yuan from the Chinese government to upgrade the rural electric grid in the province in 1998. Fifty-four individuals were involved. Among other things, executives of the firm took bribes for purchasing shoddy equipment from suppliers at inflated prices. The president, Wang Wenxue, was convicted of taking bribes totaling 7.1 million yuan.[22] A corruption case in a refinery of Yanchang Oil Corp., the fourth largest oil company in China, involved four coconspirators who received large sums of bribes for awarding contracts. The lead culprit, a deputy chief engineer named Li Xin, was convicted of receiving 5.3 million yuan in bribes for two transactions in 2012.[23]

The second most frequent form of corruption is embezzlement and misappropriation. The two categories are, according to the Chinese criminal code, distinct crimes, although in practice this distinction is often blurred since both acts involve the theft of SOE funds. Chinese prosecutors distinguish the two acts by defining embezzlement as stealing public funds and misappropriation as unauthorized temporary use of public funds for private benefit. If a government official or SOE executive spends public funds with no intention of repayment, this constitutes embezzlement. If the same individual temporarily appropriates public funds for an unauthorized purpose but eventually returns the funds to the government after reaping the benefits (typically the income generated by the unauthorized use of the funds), this is misappropriation. Both are profitable activities carried out by senior SOE executives, often in close collaboration with directors of finance. In some cases, senior executives pocket the stolen funds themselves, but in many instances they share the embezzled funds with other executives as bonus payments or fringe benefits.[24] Embezzlement and misappropriation frequently occur inside Chinese SOEs mainly because of poor financial controls, which allow senior executives to cook the books, conceal profits, and keep slush funds that they can tap for personal benefit.

A simple but representative method of embezzlement in SOEs is the use of their funds to reimburse personal expenses. One example is Xu Minjie, a senior vice president of China Ocean Shipping Group (COSCO), which was rocked by the arrests of seven senior executives in late 2013. Xu was convicted of getting the firm to reimburse him 308,000 yuan for his wife's dining and beauty treatment expenses over a four-year period.[25] An equally simple method is to pocket unexpended funds not recorded on the books. During 1998–2002, Hou Ximing, general manager of Qilu Petro Chemical Corp., Sinopec's branch in Shandong province, embezzled 280,000 yuan from the funds left over from employees' benefits and capital projects.[26] Another routine method of embezzlement is fabrication of an SOE's finances. When Zhongshan Huaqiao Real Estate Co. was about to be privatized in 1997, five executives, including the firm's general manager, his deputy, and the chief accountant, faked the firm's ledgers and stole 4.5 million yuan, which they later shared among themselves.[27] A similar case occurred in 1998 in Chongqing. During the privatization of Pengshui Food Services, a struggling small SOE, four of its senior managers, including the manager, the party chief, and the finance chief, conspired to hide three real estate properties owned by the firm and to later sell them, sharing the proceeds among themselves.[28]

Embezzlement can assume more subtle forms. In the corruption case at the Capital Highway Development Corp., the chairman, general manager, and chief financial officer were all involved in using 3.17 million yuan in refunded insurance premiums in 1996, which were not recorded on the company's books, to purchase private investment products for the senior executives of the firm.[29] In the Qinghai Energy Development Group scandal, with the endorsement of the firm's president, the director of finance and his deputy engaged in an elaborate scheme of fabricating the firm's financial statements and hiding 32 million yuan in profits, which they used to pay extra bonuses to senior and mid-level executives during 2005–2013. In one instance, the president asked the newly appointed party chief and chairman of the firm whether senior management should get extra pay ahead of the Chinese New Year in 2013. After receiving permission, he ordered the financial chief to dip into the slush fund to pay out 270,000 yuan to twelve senior executives of the company.[30] Nanping Mining Development Corp. had several joint ventures with private firms during 2004–2007. Under the direction of the general manager of the SOE, the executives fabricated accounts, illegally shared the hidden profits of the joint ventures, and misused their funds for personal purposes.[31]

In the simpler cases of misappropriation, perpetrators use SOEs' funds for unauthorized purposes but later quickly return them. Xue Yuquan, chairman of Shandong Gold Corp., needed 4 million yuan in capital to register a private firm he and another accomplice were setting up in 1997. He ordered the director of finance to transfer 4 million yuan of the company's funds into the bank account of his private firm, assuring him that the funds would be repaid once the registration was completed. Working with a local branch manager, the director of finance carried out the scheme, depositing the 4 million yuan in the account owned by Xue's private firm and transferring the funds back in three weeks.[32] But the thin line between misappropriation and embezzlement is crossed when misappropriated public funds generate income which SOE executives keep for themselves. Zhang Shen, chairman of Qilu Petro Chemical Corp., misappropriated more than 6.5 million yuan between 1999 and 2001, and deposited some of the funds in bank accounts controlled by his mistresses, one of whom transferred the funds into a company she owned.[33] Ying Guoquan, chairman of Wenzhou's largest state-owned grocery store chain, misappropriated 38.9 million yuan of his firm's funds between 2006 and 2010 to finance the operations of a private company owned by his son and a friend.[34] In some cases, when SOE executives misappropriate public funds to speculate in risky investments, they may incur heavy losses. Liang Jingli, chairman of Liuzhou Iron and Steel Group, directed the deputy finance chief of the company in 2009 to provide him with 20 million yuan in company funds for personal investments in the stock market, although it is not known what happened to his investments.[35] The finance director of a subsidiary of Qinghai Energy Development Group was much less lucky. He misappropriated 80.8 million yuan of the firm's money to buy lottery tickets during 2010–2013. Not a cent was recovered.[36]

Insider Privatization through Collusion

Crimes such as bribery, embezzlement, and misappropriation of public funds may generate impressive corruption income for their perpetrators, but the amount of wealth gained from such activities pales in comparison with the windfall profits through illicit privatization of SOE assets. More complex and demanding, illicit privatization requires collaboration among numerous executives who may have direct or indirect influence in the acquisition and disposal of state-owned assets. In nearly all cases, the participation of the most senior executive, the chairman or president of the SOE, is a prerequisite. But even his power may not be enough to ensure the smooth execution of his schemes because he alone does not control all the necessary procedures required to complete such transactions. The cases in this study show that incipient forms of illicit privatization emerged in the early 1990s, and over the years SOE executives engaging in this activity have acquired increasingly sophisticated means to seize control of state-owned assets for free or at a nominal cost. In this section, we identify and analyze these methods.

Self-Dealing

One relatively easy way for executives to benefit from their power in SOEs is to channel their firms' business to companies owned by themselves or their family members. Such activities do not require the transfer of the legal title to the SOE assets but do produce plentiful benefits. The nature of such activities is similar to giving SOE business to private businessmen and then demanding bribes in return. Of course, one may question whether such activities should be classified as "illicit privatization." We group them in this category mainly because the SOE executives who knowingly and systematically give their companies' business to private firms directly owned or controlled by their family members effectively act for the benefit of these private companies, not for that of the SOEs they manage. The SOE assets, which in this case include profitable business, funds, and supplies, are deployed by the corrupt SOE executives to generate income for private firms owned by themselves or their family members at steep discounts or at no cost.

For example, one mid-level manager of Hengshan Iron Corp., a Zhejiang-based SOE that went bankrupt in 2003 due to mismanagement, set up his own private company and gave 500,000 shares to the president of Hengshan Iron. The private company purchased iron ore at low prices and then resold it to Hengshan Iron at higher prices.[37] In the mega scandal that embroiled fifteen senior executives at China Mobile, the party secretary and vice chairman of China Mobile, Zhang Chunjiang, accepted bribes totaling 7.46 million yuan for giving the company's ad and consulting business to two private companies before he was caught in 2010. Zhang's wife owned a 15 percent stake in one of them.[38] One of the criminal charges leveled against Lin Kongxing, chief of Huazhong Electric Power, was that he gave contracts to a firm formed by his daughter and son-in-law during 1995–2000. Because Huazhong Electric Power was one of the largest electric power generators in the country at that time, Lin could demand deep discounts from suppliers. He thus ordered suppliers to provide materials to the private firm owned by his daughter and son-in-law at large discounts and then his daughter and son-in-law would resell the same materials to Huazhong Electric Power at full price, pocketing nearly 83 million yuan in illegal gains.[39] In the corruption case at the Agricultural Development Bank of China, the son of the chief culprit, a vice president, owned half of a private firm (even though he contributed no capital). The bank purchased equipment worth hundreds of millions of yuan from this private company between 1996 and 1999.[40]

Bao Shijia, a senior executive at COSCO in charge of shipping crude oil, allegedly helped a firm owned by his son and daughter-in-law to reap huge profits by trading oil.[41] Liang Jingli, the disgraced chairman of Liuzhou Iron and Steel Group. in Guangxi, helped his daughter set up a trading firm in Hong Kong and bought fourteen shiploads of coking coal from her firm, netting her a profit of $5.42 million in 2012–2013. Liang and thirty-four of his fellow executives of the SOE also owned two private firms, to which they transferred the SOE's waste disposal business. They received dividend payments from these two firms.[42] Wu Rijing, chairman of Xinguang International Group, one of the largest SOEs owned by the Guangdong provincial government, established a subsidiary in 2006 which was controlled by an accomplice. Wu helped the subsidiary raise funds and gave it the contracts won by Xinguang International. A year later, Wu asked his crony to loan 25 million yuan to a company owned by Wu's two brothers.[43]

Asset Stripping and Theft

Taking legal control of state-owned assets at deep discounts or no cost is the surest way for SOE executives and their families to amass a fortune. In our sample, SOE executives who managed to seize state-owned assets in this way gained the most corruption income. Given the lax control over SOEs and enormous discretionary power enjoyed by SOE executives, asset stripping and theft can be creatively accomplished through collaborative efforts among SOE executives. One of the most popular ways of stripping SOE assets is to form a joint venture between the SOE and private companies owned by friends of the SOE executives. The SOE executives then transfer assets to the joint venture at a discount or inflate the equity contribution from the private company. When the scandal at Shaanxi Electric Power Group came to light in 2005, investigators discovered that in a joint venture formed between one of its subsidiaries with a private real estate company, the SOE's contribution was undervalued by 100 million yuan.[44] Li Yongxin, chairman of Hebi Coal Group in Henan, helped another SOE executive turn one of its subsidiaries into a private company registered in Hong Kong in 2003–2004. In return, he received 14 percent of the shares in the new company (worth 3.3 million yuan).[45] In the corruption case of Guangzhou Yangcheng Group, which went bankrupt in 2001, the chairman of the SOE sold the company's assets to a private entrepreneur at a steep discount. Guangzhou Yangcheng invested 178 million Hong Kong dollars (HKD) in 1997 for a 55 percent stake in a joint wood-processing plant with a private firm. When the firm began production and was valued at 1 billion HKD, Luo Hong, the chairman of Guangzhou Yangcheng, "sold" the 55 percent stake to the private businessman at the original price of 178 million HKD. In return, Luo received 2.5 million HKD and 200,000 yuan from the private businessman as a bribe. The private businessman also gave 1.04 million yuan and 100,000 HKD to the vice chairman and general manager of Guangzhou Yangcheng. Another deputy general manager received 4.82 million HKD and 200,000 yuan in bribes.[46]

A form of reverse asset stripping is to overpay for private assets owned by well-connected businessmen who set up joint ventures with SOEs, as in the case of Lanzhou Liancheng Aluminum Corp. in 1994. The director of the factory, Wei Guangqian, became a friend of a private businessman from Guangdong. In addition to receiving kickbacks from this private entrepreneur in a land deal, Wei directed his factory to form a joint venture with the private businessman, who contributed wildly inflated assets (assessed by three people from an intermediary agency who were also bribed). The reported value of the private businessman's assets in the joint venture was booked at 91.9 million yuan, even though they were really worth 20 million yuan. Then Lanzhou Liancheng Aluminum made a cash investment of 31.7 million yuan in the joint venture (one key executive of Lanzhou Liancheng received 5 million yuan in kickbacks from this deal).[47]

The most sophisticated form of theft usually involves the establishment of a private company owned by the SOE executives themselves. In these schemes, the executives jointly set up a private company as a first step. They then proceed to transfer assets of their SOE into this private company either for free or at a deep discount. Five executives at an unnamed small SOE in Taizhou, in Jiangsu, followed this strategy. They first illegally used 400,000 yuan of the SOE's funds to set up a private firm in March 2000 and then, through a variety of illegal means, systematically transferred earnings of the SOE to their private firm.[48] In the case of Chongqing Haikang Group, its chairman, Xiang Daocheng, first formed a private firm with a private businessman as a vehicle for purchasing assets owned by a bankrupt SOE in 2000. Xiang used his power to force Haikang Group to extend a loan of 7 million yuan to close the transaction. After three years, the assets (mainly land) purchased by Xiang's vehicle appreciated greatly in value, and his partner sold the land back to the local government for 39 million yuan.[49] With the help of two executives and a local party chief, Wang Chengming, chairman of Shanghai Electric

Group, was able to inject, as equity, a prime piece of land acquired by the SOE at 200 million yuan in 1999 into a subsidiary it partially owned. Then the SOE sold its equity in the subsidiary, without any markup, to a private firm owned by one of Wang's accomplices, thus repaying the SOE its original investment and making the subsidiary totally private. Wang's accomplice then gave Wang a 50 percent equity stake in the now private firm, which owned the land. By 2003, the value of the land rose to more than 500 million yuan, giving Wang and his accomplices a paper profit of over 300 million yuan.[50]

The colluding executives at Guangzhou Baiyun Nonggongshang Corp. applied the same strategy. The president of the SOE, Zhang Xinhua, set up a joint venture between Guangzhou Baiyun and a private company, Guangye Property, which Zhang actually controlled through majority ownership. After this joint venture was formed, Zhang transferred various assets of Guangzhou Baiyun (factory buildings and land) to the joint venture. In 2006, Zhang formed a new private company and recruited some of his colleagues in Guangzhou Baiyun to this new company and gave them shares. The new company then purchased the minority stakes (valued at the original price of 120,000 yuan) held by Guangzhou Baiyun in the joint venture—even though the real market value of the joint venture had risen to 284 million yuan due to the injection of undervalued assets owned by Guangzhou Baiyun. Zhang himself owned 25 percent of the new firm (worth 75 million yuan).[51]

Ying Guoquan, chairman of Wenzhou Cailanzi Group, an SOE based in Wenzhou, used a nearly identical scheme to steal state-owned assets (mainly land) worth more than 100 million yuan between 2003 and 2006. Ying and several of his fellow executives first formed a new mixed-ownership firm called "Cailanzi Development Corp. Limited." In Chinese, with the exception of two characters, the name of the new company is nearly identical to the name of the SOE that Ying headed (Cailanzi Group Corp.). After successfully lobbying the Wenzhou city government to allocate, at a deeply discounted price, a valuable plot to the SOE (Cailanzi Group Corp.), Ying and his coconspirators then bribed two city officials, who changed the two characters in the relevant documents of the municipal government and named the new firm, Cailanzi Development Corp., as the recipient of the land. The fraudulent scheme netted Ying and his fellow executives, who were majority owners of the new firm, more than 110 million yuan in paper profits before it was uncovered.[52]

The best opportunity for SOE executives to acquire valuable state-owned assets is *gaizhi*.[53] Literally translated as "ownership system change," *gaizhi* is privatization in all but name. Through *gaizhi,* a previously wholly owned SOE may be transformed into one of mixed ownership (state–collective or collective–private) or full private ownership. Two groups of officials are in charge of *gaizhi*. The members of the first group are local government officials (party chiefs, mayors, and members of development and reform commissions). The second group consists of senior executives in SOEs. If they buy off local officials, the SOE executives can acquire the state-owned assets cheaply. This was the case in the privatization of Huangyan Real Estate Development Corp. owned by the district government of Huangyan in Zhejiang. Chen Xi, the SOE's chairman, who was also a deputy director of the district's bureau of land resources, bribed the district mayor, executive vice mayor, and three other local officials, who in turn helped him carry out his scheme. After the assessor hired by Chen concluded that the SOE was worth 33.4 million yuan, the local government agreed to this valuation and authorized the ownership change in December 2002. Chen and his son subsequently owned 85 percent of the new firm. Because the assets were so severely undervalued, Chen and his son reaped huge profits. In 2003 alone the newly privatized firm generated a profit of 60 million yuan and claimed assets of over 1 billion yuan.[54]

However, even without the help of local officials, SOE executives can steal valuable assets by keeping them concealed during *gaizhi*. When Pengshui Food Services was privatized in 1998, its four top managers hid three real estate properties and later sold them, sharing the proceeds of 1.85 million yuan.[55] Compared with executives at large SOEs in control of far more valuable assets, these four executives were petty thieves. Wang Yongchun, general manager of a government-owned real estate firm in Lanzhou, succeeded in hiding more than 84 million yuan in SOE assets when his SOE was privatized in 2007. His method involved misclassifying three subsidiaries during the valuation phase as "collective" rather than "state." According to the regulations, collectively owned assets could be kept in the newly formed entity. As a result, Wang owned 2.4 percent of the new "collective" firm, worth millions of yuan.[56] Wu Xiaoli, general manager of a Shanghai SOE, applied a slightly different method to gain control of valuable real estate owned by her SOE. When her SOE went through an ownership change in 2010, Wu concealed the real estate assets and later owned 49 percent of the newly formed private firm. The value of the real estate was roughly 42 million yuan.[57]

Looting through Ostensibly Legitimate Asset Transactions

The third form of looting SOEs is through sweetheart, albeit ostensibly legitimate, asset transactions with favored private businessmen. In these deals, the SOEs typically purchase assets owned by private businessmen at inflated prices or sell them SOE assets at deep discounts, thus transferring large amounts of state-owned wealth into private hands. The scandal at China National Petroleum Corp.

(CNPC) revealed how profitable such transactions were for private businessmen who had befriended powerful politicians and SOE executives. Jiang Jiemin, the former chairman of CNPC and a protégé of Zhou Yongkang, was accused of, in addition to pocketing 14 million yuan in bribes and possessing another 14 million yuan in unexplained wealth, helping private businessmen obtain exploration and production rights in state-owned oil fields at the behest of Zhou Yongkang.[58] According to investigations carried out by Caixin, CNPC sold Zhou's elder son, Zhou Bin, the rights to two blocks in an oil field in 2007–2008, which Zhou Bin quickly resold for a reported profit of 550 million yuan. Cao Yongzheng, allegedly Zhou Yongkang's personal fortune-teller, was made a joint venture partner with CNPC, and Cao's firm shared hundreds of millions of yuan in revenue from a high-yielding block in an oil field owned by CNPC. Caixin's reporters found that Cao's firm had undistributed profits of 1.1 billion yuan at the end of 2012.[59]

Huang Xiaohu, chairman of Anhui-based Jungong Group, made millions of yuan in profits by purchasing state-owned mines at deeply discounted prices. One of the transactions he completed was the purchase of two coal mines owned by Xinwen Mining Group, a giant SOE in Shandong. The transaction must have yielded huge profits for Huang, who gave 11.38 million HKD in 2009 as an "appreciation" to the chairman of Xinwen, Lang Qingtian (who received a suspended death sentence for his role in another mega corruption scandal). Separately, Huang also gave 4.5 million yuan in bribes to a local deputy mayor in Anhui who helped him purchase a majority stake in a coal mine.[60] The corruption case that led to the arrests of multiple senior executives at China Resources, a giant state-owned conglomerate with $66 billion in revenue in 2014, also centered on questionable large asset transactions between the conglomerate and private businessmen.

According to press reports, Song Lin, chairman of China Resources, overpaid several billion yuan for coal mining assets owned by a heavily indebted Shanxi coal tycoon in two transactions in 2010. After Song was arrested in 2014, several of his closest aides involved in the purchase, including the firm's chief auditor, the chairman, and the CEO of the subsidiary that made the purchase, were all detained.[61]

Mechanisms of Collusion

It is hard for SOE executives to steal successfully without aligning their interests and assessing the benefits and risks of participation in illegal acts. Analysis of the evidence from the sample cases suggests that these executives depend on three mechanisms in the formation of collusive alliances and the commission of criminal acts inside the SOEs.

The first is *maiguan maiguan,* the buying and selling of appointments and promotions. A vital mechanism in vertical collusion, this widespread practice in local governments has also pervaded large SOEs, where the top executives have great influence, if not a monopoly, on personnel decisions. *Maiguan maiguan* performs a key function in aligning the interests of corrupt SOEs and facilitating their collusion. One obvious reason for the existence of *maiguan maiguan* in large SOEs is that mid-level and senior executive positions are desirable because they carry high status, offer better compensation, and can generate greater corruption income. By contrast, smaller SOEs have flatter organizations, and mid-level or senior executive positions may not be desirable enough to warrant bribes. Another reason that *maiguan maiguan* facilitates collusion in large SOEs is that this practice enables top executives and their subordinates to develop deeper personal ties, align their interests, and share risks. Evidently, a top executive will have greater trust in a subordinate who has bribed him for a promotion. The last reason that *maiguan maiguan* breeds collusive corruption in large SOEs is that those who have purchased their executive positions have strong incentives to recover their investments by participating in theft.

In the fifty sample cases, executives in nine of them, all with large SOEs, engaged in *maiguan maiguan*. During his trial in 2015, Jiang Jiemin, the former chairman of CNPC, was accused of taking bribes to help others to receive promotions. The head of the finance department at the Agricultural Development Bank of China paid a bribe of 300,000 yuan in 1999 to the vice president of the bank to advance his career prospects (he was later promoted to vice president of the bank).[62] During his long tenure (2000–2012), Li Changxuan, general manager of Sinograin Corp.'s Henan branch, received 3 million yuan in bribes (all from public funds) from twenty-five subordinates who were directors of the firm's municipal and county affiliates.[63] Li Renzhi, chairman of the Yao Coal Group in Gansu, received 800,000 yuan in bribes from fifteen mid-level executives who later received better jobs and promotions in 2007–2009. They included the head of the power division, director of supplies, deputy director of audits, director of safety, and three managers of local coal mining subsidiaries.[64]

The second mechanism is the direct sharing of the illicit income from corrupt activities, a common practice in horizontal collusion. In most cases, the illicit income consists of bribes and embezzled or misappropriated funds. The case involving three managers of the Sanming City Materials Group is the most representative. Between 2005 and 2007, the general manager, his deputy, and the CCP secretary for discipline inspection at the firm consulted with each other and collectively agreed to make loans totaling 2 million yuan to another firm using the SOE's funds. They split the proceeds among themselves.[65] In some cases, such income is derived from dividends generated by the ownership of shares (either voting or nonvoting) in private firms that benefit from business with the SOEs. For example, four executives caught for corruption at Nanjing Changta Coal Co. in Fujian collectively decided in 1997 to lease part of a coal mine to a private businessman in return for receiving nonvoting shares and dividend income.[66] Finally, participation in collusive corruption can be motivated by the prospect of partial ownership of a new private firm set up with assets stripped from the SOE. Since theft of a valuable asset—usually land—is a complex act procedurally, key individuals in the firm can be persuaded to participate only with the inducement of shares in the new company. The executives at Guangzhou Baiyun and Wenzhou Cailanzi who took part in the scheme all owned shares in the new firms that were set up with the stripped state-owned assets.[67]

The third and last mechanism of collusion is the knowledge or information about corrupt activities carried out by fellow executives. In these cases, executives caught by anticorruption investigations did not collude directly with each other, but they nevertheless seemed to be knowledgeable or aware of their colleagues' criminal activities. As we hypothesize, such knowledge can motivate an official inside the Chinese party-state to start his own corrupt activities because, in an organization led by corrupt individuals, not only are norms subverted but also detection risks tend to diminish (as top corrupt leaders do not wish to attract attention by alerting the authorities to the possible criminal acts committed by their subordinates). Such knowledge gives the perpetrators of corruption some bargaining power with the prosecutors when they are caught. The clue to such implicit knowledge can be found in the sentencing documents or their summaries in the press when a convicted official or a SOE executive is credited with "exposing crimes committed by others" (*jianju taren fanzui*) or "earning a major merit" (*zhongda ligong*). Occasionally, press coverage of corruption in SOEs and local governments provides greater detail on the role played by executives and officials in uncovering criminal acts committed by their colleagues who are not their partners in crime. In our sample, there are six instances in which corrupt SOE executives received lenient punishment because they provided tips to investigators that led to the arrests of other executives who were not their coconspirators. One representative example was Huang Xiaohu, chairman of Anhui Jungong Group. After his arrest in 2013, Huang gave investigators information that his predecessor and another senior executive had engaged in bribery and embezzlement. Huang received nineteen years, instead of a harsher sentence. At Capital Development Corp., a senior executive investigated in 2004 for illegal distribution of state-owned assets, tipped off the prosecutors about his boss's corrupt activities.[68]

Causes of Collusive Corruption

Large-scale and persistent theft in SOEs is no accident. Such activities can best be understood in the institutional context of the Chinese political economy in general, and that of the SOEs in particular. Here we briefly discuss three institutional features that make collusive corruption in SOEs not only possible, but highly profitable.

Politicized and Weak Corporate Governance

Of the fifty sample cases, forty-four involve the highest-ranking executive in the company, the chairman, president, or party secretary. The participation of the most senior executives in large corruption cases involving SOEs, collusive corruption cases in particular, is easy to explain. Because the most senior executives in SOEs have near-total control in making important business decisions, corruption is impossible without the support and participation of these individuals. Senior executives in SOEs are also well positioned to collude with their underlings because most of the latter are their trusted loyalists and supporters (some of the top executives in this sample promoted or appointed their subordinates in exchange for bribes). The combination of the executive power vested in their positions and the personal relationships with their junior colleagues greatly facilitates collusive activities.

Additionally, corporate governance in most Chinese SOEs is only rudimentary. As revealed by the sample cases, the entities that are supposed to have oversight over the chairmen or presidents of the SOEs, such as the board of directors, local governments, or local state-owned assets supervision and administration committees, exercise little control over the major decisions made by the senior executives of the SOEs. These entities have little knowledge of the operations of the SOEs and conduct only infrequent and cursory inspections of the facilities. According to Li Changhan, the president of Sinograin Corp. (Henan) who carried out an elaborate scheme to defraud a government-sponsored grain subsidy program to the tune of 700 million yuan, Sinograin Corp. rarely looked into the management of its Henan subsidiary. When it occasionally sent down inspectors, they would be taken to a few well-managed granaries. In fact, in 2008, after the Beijing headquarters of the firm received tips about the ongoing fraud in Henan, it dispatched auditors to Henan, but they uncovered suspect transactions involving only several thousand tons of grain, and nothing came of the audit.[69]

Corporate governance is particularly weak in SOEs owned by local governments. One reason is the long tenure of their top executives.

Unlike giant SOEs directly administered by the State-Owned Assets Supervision and Administration Commission (SASAC), which have stricter limits on age and tenure (although these restrictions have not prevented major corruption scandals), locally owned SOEs do not have such restrictions.[70] In the case of Gansu Lanzhou Tansu Group, the chief perpetrator was the president of the company from 1987 to 2002. Wang Xiaojin, chairman of the Anhui Gujing Group, headed the company for over twenty years. Li Changxuan, who presided over the 700 million yuan fraud at Sinograin Corp. (Henan), headed the subsidiary for twelve years. Zhang Xinhua, who organized a sophisticated scheme to gain state-owned assets valued at over 284 million yuan, was the president of a local SOE for fifteen years. Ying Guoquan, the chairman of a food group in Wenzhou who also engineered a similar asset-grabbing scheme, headed his SOE for twelve years. In many ways, top executives in Chinese SOEs are "dirt emperors" who exercise unchallenged control within their fiefdoms. The concentration of such managerial power in the hands of poorly supervised executives is behind the widespread phenomenon of collusive corruption in Chinese SOEs. In vertical collusion, as we know, even "dirt emperors" need coconspirators to execute more sophisticated schemes involving the theft of nominally state-owned assets.

Lack of Effective Financial Control

Chinese SOEs are particularly vulnerable to looting by their executives because of lax financial control. In most of the fifty sample cases, executives were able to embezzle large amounts of company funds, illegally use company funds to invest in securities and reap the gains, and set up off-budget slush funds to cover unauthorized expenses (including bribery). Poor financial controls inside Chinese SOEs allow executives to collude with each other to extract large sums of money for personal use. As mentioned earlier, embezzlement is the second most frequently committed crime among SOE executives. Evidence from the sample cases shows that, in addition to theft, embezzlement in Chinese SOEs is frequently disguised through bogus "loans" and slush funds. Using fake loans to steal SOE funds gives executives at least some plausible legal cover even though they do not intend to repay the loans. In the case of Hengshan Iron Corp., one president borrowed 600,000 yuan from the company as a "loan" in 1998 but never paid it back. In the corruption probe of Qingqi Group, a Shandong-based motorcycle manufacturer that later went bankrupt, investigators found that the company chairman took 6.5 million yuan for personal use but did not pay it back.[71] The chairman of Henan-based Hebi Coal Group, Li Yongxin, illegally authorized a loan of 64.5 million yuan to a personal friend in 2003.[72]

A much more prevalent form of theft is the use of slush funds—income generated by SOEs but deposited in hidden accounts that do not show up on the corporate balance sheets. Executives have complete control over these slush funds. In the case of Hengshan Iron Corp., slush funds in excess of 3 million yuan were used to pay for large bonuses and discretionary spending (usually extravagant entertainment or travel expenses disallowed by government policy) for company executives before the firm went bankrupt in 2003. In the probe of the scandal at Huishang Group in Anhui in 2007, investigators discovered that its executives had a slush fund of over 2 million yuan from profits gained from the company's off-book investments and hidden in a brokerage account not included on the company's books.[73] In 2002, the top three executives of Qingqi Group hid in a slush fund 35.2 million yuan in profits generated by a plot of land owned by their company; they used the money to purchase stocks for their own investments.[74]

By far the biggest financial loophole in SOEs is control over the use of its cash. "Unauthorized use of public funds," a serious crime in China, is endemic in SOEs. It normally refers to the use of an SOE's funds for purposes that are either unauthorized or explicitly prohibited. In these cases, the perpetrators do not actually embezzle the funds. Instead, they use the funds mostly to generate undeclared income for themselves (such as investing in the stock market and pocketing the gains). Nearly all the instances of "unauthorized use of public funds" in our sample are connected with investments in securities made by executives using company funds without proper approval or in explicit violation of company and government rules. One executive at Lanzhou Liancheng Aluminum Corp. misused 13 million yuan in stock market speculation in 1994.[75] The worst offenders in terms of unauthorized use of public funds were executives of Huishang Group, a large Anhui SOE in the logistics business. Cai Wenlong, its chairman for more than ten years, filled his company's senior positions with friends from his hometown. Cai himself was responsible for massive losses in his unauthorized and ill-fated investments in stocks and commodities. In 2001, without board approval, he authorized using company money to speculate in the stock market, losing 155 million yuan (these transactions netted him a bribe of 800,000 yuan from a private broker who executed the trades). Undeterred, Cai gambled on commodities even though government regulations prohibit such investments. He lost another 180 million yuan. Many of his subordinates took part in similar schemes. Three executives got lucky when their 12 million yuan of investments in stocks funded by the company's money produced a profit (which they shared). But two of their colleagues were not so fortunate. One deputy manager in charge of the company's funds misused 18.8 million yuan to speculate in options for commodities and lost 16.5 million yuan.

Another lost all of the 15 million yuan of the company's funds used in his ill-timed bets on commodities.[76] The biggest case of unauthorized use of public funds occurred at the Agricultural Development Bank. According to government investigators, during 1996–1999 executives at the bank used 810 million yuan of the bank's money to speculate in stocks, with the gains disappearing into their own pockets.[77]

Unclear Property Rights

As illustrated by the description and analysis of collusive corruption in SOEs, it is evident that changes in the property rights in state-owned assets have created ideal conditions for the agents of the state to loot valuable assets over which they then can exercise direct control. The progressive decentralization of the control rights to state-owned property without real clarification of ownership has given those with control rights effective ownership rights because they have the ability to transfer to themselves and to their cronies the control rights, physical possession, and income streams from the state-owned property. Three groups have benefited from the decentralization of control of property with no real owners. SOE executives are the biggest beneficiaries since they exercise the control rights directly and possess a wide variety of means to extract wealth from the state. Political elites, both local and national, have also reaped enormous ill-gotten gains from this institutional arrangement. Although they do not directly control the SOE assets, they do control the appointment of SOE executives, who must please their political superiors with bribes or access to underpriced state-owned assets. The third group consists of well-connected private entrepreneurs who use bribery to turn SOE executives and local political elites into their patrons. The victims of the looting by colluding elites are the nominal legal owners of these assets, the Chinese people, who exercise little oversight or control over either the agents or the property of the state.

The evidence illustrates how the combination of decentralization of executive authority and partial property rights reform has enabled executives in SOEs to misappropriate nominally state-owned assets to benefit themselves, their families, and friends in the private sector. Three of our findings warrant special attention.

First, while looting by SOE insiders exists at all levels, the amount of wealth available for looting is far greater inside the colossal SOEs directly controlled by the central government. The scandal at CNPC, the country's largest energy firm, which came to light in 2013, shows that family members of the top ruling elites can steal hundreds of millions of yuan of wealth with relative ease. Of course, lower-level elites in China's state-owned sector have access to considerable wealth that can also be stolen. However, such looting requires greater effort and ingenuity because they lack the requisite political power to seize the most valuable assets owned by the state.

Second, SOE executives who loot state-owned property have demonstrated a remarkable adaptability in seeking out the opportunities offered by China's hybrid economy. To be sure, many of the activities they engage in are garden-variety forms of theft, such as bribery and embezzlement. But as they gain greater control over the finances and operations inside the SOEs, they have learned to maximize the income potential of their newly found discretionary power. In particular, through "insider privatization," SOE executives can form private companies or joint ventures with their cronies to which they then transfer valuable assets from the SOEs that they control at deeply discounted prices or at no cost.

Third, although looting by senior officials and their family members attracts headlines, mid-level officials in Chinese SOEs are almost equally capable of accumulating significant private fortunes. This suggests that China's crony capitalism differs from the oligarchical cronyism in Russia and other former Soviet republics in one critical dimension. The social base of crony capitalism may be narrow, but given the large number of mid-level officials (including SOE executives) who actively participate in the looting of the state, the size of this group is large and the damage done by this group to China's socioeconomic well-being may be even more substantial than that of the small number of oligarchs. Since they are entrenched in all sectors and reaches of the economy, they are also more difficult to dislodge.

6

In Bed with the Mafia: Collusion between Law Enforcement and Organized Crime

In some of the recent major cases involving officials, the egregiousness of their crimes and the amounts of money involved are simply shocking. They trade power for money and sex with utter brazenness and recklessness!

—Xi Jinping, April 19, 2013

IT NOW has become a routine ritual for senior Chinese leaders to express outrage, as Xi did in April 2013, over the depravity of their underlings. However, the greed, decadence, and lawlessness of the agents of the party-state should not surprise us if we consider the intrinsic attractiveness of collusion for its perpetrators, who can with great ease convert their public authority into illicit instruments for accumulation of private wealth. Since the benefits of forming close personal relationships with government officials are obvious and bountiful, the world of crony capitalism inevitably beckons criminal elites to scramble for its spoils. Consequently, it is not unusual to encounter the presence of politically protected organized crime in societies ravaged by crony capitalism. In other words, the collusion between organized crime and government officials, law enforcement in particular, is also an identifying characteristic of crony capitalism.

In the case of post-Tiananmen China, rapid growth and changes in property rights have created irresistible opportunities for elites of the criminal underground.[1] Amid rising prosperity, not only are their traditional businesses such as gambling, prostitution, and drug trafficking booming; they can also extend their reach into new sectors with higher profit margins and potential for instant large fortunes, such as real estate, mining, construction, and transportation. In both cases, however, protection from local authorities, in particular from law enforcement officials (LEOs), is vital. Fortunately for China's aspiring mafia bosses, recruiting willing accomplices from the ranks of LEOs has turned out to be much less challenging than they might have feared because these officials are subject to the same economic incentives that have made corruption endemic. In this chapter, we investigate the collusion between organized crime and LEOs by analyzing well-publicized cases of organized criminal groups that have received protection from multiple LEOs. We attempt to understand the market dynamics in the darkest corner of crony capitalism in China and probe the decay of a key institution in the Chinese party-state. The objective is to further substantiate the claim that crony capitalism is generating the same governance pathologies in critical state agencies and that the capabilities of the Chinese state, despite its outward appearance of strength and efficacy, have been seriously degraded.

Corruption and Mafia Influence in Law Enforcement

Corruption in Chinese law enforcement agencies is a well-publicized fact. A partial and perhaps imperfect gauge of the extent of rot in this vital part of the Chinese state is the large number of senior police officers who have been arrested and sentenced for corruption and other criminal activities (including murder and protection of organized crime). One incomplete list of chief LEOs who had been arrested, prosecuted, and sentenced for criminal activities as of November 2011 includes 197 senior police officers (defined as police chiefs and deputy police chiefs).[2] Among them were one deputy minister of public security, one assistant minister of public security, four directors general in the departments of the Ministry of Public Security, seven directors of provincial departments of public security, nine deputy directors of provincial departments of public security, 99 directors of prefecture and county bureaus of public security, and 76 deputy directors of prefecture and county bureaus of public security. Also notable is the fall of police chiefs in major cities and provincial capitals, such as Tianjin, Shenyang, Qingdao, Taiyuan, Nanchang, and Fuzhou. The seriousness of their crimes can be measured by the severity of the punishment they received. Of those whose sentences were publicly announced, fourteen were sentenced to death, nine received a suspended death penalty, and ten received life imprisonment. Five committed suicide. Among the 197 disgraced police chiefs, thirty-nine, or 20 percent, were explicitly linked to organized crime.

Theoretically, collusion between law enforcement and organized crime is not difficult to understand. In spite of their use of violence and committing of crimes, mafia bosses seek the same benefits from collaborating with LEOs as private businessmen seek from colluding with government officials. One of them is a reduction of the uncertainty in their overall business environment. Private businessmen successful in bribing government officials gain greater certainty in securing desired transactions at a lower cost. Crime bosses who put senior police officers on their payrolls need not worry about actions that will disrupt their profitable criminal operations, such as gambling and prostitution. Another benefit is the elimination of competition. Private businessmen, particularly those in pursuit of undervalued state-owned assets, can remove their competitors from the bidding process by bribing the officials in charge. Similarly, a crime boss who has gained the protection of the local police chief can count on him to keep other organized criminal groups off his turf.

Political and social status, for instance membership in the local people's congress or people's political consultative conference (PPCC), is a third benefit that crime bosses can gain by their association with powerful local politicians. Such a status not only provides a useful legitimate cover for their illegal activities but also facilitates the building of political networks and expansion of their criminal operations. Among the fifty sample cases selected for this study, thirteen crime bosses, or one-quarter of the total, were members of their local people's congresses or the PPCC. Among the thirteen, four were members of the local people's congress (Li Zhengang in Maoming, Ou Jian in Xiangtan, Lan Linyan in Hengfeng, and Xie Wensheng in Heyang), five were members of the local PPCC (Zhang Zhixin in Qiqihaer, Chen Kai in Fuzhou, Xiong Xinxin in Fuzhou, Liao Fudong in Wuxuan, and Jiang Qixin in Dongan), two were members of the standing committee of the local PPCC (Yao Zhihong in Shaoyang and Zhang Wei in Wenling), and one was a member of both the local people's congress and the PPCC (Liu Yong in Shenyang). What sets these crime bosses apart from the others in the sample is the large size of their criminal enterprises and their personal wealth. Without exception, they all owned and operated profitable businesses in real estate, mining, loan sharking, and prostitution. Their financial resources gave them the means to bribe local government officials, whose sponsorship was indispensable to induction into these two bodies. At the same time, the large size of their business operations also motivated them to purchase additional political insurance, the kind provided by membership in these two bodies.

The most important benefit for organized crime seeking protection from LEOs is realization of the huge profit potential offered by the opportunity to gain control of severely underpriced state-owned assets, almost exclusively land and mines. However, unlike an average private entrepreneur who typically resorts to bribery, a crime boss mixes bribery with intimidation and violence. In press accounts of the involvement of organized crime in China's real estate and mining sectors, crime bosses, after paying off senior LEOs, rely mainly on violence, such as assaults and even murder, to drive out the competition in these sectors. Once they gain control of these assets, they continue to pay the same government officials and LEOs, practically putting them on retainer.

However, there is one vital difference between a crime boss and a private entrepreneur seeking favors from government officials. The task for a private entrepreneur is far more complicated because he must gain access to—and then bribe—officials in multiple government agencies, which have overlapping authority over the disposal of state-owned assets or the enforcement of business regulations. On most occasions, a crime boss normally needs to befriend and bribe officials in only one government agency—the bureau of public security. A gangster has no need to bribe a large number of officials in several agencies unless he turns his criminal enterprise into a conglomerate with multiple business lines (such as finance, transportation, and real estate). As we shall see in our cases, only a small number of crime bosses have managed to build large and complex operations. Consequently, the majority of crime bosses, even the most flamboyant ones, generate lower profits from their criminal activities because their conventional illegal businesses, such as gambling and prostitution, lack the economics of scale or have much lower profit margins than the real estate, mining, and construction deals struck between private businessmen and government officials. As the data in the Appendix indicate (see Table A.4), this economic reality forces crime bosses to keep the number of officers on their payrolls relatively small to economize on the amounts of bribes they have to pay. In addition, the sum of their bribes is much smaller than that paid by private businessmen.

Yet, for LEOs, even relatively small bribes are attractive enough for them to offer protection to organized crime. The most plausible explanation is that the market value of their power is essentially zero since there is no other buyer for their protection and they have little power to extract large bribes from private businessmen whose commercial activities do not require assistance from the police under normal circumstances. As a result, they are willing to accept the price offered by a buyer who operates a monopsony. Despite this crucial difference, the emergence and growth of collusion between organized crime and LEOs closely resembles the relationships between private businessmen and government officials in that both types of collusion have risen and taken root in Chinese society.

One obvious cause of the rise of this type of collusion is the growth of organized crime since the 1990s. As a social phenomenon, organized crime did not exist as a special category in the 1980s. A keyword search for the Chinese term *heishehui* (organized crime) in the China Knowledge Reserch Integrated Database (cnki.net), which includes electronic copies of all the major publications in China, finds that the first time this term was used in a specific Chinese context was in 1990. But the number of references to *heishehui* increased dramatically thereafter (peaking at about 1,000 in 2010). This development has stimulated considerable scholarly research, most of which is focused on the links between organized crime in China and international human and drug trafficking. Research conducted outside of China that focuses exclusively on the growth and impact of organized crime in China remains relatively rare.[3] The collusion between LEOs and organized crime, also a post-1989 phenomenon, has received even less scholarly attention.[4]

Based on press reports and data collected for this study (Table A.4), collusion between LEOs and organized crime is widespread geographically and has persisted despite repeated crackdowns by the Chinese government. The cases collected for this study indicate that this phenomenon exists in a majority of Chinese provinces. The fifty sample cases occurred in eighteen provinces. Hunan topped the list with nine; five cases occurred in Liaoning; Jilin and Guangxi each had four cases; Fujian, Jiangxi, Shaanxi, and Shanxi had three cases each; Henan and Zhejiang had two cases each; and Guizhou, Heilongjiang, Hubei, Jiangsu, Shandong, Sichuan, and Yunnan had one case each. While the size of the sample is too small to establish which provinces or regions had the most serious problem of collusion between LEOs and organized crime, the presence of such collusion in more than half of China's provinces shows that this scourge is widespread, and additional research should yield additional evidence to confirm this observation. What is important to note here is that this type of collusion takes place in regions regardless of their levels of socioeconomic development. More developed coastal provinces, such as Guangdong, Zhejiang, and Fujian, have reported such collusion, just as the poorer agricultural or resource-rich provinces of Shaanxi, Shanxi, Hunan, Henan, Guangxi, Yunnan, and Guizhou. Provinces with high concentrations of state-owned enterprises, such as Liaoning, Heilongjiang, and Jilin, are as likely to be victims of such collusion as provinces with a large presence of private firms and foreign companies, such as Guangdong, Jiangsu, Zhejiang, and Fujian.

However, to the extent that organized crime follows the same imperative of chasing profits, we can detect two patterns in our cases. Crime organizations operating in poor but resource-rich regions are more likely to get into the mining sector because it yields high returns, as shown in our sample. The crime boss in Tongguan in Shaanxi, for example, operated illegal gold mines. In Xinhua, Hunan, the criminal organization headed by Liu Junyong also owned gold mines, as did the criminal organization run by the Zhu family in Qianshan, Jiangxi. Dong Baojun, the gangster in Jinzhou, Liaoning, had a joint venture in molybdenum mining. Zhang Xiuwu, a crime boss in Lingyuan, Liaoning, used his thugs to seize control of a local iron ore mine. Several organized criminal gangs in our sample, such as those led by Lan Linyan in Hengfeng, Jiangxi, Xie Wensheng in Heyang, Hunan, and Song Kuixiang in Gaoping, Shanxi, all operated coal mines.[5]

By comparison, heads of criminal organizations operating in more wealthy urban centers prefer to set up front businesses (often real estate companies, transportation companies, logistics firms, and conglomerates) because the use of violence and intimidation gives them a significant competitive edge in these sectors. Hao Wanchun, a crime boss (active in 2000–2006) and a close friend of a deputy police chief of Shenyang, owned a real estate development company. Zhang Zhixin, who ran a mafia ring with his brother during 1993–2003, operated both a prostitution ring and a string of taxi companies in Qiqihaer in Heilongjiang. Nie Lei, who managed to recruit Qingdao City's deputy police chief as his protector, owned a real estate development company as well as illegal casinos and brothels during 2000–2010. Li Zhengang, the head of a criminal gang in Maoming, Guangdong, ran underground casinos and a loan-sharking business between 2001 and 2010. Song Pengfei, another crime boss active in Shenyang during 1995–2006, operated a logistics company that controlled a large portion of the cargo business in Zhejiang, Shenyang, Changchun, and Ha'erbin. The most wide-ranging and sophisticated operation in our sample was run by Chen Kai, a crime boss active in Fuzhou, Fujian, during 1991–2003. He owned Fujian Kaixuan Group, which operated brothels and casinos, and engaged in money laundering and drug trafficking. In addition, he was a real estate developer and owned several hotels, from which he ran his gambling and prostitution businesses. Hao Weicheng, whose criminal gang operated for two decades in Changchun (1990–2010), engaged in illegal loan collections, real estate, construction, and forced evictions. When he was sentenced to a twenty-year term in 2010, the court confiscated his personal assets worth 40 million yuan. Jia Jianjun, a crime boss in Yiwu in Zhejiang during 1993–2001, monopolized the local cargo shipping business and his company controlled assets in the amount of close to 100 million yuan. Ou Jian, whose businesses in Hunan during 1989–2010 included gambling, loan sharking, and logistics, reportedly earned over 100 million yuan in illegal profits.[6]

The Sociology and Economics of Collusion with Organized Crime

Despite its use of violence, organized crime is fundamentally a profit-seeking activity. As such, organized crime in China follows the same economic principles that dictate legitimate business operations. If legitimate businesses generate profits through superior products, management, and efficiency, organized crime makes money by utilizing its comparative advantage—its capacity for using violence to drive out the competition or to seize assets. The economic logic that animates organized crime in China can be seen in official documents identifying its key areas of operation. Chinese law enforcement authorities have repeatedly launched anti-mafia campaigns called "*dahei chu'e*" (strike at black and root out evil). When such campaigns are initiated, the authorities usually identify areas as priorities for crackdown. In June 2008, for example, the provincial department of public security in Liaoning issued a list of specific priority targets and a quota for a new anti-mafia offensive on the eve of the Beijing Olympics. The department demanded that every city must eliminate one criminal organization; each county and district must destroy five such organizations. In particular, the order singled out five types of organized crime that should be priority targets:

1. Groups that monopolize markets through the use of violence, engage in illegal mining and exploration for oil, and loot the state's natural resources.

2. Groups that use violence and intimidation to monopolize the transportation, logistics, wholesale, and construction industries, and use violence to evict urban residents and disrupt markets and regulatory enforcement actions.

3. Groups that manipulate and control elections to seize control of local governments.

4. LEOs who leak tips to organized crime, cover up their crimes, and collude with them in criminal activities.

5. Groups that use hotels and entertainment venues to engage in gambling, prostitution, drug trafficking, and loan sharking.[7]

What is notable in this list is that of the five mafia activities identified by Liaoning's provincial department of public security (and presumably similar departments in other provinces), three are economic in nature. This list confirms that organized crime has pervaded a wide range of political and economic activities. Especially worrying for the authorities is the impact of organized crime on the integrity of law enforcement agencies, the control of grassroots political power, and important economic sectors such as natural resources, construction, transportation, and logistics.

Our sample offers evidence in support of such concerns. Among the fifty criminal groups profiled here, sixteen operated mining businesses; six owned real estate development companies; twelve ran businesses in logistics, construction, transportation, wholesale seafood, illegal loan collection, and others.[8] Altogether, thirty-four of the fifty criminal groups had profitable businesses alongside their more conventional criminal activities, such as extortion, gambling, prostitution, and drug trafficking. The demand for protection from local government and law enforcement officials thus originates from two sources. Obviously, conventional criminal activities require such protection. But more importantly, sophisticated and lucrative criminal operations necessitate reliable and sustained protection since they have valuable fixed assets (hotels and mines in particular) and regular income streams, all of which are vulnerable to competition from legitimate businesses and other criminal organizations, and to crackdown by law enforcement.

The Sociology of Collusion

To gain protection from LEOs, organized crime has several means to establish long-term relationships with their protectors. Like private businessmen skilled in exploiting the Chinese gift-giving culture in recruiting corrupt officials, leaders of organized crime also resort to small gifts to initiate their relationship with LEOs. Technically, this is not difficult to do because most crime bosses have covers as generous private businessmen eager to please local officials. One typical example is how the police chief of the city of Wenling in Zhejiang was recruited. One of the leaders of the criminal group whose cover was "general manager" of a conglomerate first met the local police chief, who was staying at a hotel owned by the conglomerate in 1996. He offered the chief a basket of fruit as a token of appreciation for his patronage. Then a few days later, he purchased an expensive suit and other accessories for the police chief, who accepted the gifts. Six months later, the crime boss placed a plastic bag containing 50,000 yuan in cash in the police chief's room, telling him that this was the "dividend" from his equity shares in their company. Although initially reluctant to take the cash gift, the police chief nevertheless accepted the money—and then started performing protective services for the crime boss.[9] Hao Wanchun, a crime boss in Shenyang, first befriended a rising star in the city's public security bureau by giving him two expensive watches upon hearing the news that the police officer, Zhang Jianming, was being considered for promotion in 2002. Claiming that he knew municipal leaders well, Hao offered to use his contacts to help Zhang improve his chances.[10]

Besides offering gifts, crime bosses also take advantage of China's dining culture to approach their prospective protectors. Xiong Xinxin, Fuzhou's crime boss, first established his ties with Xu Xiaogang, a deputy director of the Jiangxi provincial public security department, by inviting him to dine at a fancy restaurant in a five-star hotel in the provincial capital in 2000. Xiong had legitimate cover: He was both a successful businessman and a member of a district PPCC.[11] Liu Zhiduo, the police chief of Yiwu in Zhejiang, began his association with organized crime by attending a dinner in 1995 hosted by a woman who was a member of the criminal organization and who later became his mistress.[12] Song Kuixiang, leader of a criminal gang in Gaoping, Shanxi, befriended the city's party chief, Zhang Xilai, initially with a dinner hosted in his own hotel in 1995 and, to show his appreciation, Zhang promised to help nullify the Gaoping public security bureau's preliminary decision to send Song off to "education through labor" for his involvement in a fight.[13]

For crime bosses, the most effective and reliable way of securing long-term support from local government and law enforcement officials is by giving them free sex in their brothels or providing them with prostitutes. One example in our sample is Zhang Zhixin. The Heilongjiang gangster (active in 1993–2003) recruited a deputy party chief and the secretary of the discipline inspection committee of the municipal bureau of public security by giving him a "gold card" which entitled him to free access to Zhang's hotels and bathhouses. There the police officer patronized prostitutes free of charge. Zhang used the same tactic to befriend several LEOs and local politicians. Their dalliances with prostitutes were secretly recorded on video.[14] Li Yang, a deputy police chief in Huai'an, Jiangsu, frequently patronized the brothel run by Shi Chuanhai, leader of a criminal organization engaged in prostitution and drug trafficking (during 1992–2001). Eight of his fellow police officers also received free sexual services at the establishment, one of them on ten separate occasions.[15] Xu Jie, who presided over a criminal gang in Shunchang in Fujian for a decade (1991–2001), not only delivered a mistress to the deputy police chief but also arranged two trips for the deputy party chief in charge of law enforcement and a group of police officers to patronize prostitutes in a fancy hotel in Fuzhou.[16] Ou Jian, a crime boss in Xiangtan, Hunan, during 1989–2010, solidified his ties with the local deputy police chief, his primary protector, by providing prostitutes and drugs.[17] Yao Zhihong, whose criminal enterprise during 1994–2002 included a large brothel in Shaoyang, Hunan, provided local government and law enforcement officials with complimentary services to obtain their protection.[18]

Another way of forming a long-term relationship is to offer LEOs a share of the profits from criminal activities. Feng Yongqiang, a mafia boss operating gold mines in Tongguan, Shaanxi, between 1998 and 2007, gave shares in his mines to local police officers. The deputy police chief had shares in two mines. The brother of the secretary of the local CDI was a business partner in gold mining with the mafia boss.[19] Liu Junyong, a gangster operating a gold mine and a construction company in Xinhua, Hunan, during 1995–2005, allowed a local police chief to invest 80,000 yuan in his businesses.[20] Chen Kai, the Fuzhou crime boss, actively befriended the son of the city police chief in the early 1990s and then managed to become the godson of the police chief himself. The son of the police chief was made a business partner and vice chairman in Chen's conglomerate.[21] Putting local officers on a regular retainer can secure their long-term protection as well. Fuzhou's deputy police chief, who had responsibility over the city's entertainment industry, received a monthly payment from Chen Kai for allowing him to freely operate his drug, gambling, and prostitution operations in his hotels and clubs.[22] A particularly egregious case was the joint prostitution venture established between Yao Zhihong, a crime boss, and local authorities in Shaoyang, Hunan. With the support of two local officials, the deputy director of the anticorruption unit in the prosecutor's office and a deputy director of the city's economic commission, Yao succeeded in making a security firm run by the local public security bureau a joint venture partner in his brothel in 1997.[23] In a similar instance in 1999, the manager of a local casino owned by Ou Tao, a crime boss in Rucheng, Hunan, met with the local police chief, the CCP secretary in charge of law enforcement, and another local government official to hammer out an agreement which would pay the local public security bureau a fixed protection fee.[24] The party chief of Zhumadian in Henan owned shares in the largest and most luxurious mafia-operated brothel (shut down in 2013) in Zhengzhou, the provincial capital.[25] Xie Kongbing, the deputy CCP secretary of politics and law in Chenzhou, Hunan, became a protector of the local crime boss after he was promised dividend-only shares in a coal mine operated by the gangster in 1998.[26]

On occasion, protection is much easier to obtain when the mafia boss himself is a police officer, a family member of a powerful local politician, or a local official. Police officers who have become crime bosses have unique advantages in carrying out criminal activities under the protection of his colleagues. Their intimate knowledge of the operational tactics of law enforcement allows them to conceal their involvement or to commit their crimes with reduced risks of detection. Unlike average gangsters, police officers who have turned to organized crime can use their cover to disguise criminal acts as official law enforcement actions. Their contacts inside the law enforcement agencies and personal relationships with superiors provide additional protection and access to confidential information critical to their survival. We have three such examples: Guan Jianjun, head of the patrol brigade of an urban district, formed a criminal organization in 1999 and seized several coal mines in Yangquan, Shanxi. His father was a deputy police chief.[27] Wang Yufan, a deputy police chief in Tonghua, Jilin, was also the head of a criminal organization before his arrest in 2009. His official driver was his closest partner in crime.[28] Long Jiefeng, a police officer who headed a violent criminal organization, terrorized Sihui City in Guangdong between 1999 and 2005 before he was shot dead by a rival gang.[29]

In several cases in our sample, the leader of the criminal gang was either a family member of a powerful local official or an official himself. Their family backgrounds or contacts inside the government provided them with political and social capital to gain protection from the local authorities. The father of Liu Yong, Shenyang's well-shielded gangster (active 1995–2000), was a retired chief of the criminal tribunal in the municipal intermediate court. Among Liu's most important patrons were a former president of the court and a sitting vice president.[30] Tang Hong, a gangster active during 1993–2000 in Suining, Hunan, relied on his father, the chairman of the county people's congress, for protection. Tang himself was an official in the local tax bureau. Tang's brother, also a gangster, was an official in the local administration of industry and commerce.[31] The father of Tian Bo, leader of a criminal organization active during 1995–1999 in Meihekou, Jilin, was a former vice magistrate of the city and promoted the official who later served as Tian's principal protector.[32] Zhu Haiquan, the head of the Zhu family that led a criminal gang during 1989–2001 in Qianshan in Jiangxi, was the township party secretary.[33] Before his fall in 2010, Lan Linyan, the crime boss in Hengfeng, Jiangxi, was his village's party chief and a delegate to the provincial people's congress. Another leader of his gang was a member of the county people's congress; two other gangsters were members of the county PPCC.[34] Tan Heping, the head of a criminal organization in Lianyuan, Hunan, was the deputy director of a local rural credit co-op until his arrest in 2001.[35] Zeng Shaolin, who during 1997–2001 led a gang of more than thirty criminals in Fushun, Sichuan, was a deputy director of the county housing bureau.[36]

An intriguing puzzle in the sociology of collusion is how bonding, trust, and cooperation were established and facilitated within local governments and law enforcement agencies. In most published accounts of the cases in the sample, Chinese authorities released few details about how local government and law enforcement officials colluded with each other while they provided much greater amounts of information about how leaders of criminal organizations befriended and corrupted these officials. However, in a few instances, official press coverage did disclose enough information to allow us to piece together the puzzle. One mechanism through which local government and law enforcement officials develop trust and collaborative relationships in their activities is the practice of *maiguan maiguan,* or the buying and selling of offices. As we have seen, this practice also plays a crucial role in facilitating collusion among local officials and private businessmen as well as within SOEs. The same practice is also widespread inside Chinese local law enforcement agencies, where it functions as a bonding mechanism among crooked cops. Obviously, police chiefs who take bribes from their subordinates are not only corrupt and easy targets for organized crime, but also are more able to rely on the officers who have bribed them to protect gangsters. Similarly, those who have bribed their way up the ladder inside the public security bureaus are more likely to accept bribes from organized crime to recover their investment.

Several LEOs in our sample were explicitly accused of selling offices to junior police officers. Yang Qiang, the police chief of Maogang District in Maoming, Guangdong, took 3.45 million yuan in bribes from thirty-six officers during 2004–2009.[37] Between 1996 and 2001, Liu Zhiduo, the police chief of Yiwu in Zhejiang, also sold offices to his subordinates, one of whom, deputy police chief Wu Xinhua, was involved in protecting the same crime boss Liu shielded.[38] Zhou Tingxin, the deputy police chief of Zhengzhou arrested in 2014 for protecting a mafia-run brothel, was also a seller of offices.[39] Li Jian, the CCP secretary of politics and law in Shunchang, Fujian, took bribes from subordinates seeking office. More than ten officers who had bribed Li were also involved in protecting the same gangster, Xu Jie, who ran a mafia-style group during 1991–2001.[40] In 2006, Cai Yabin, deputy police chief of Xiangtan in Hunan, who was the "umbrella" of the city's crime boss, Ou Jian, paid 70,000 yuan to the city's police chief, who was himself later arrested for taking bribes from subordinates and protecting drug traffickers during 2002–2009.[41]

Bonding among colluding officers can also be established through joint participation in illegal activities. In two cases in our sample, police officers patronized local brothels together. Xu Jie, the gangster in Shunchang in Fujian, organized two trips for one of his chief protectors, a local party official in charge of law enforcement and a group of police officers, to have sex with prostitutes in a luxury hotel in Fuzhou, the provincial capital. Li Yang, a deputy police chief in Huai'an in Jiangsu and protector of a crime boss who operated a brothel, participated in three group sex orgies with prostitutes and several other police officers during 2000–2001.[42] In two other cases, key local government and law enforcement officials collectively conspired with organized crime to negotiate the terms of protection. This happened in 1996 in Shaoyang, Hunan, when the deputy director of the anticorruption unit in the prosecutor's office and a deputy director of the city's economic commission negotiated with Yao Zhihong, the gangster running a brothel, for a partnership between the criminal organization and a security firm run by the local public security bureau.[43] In Rucheng, also in Hunan, the local police chief, the CCP secretary in charge of law enforcement, and another local government official met a representative of the local crime boss in 1999 to hash out the terms of protection for the gangster's casino.[44]

The Economics of Collusion

Once a long-term relationship is cemented, crime bosses can expect many favors from LEOs. The most basic is protection for their conventional criminal activities, such as gambling, prostitution, and drug trafficking. As far as LEOs are concerned, the costs for delivering such services are relatively low because all they need to do is to turn a blind eye. By comparison, the costs of covering up violent assaults and even murder are much higher because that requires more elaborate steps and may leave behind incriminating evidence. Nevertheless, police officers working for organized crime take such risks and often manage to shield the criminals from arrest and prosecution. In Tongguan, Shaanxi, due to interference by dirty police officers (one of whom faked evidence), the death of a peasant worker, presumably murdered by a criminal gang, went unresolved for eight years.[45] In Wenling, Zhejiang, the crooked police chief directed his subordinates not to formally arrest members of the gang involved in three violent assault incidents and set free a suspect charged with sheltering a murderer in 1998.[46] Corrupt LEOs also routinely give advance warnings to crime bosses to enable them to elude capture. Zhang Jianming, Shenyang's deputy police chief, learned that the provincial department of public security was about to intensify its crackdown on organized crime in 2006, so he warned his friend, Hao Wanchun, leader of a criminal gang, to "get the hell out." Hao subsequently took several overseas trips.[47] Xie Donggong, who co-led a criminal gang with his brother in Heyang in Hunan, was also given advance warning to flee by a crooked police officer who knew of his pending arrest in September 2006.[48]

Local officials who have no responsibility over law enforcement can help organized crime gain access to loans from state-owned banks, government contracts, and land. As many criminal organizations have covers as private companies, local officials who have received bribes from these groups treat such favors in the same way as helping average private businesses. Based on press reports, this problem is especially serious in the real estate sector. Liao Fudong, a gangster in Wuxuan, Guangxi, bribed the county party chief Li Qiliang with 40,000 yuan and was able, with Li's help, to obtain a loan of 6 million yuan from the local branch of the China Agricultural Bank in 2007. Liao also gave a 50,000-yuan bribe to the director of the county bureau of land resources, who helped him to obtain mining licenses cheaply.[49] In 1999, Hu Dongchun, a county CCP secretary in charge of law enforcement in Hunan, awarded a contract for a highway project to Jiang Qixin, a local gangster, even though Jiang's firm lacked the qualifications and its completed project failed to pass inspection.[50] Wang Changlin, an owner of mining businesses connected with organized crime, was able to purchase most of the iron ore mines in Lingyuan, Liaoning, in 2006 for only 20 million yuan due to the help of his patron, local party chief Song Jiulin.[51] Chen Kai, the Fuzhou crime boss, paid a district party chief 100,000 in Hong Kong dollars in 1998 and obtained a plot of land in the official's district for 6 million yuan less than its value.[52] From the sentencing document of Liu Yong, a one-time high-flying gangster in Shenyang in the late 1990s, we can gain a glimpse of the extensive dealings between organized crime and local officials that result in significant profits for the crime bosses. Liu was accused of bribing a number of local officials who then helped him obtain contracts and state-owned assets. The director and a deputy director of a district labor bureau helped Liu lease a shopping mall from the district government; another director of the district labor bureau helped Liu change the ownership of the leased shopping mall into a private firm, which later became Liu's holding company; the deputy executive mayor of Shenyang authorized exemption from land transfer payments and associated fees for a large shopping plaza Liu planned to build; and a deputy general manager of the provincial branch of the China Agricultural Bank misappropriated 20 million yuan to help Liu purchase commercial real estate.[53]

Another insidious service that can be provided by crooked LEOs (and judges) is the use of their authority to help criminals gain the upper hand in commercial disputes or to become their enforcers. The Maoming, Guangdong, case in our sample is typical. In 2005, the police chief of a district bureau of public security, Yang Qiang, assisted a crime boss, Li Zhengang, in kidnapping a businessman who owed Li 20.48 million yuan in high-interest loans. Yang sent his police officers, who rode in Li's Mercedes-Benz SUV from Guangdong to Jiangsu, grabbed the businessman, and took him back to Maoming. Li had paid Yang 430,000 yuan in bribes.[54] In 2005, Shenyang's deputy police chief, Zhang Jianming, issued a warrant for a businessman on false charges of fraud after the businessman began to petition local authorities to investigate a transaction conducted by a gangster who was Zhang's friend.[55] Judges in the pay of organized crime can render rulings favoring the criminals as well. In the Maoming case, the crime boss, Li Zhengang, forged a loan document in 2005 and used it to sue the owners of a commercial complex in Guangzhou for defaulting on the loan. The judge, who had been bribed by Li, ruled in his favor and ordered that the complex be auctioned off to pay off the loan, netting Li a profit of 28 million yuan.[56] In 1999, Liu Yong, the Shenyang gangster, paid more than 200,000 yuan in bribes to a vice president of the municipal intermediate court after she rejected the filing of an administrative lawsuit that would have harmed Liu's business.[57]

The data in Table A.4 show that the number of officers involved in collusion with organized crime is relatively small. However, it is worth noting that they are typically police chiefs, deputy police chiefs, or other senior police officers who control enough power to protect crime bosses who have bribed or befriended them. In the fifty cases included in this sample, the principal protectors of organized crime include sixteen police chiefs, seventeen deputy police chiefs, five other senior LEOs (judges, prosecutors, political commissars in the public security bureau), and twelve local party and government officials (including five local party chiefs and four secretaries or deputy secretaries of the CCP law and politics committee, which oversees law enforcement in local jurisdictions). In terms of the seniority of these principal protectors of organized crime based on jurisdiction, two were provincial-level LEOs, fifteen were prefecture-level LEOs, and twenty-two were county-level LEOs. The data from the sample suggest that the majority of officials colluding with organized crime (thirty-eight out of fifty) are mid-level LEOs. The prominence of mid-level LEOs among those involved with organized crime is largely the result of the economic calculations behind this particular kind of collusion. As the operator of a criminal enterprise, a gangster's capacity to offer bribes is constrained by his relatively small revenue streams. He cannot afford to bribe very senior LEOs (provincial-level ones), who probably will demand larger bribes; this is in addition to the difficulty in establishing access to them. But on the other hand, he needs to bribe only a small number of LEOs to obtain the necessary protection in his locality. The hierarchical nature of a law enforcement organization enables a crime boss to bribe only a few key officials to acquire the requisite protection, in the pattern of vertical collusion we have encountered in other chapters. Consequently, as shown in our sample cases, the average number of LEOs involved in collusion with organized crime is five (the average number of all kinds of officials involved is ten). But nearly all of the LEOs are police chiefs, deputy police chiefs, or other key officers who can provide the most dependable protection sought by organized crime.

Evidence in support of this observation can be found in three cases in this study. Liu Junyong, a crime boss whose criminal enterprise during 1995–2005 included gambling, murder, and coal mines in Hunan, had four police officers as patrons. One was a deputy police chief of the county; two were, respectively, the director and the deputy director of the criminal investigation unit of the police; and the last one was the chief of the police station in Liu's hometown, where he had extensive criminal operations.[58] The list of senior LEOs who shielded Nie Lei, a crime boss in Qingdao arrested in 2010, is even more impressive. Of the eight officers implicated in his case, one was a deputy director of the municipal bureau of public security who also served as the municipal executive deputy secretary of politics and law, three were district police chiefs, one was the head of the Communist Youth League of the municipal bureau of public security, one was the deputy chief of the special force unit of the municipal police department, and the other two were senior police officers in charge of criminal law enforcement units in two districts.[59] Zhang Wei, the Wenling crime boss who managed to recruit sixty-six officials (including the city mayor, police chief, and thirteen other LEOs) during 1995–2000 to protect his criminal enterprise, did so out of necessity. Zhang ran a sprawling criminal empire with operations in several sectors: financial fraud, tax fraud, extortion, kidnapping, and real estate. The cover for Zhang's criminal organization was a conglomerate, Zhejiang Donghai Group, of which Zhang was the chairman of the board. The multiline nature of Zhang's criminal enterprise necessitated protection by officials in a wide range of government agencies. However, the income it generated (the case involved 500 million yuan in forfeited assets, as well as tax and banking fraud) was more than enough to fund the bribes to these officials. For example, Zhang's criminal organization paid 470,000 yuan in several bribes to the director of the bureau of public security of Wenling City, and 350,000 yuan to the mayor of the city.[60]

Chen Kai, the Fuzhou crime boss who operated a large conglomerate with income from many illegal businesses during 1991–2003, was also able to reward his numerous protectors handsomely. According to press reports, he paid about 10 million yuan in bribes to various officials. His chief protector, the city's police chief, received a total of 6 million yuan in bribes. An official who had authority to regulate the city's entertainment industry was bought off with 470,000 yuan. The head of the Bank of China's Fuzhou branch received over 700,000 yuan in bribes so that Chen's criminal organization could get loans from the state-owned bank. In a rare feat, Chen even ensnared the deputy chief of the provincial department of state security (the Chinese equivalent of the KGB) in Fujian with a bribe of more than 100,000 yuan.[61] By comparison, criminal organizations operating smaller and less lucrative illegal businesses could afford less generous bribes to their protectors. Dong Tianyun, who controlled a highway rest stop in Shaanxi where he forced truckers hauling crude oil to local refineries to pay him a transit fee, generated a total of 4 million yuan in profits from his crimes during 1995–2001. His bribes to five police officers totaled 132,800 yuan. The county police chief, who drew a seven-year sentence, received only 30,000 yuan.[62] The deputy police chief of Xishuangbanna in Yunnan apparently was rewarded better for protecting a criminal organization that engaged in smuggling cigarettes and gambling during

2002–2006. He was paid 120,000 yuan by the head of the criminal organization in four installments.[63]

Data on corruption income gained by the chief protectors of organized crime indicate that collusion with organized crime may not be a particularly profitable activity. The average corruption income of the thirty-one officials for whom the amount was reported was 2.15 million yuan, and the median was 0.66 million yuan, a fraction of the corruption income gained by local officials selling offices or colluding with private businessmen (Tables 3.1 and A.2) and SOE executives colluding with each other (Table A.3). The principal factor behind the relatively small amounts of corruption income generated by LEOs colluding with organized crime is their lack of power over the economy. In addition, most LEOs have a lower political status in the hierarchy of the party-state. A county police chief is usually a sub-*chu* official, half a level below a county party secretary. Of the fifteen officials with corruption income below the median, eight were county police chiefs or deputy police chiefs and four were prefecture police chiefs and deputy police chiefs, and few of them had diversified sources of income outside of taking bribes from organized crime or their junior colleagues.

By comparison, those who gained corruption income above the median had more diversified sources of income. Four of the five county party secretaries who collected bribes from both businessmen and crime bosses had total corruption income ranging from 1.08 to 1.8 million yuan. The two police officers who reported the largest corruption income were unique cases. Wang Yufan, whose 18.1 million yuan in corruption income tops the list in Table A.4, was himself a crime boss, owned a coal mine, trafficked in narcotics, and organized prostitution. But half of his corruption income came from two criminal acts: embezzling 2.4 million yuan together with a businessman in 2009, and collecting 7 million yuan in kickbacks from a real estate developer who built a housing complex for the public security bureau, which Wang directed.[64] Yang Qiang, the police chief of Maogang District in Maoming, Guangdong, had total corruption income of 14.19 million yuan. Of this amount, 3.45 million yuan was in bribes from his subordinates in return for appointments and promotions. In addition, he had more than 9 million yuan in "unexplained wealth." In other words, assuming his "unexplained wealth" did not involve bribes from organized crime, Yang's corruption income from activities unrelated to organized crime was at least 12.45 million yuan, more than ten times the amount of the bribe—1.18 million yuan—he received from a crime boss who was operating forty illegal gambling joints in his district.[65]

Duration of Crime and the Penalty
for Colluding with the Mafia

The data on the duration of organized crime groups suggest that, due largely to the protection provided by senior local LEOs, these groups can expect to survive almost a decade (the average and median number of years of survival are eight and nine, respectively). If most protected criminal gangs in China can operate for nearly a decade before they are destroyed, the harm inflicted on Chinese society is incalculable. As shown by our description of the extensive criminal activities in which organized crime is engaged, not only will law and order suffer as a result of such persistent criminality, but also the overall socioeconomic well-being of ordinary citizens will fall prey to organized crime that extends its presence well beyond its conventional areas of operation.

Fortunately, even in a party-state where local LEOs can be hopelessly corrupt, the top leadership of the regime retains the capability to reassert control over its wayward agents. In fact, the central authorities of the party-state have every incentive to eradicate collusion between law enforcement and organized crime simply because this scourge undermines their authority over a vital instrument of state power. As a result, the Chinese government has launched repeated campaigns against organized crime. These periodic crackdowns may not completely destroy mafia-style groups, let alone change the political and economic environments in which these groups operate and thrive. However, such efforts do produce some modest successes, at least in terms of dismantling criminal gangs that have grown too powerful or have attracted too much attention.

Besides periodic "strike black" campaigns during which mafia-style groups are most vulnerable, Chinese crime bosses are usually brought down in the following ways. First, tips provided by ordinary citizens and victims' families can occasionally trigger investigations from higher authorities. In the case of Zhang Wei, Wenling's criminal gang leader, an ordinary citizen persisted in his efforts in the late 1990s to report his criminal activities to the higher authorities. He went directly to the Ministry of Public Security in Beijing and, with the help of several retired officials, managed to get the attention of LEOs unconnected with the local police. The central authorities then directed Zhejiang's law enforcement authority to investigate the allegations.[66] Leads were also provided by the victims' families. After Liu Junyong's thugs killed a local peasant in 2003, the family of the victim went to Beijing and petitioned the Ministry of Public Security, prompting an investigation that resulted in the unraveling of Liu's crime organization in Hunan.[67]

Second, confessions by a member of the criminal organization can lead to the arrest of the other members. When a junior member of a criminal gang is arrested by LEOs untainted by organized crime, he often provides the interrogators with information about his criminal organization, leading to the fall of the crime boss and uncovering his protector. This was the case in the fall of Xiao Qiang, the police chief of Heyang in Hunan. After a member of the criminal gang protected by Xiao was arrested in 2006, the suspect gave the police enough information to lead to the arrest of the two leaders of the criminal gang and their protector, Xiao.[68] In some cases, the crime boss reveals to the investigators the identity of his protectors in the hope of gaining leniency. Shortly after he was sentenced to death in 2004, Li Manlin, a crime boss in Taiyuan, told the authorities that Shao Jianwei, a former deputy police chief of the city, had been protecting him for years. Shao was then arrested. To gain leniency for himself, Shao told the investigators that he had paid a bribe of $100,000 to the provincial secretary of politics and law (the third most senior party official in the province), Hou Wujie, to seek a promotion. Hou was then detained.[69]

Third, accidental discovery, often resulting from an investigation into the fraudulent activities of the front companies operated by organized crime, can yield the initial lead. The fall of Xiong Xinxin, the crime boss in Fuzhou, Jiangxi, began with an investigation into a major case of financial fraud conducted by the CCDI in 2004. The company owned by Xiong was implicated, thus triggering a special investigation that resulted in his arrest in 2005.[70]

Fourth, a particularly egregious act of violence and criminality committed by the criminal gang receives high-profile media coverage and causes public outrage that forces the top leaders to take action against the criminal gang. In Qingdao, Nie Lei's thugs attacked a local Crowne Plaza Hotel and stabbed its manager on a night when the city's top leaders were entertaining participants in an international sports event at the hotel in 2010. The incident was covered by the local press and in less than three months an arrest warrant for Nie was issued.[71]

Finally, higher-level law enforcement authorities may have independent sources of information to launch an investigation. Typically in these cases, both the criminal leader and his protectors are the targets. In the case of Li Zhengang in Maoming, Guangdong, the provincial procuratorate in 2010 directed the Guangzhou Municipal Procuratorate to investigate Li Zhengang's crime organization. The officers sent by Guangzhou to Maoming spent six months to uncover his "protective umbrellas."[72] The Chen Kai case in Fuzhou was apparently cracked in 2003 after a rare joint investigation into a drug-trafficking ring that appeared to have used Chen's business to launder its money by the central Chinese law enforcement authorities and the U.S. Drug Enforcement Agency.[73]

LEOs convicted of colluding with organized crime, contrary to expectations, receive relatively light punishment, while convicted crime bosses are punished severely (Table A.4). Of the fifty convicted crime bosses for whom the penalty was reported, twenty-one were sentenced to death and executed immediately, three received suspended death sentences, seven got life in prison, and fourteen got twenty years in jail. One obvious explanation is the deterrence signal that the Chinese authorities want to send. Since organized crime is seen as a grave threat to social stability and public safety, severe punishment is intended to deter future criminals from engaging in similar activities. The other reason is that crime bosses have committed serious crimes, such as murder and drug trafficking, which carry the death penalty.

By comparison, LEOs convicted of shielding organized crime receive more lenient treatment. Of the thirty-six chief protectors of organized crime whose penalties were reported, the most severe penalty was a suspended death sentence, given to Wang Yufang, a deputy police chief turned crime boss. Four received life sentences. One of these was a deputy police chief of Jiangxi province. He was punished more severely because of his seniority in the law enforcement apparatus. The Chinese authorities are particularly concerned about the penetration of organized crime into the upper reaches of the country's law enforcement system. Yang Qiang, the district police chief in Maoming, drew a life sentence, most probably due to the very large amount of total corruption income he received—14.19 million yuan.[74] For thirty-one officials who received term sentences, the average is 8.5 years and the median is eight years. The relative leniency with which these officials were treated is surprising, especially given their alleged protection of organized crime. One plausible explanation is that they were prosecuted primarily for two types of offenses—dereliction of duty and bribe-taking. Officers convicted of dereliction of duty are normally punished lightly. Those who are convicted of bribe-taking may escape harsh penalties if the amount of bribe is small. In most cases, LEOs take bribes from crime bosses that are insufficiently large to warrant a long prison term.

Assessment and Implications

The sample cases examined in this study indicate that collusion between law enforcement and organized crime has degraded the capacity of the Chinese state to maintain law and order in many parts of the country. In jurisdictions severely affected by such collusion, the deterioration of local governance manifests itself not only in the increase of crimes, such as gambling, prostitution, extortion, and drug trafficking, but also in the penetration of organized crime into important socioeconomic activities. Although additional empirical evidence will be needed to ascertain the full extent of the penetration of organized crime into China's body politic at the local levels, several tentative conclusions can be supported by the available evidence.

The Extensive Reach and Durability of Organized Crime

The protection provided by LEOs has enabled organized crime to engage in a wide range of illegal activities. In addition to conventional crimes, well-connected mafia-style groups pursue new and more lucrative illegal activities. These groups typically own large conglomerates that have been established in some of China's key economic sectors: real estate, transportation, and mining. Among the cases included here, the most successful mafia-style groups are those with multiple sources of income and the capacity to purchase protection from a large number of local officials. Chen Kai of Fuzhou, Zhang Zhixin of Qiqihaer, and Zhang Wei of Wenling all ran crime syndicates that controlled profitable businesses and assets worth tens of millions of yuan. Some crime bosses, like corrupt private businessmen, have also bribed their way into local political machines. Zhang Zhixin, Zhang Wei, Chen Kai, Xiong Xinxin (a crime boss in Fuzhou, Jiangxi) were all members of the local PPCC and, before they were arrested, mingled freely with local political and business elites. There is also some evidence that organized crime may be used by local officials in one of the most notorious activities in China—forced evictions. Chinese press reports often refer to the role of "thugs" in evicting urban residents from their houses and peasants from their land. While the role of organized crime is often suspected, there is no substantive proof. In two of our cases, the criminal organization was engaged in "violent evictions."[75] Although reports on the cases provide no details on its eviction business, it is reasonable to suspect that local governments and real estate developers (the only two customers of the eviction service) must have hired organized crime to evict residents refusing to move.

The evidence collected in this study also indicates that organized crime is active in sectors such as small-scale mining, real estate, local transportation (including taxis), wholesale, and logistics. While the true extent of such penetration is difficult to gauge and the influence exercised by organized crime in these sectors is likely modest, its presence nevertheless constitutes a serious threat to public order and the economic well-being of ordinary citizens. Even more worrisome is the durability and resilience of these organizations, due in part to the protection they receive from LEOs. The most alarming scenario, as shown in some of our cases, is the penetration of organized crime into local governments. With the funds generated from their various illegal activities, organized crime can easily afford the bribes to forge ties with local officials.

Effects on the Integrity of the Chinese State

While the effects of organized crime on local governance are harmful enough, the long-term damage done by the collusion between organized crime and law enforcement authorities to the integrity of the Chinese state is likely to be far more destructive and consequential. Obviously, such collusion degrades the capacity of the Chinese state in the areas of law enforcement and administrative effectiveness. The expansion of organized crime and the willingness of crime bosses to bribe any officials who are in a position to facilitate their criminal enterprises inevitably result in an ever-widening circle of corrupt officials in key state agencies. Several senior officers in the vaunted Ministry of State Security, China's highly regarded secret police, have been involved with organized crime or have been implicated in corruption scandals.[76] But a more subtle transformation of the local state brought about by the collusion between law enforcement authorities and organized crime is the illicit privatization of state power. LEOs who provide protection to organized crime are effectively misappropriating public authority for private gain. The essence of this behavior is identical to that of party chiefs who "sell" their power of personnel appointment for profit.

Indeed, if anything, the theme of "privatization of state power" connects both types of collusion—collusion among officials and collusion between officials and organized crime. The use of bribes in securing appointments and promotions within the Chinese party-state has created a new avenue for organized crime to extend its political influence. In several cases included in this study, corrupt LEOs used the bribes they received from crime bosses to "buy" appointments and promotions. While it is difficult to ascertain the degree to which organized crime has been able to influence the personnel appointment process, the dynamics of competitive bribery for senior appointments inside China's local law enforcement authorities are especially worrisome because officers aspiring to gain appointments or promotions to these highly desirable positions have only two sources of funding—bribery from their subordinates or from organized crime. If they accept bribes from organized crime, not only do they owe favors to crime bosses that must be repaid in the future; they also indirectly implicate their superiors and make them vulnerable to blackmail by organized crime.

7

The Spread of Collusion:
The Party-State in Decay

> In our regulatory and enforcement agencies ... some officials abuse their authority, use power for rent-seeking ... and let connections, friendship, and money decide their cases.
>
> —Xi Jinping, January 20, 2014

THE SPREAD of collusion to China's judiciary and regulatory agencies, specifically environmental protection, work safety, and food and drug administration agencies, is an inevitable consequence of crony capitalism. As confirmed by Xi's remarks above, the abuse of regulatory authority for the benefit of the friends of government officials is a common occurrence. Even though the central feature of crony capitalism is the theft of undervalued state-owned assets by officials, their families, and their cronies in the private sector, the evasion and violation of laws and regulations with impunity is an integral part of the ecosystem of crony capitalism because of the subversion of public authority by private wealth that is entailed in such behavior.

Institutions and regulatory bodies, such as the judiciary and environmental protection agencies, play a vital role in safeguarding the rights and welfare of Chinese citizens and enforcing the will of the state. The capture of these entities by collusive elites transforms them into private instruments for rent-seeking. Inevitably, agencies that have fallen prey to collusion fail miserably in performing their public functions. In addition to presenting and analyzing cases of collusive corruption in courts and three regulatory agencies, we briefly examine several provinces and prefecture-level municipalities struck by mega corruption scandals. These cases underscore the fact that, in extreme cases, collusion among elites in a large region can turn it into a local mafia state. By exploring the spread of collusion to critical state institutions and large jurisdictions, this chapter illustrates how collusion corrodes the institutional fabric of a Leninist party-state. More importantly, with its focus on the underlying dynamics of crony capitalism that make collusion both possible and profitable, our research identifies the institutional flaws of the Leninist party-state, not the moral failings of its members, as the root cause of regime decay.

Collusive Corruption in the Judiciary

In the post-Mao era, the Communist Party has devoted considerable effort to building a functioning legal system. However, the results of legal reform have been mixed at best because of the CCP's determination to maintain its monopoly of power, an objective that precludes a truly effective and independent judiciary.[1] Inevitably, the CCP's control of the judiciary results in its politicization and corruption. Like other critical components of the Chinese party-state, the judiciary, a vast bureaucracy consisting of 31 provincial high courts, 409 intermediate courts, 3,117 basic-level (county or district) courts, and nearly 190,000 judges, has been ravaged by crony capitalism.[2] According to data released by the Supreme People's Court, corruption in the Chinese judiciary has grown measurably since the early 1990s.

The number of judicial officials, including judges, criminally prosecuted for violation of rules and laws averaged thirty-nine per year in 1982–1992, but the number more than doubled in 1993–2001. In the period 2003–2013, the average number of judicial officials criminally prosecuted was ninety-five, slightly higher than that in the 1993–2001 period.[3] Judicial corruption has drawn both scholarly and journalistic attention, but no systematic research has been conducted on collusion among judges, a persistent and widespread phenomenon.[4] In this section we examine thirty cases of collusive corruption in the judiciary, defined as cases involving three or more judges in the same court, during the period 1994–2013. We first present the summary data of these cases in the Appendix (Table A.5), and then analyze the institutional setting, market dynamics, and behavioral patterns of collusive corruption in the judiciary.

The data in Table A.5 reveal, among other things, the persistence of collusive corruption in spite of the CCP's repeated crackdowns.[5] Also notable is the leading role played by senior judicial officials, such as presidents, vice presidents, chiefs, and deputy chiefs of tribunals, in these cases, befitting the pattern of "vertical collusion." They were the principal culprits in twenty-eight of the thirty cases selected here. Also worth noting is that judicial corruption is relatively difficult to detect. The average duration of corruption by the lead perpetrator in the sample is almost six years (the median is five years). However, senior judges in intermediate and high courts have longer durations of corruption (they account for ten of the thirteen judges with an above-median duration of corruption), an indication of the low detection risks for crooked judges. The average number of judges involved is seven (the median is six). By and large, judicial corruption is not a lucrative activity for most perpetrators. The median corruption income for the lead perpetrator in our sample is 760,000 yuan. However, judicial corruption is marked by high inequality of illicit income. While some senior judges could be bought for a mere 10,000 yuan, others reaped millions of yuan in bribes. A closer look at the sources of corruption income for the top earners in the sample shows that the differences in corruption income are due to the diversity of the corrupt activities and the seniority and assigned responsibilities of the perpetrators.

Generally, businessmen litigating disputes in basic-level courts are unwilling to spend large sums of money on bribes because these courts have jurisdiction over cases that are relatively simple or have small claims. More complex cases with larger claims are typically tried in intermediate or high courts. As a result, senior judicial officers in basic-level courts in our sample who pocketed outsized corruption income were those who had more diverse sources of revenue, not only bribes from litigants. Guo Shenggui, the president of the Xicheng District Court in Beijing, collected 3.67 million yuan from lawyers as "broker's fees" during 1999–2006 for recommending them to litigants whose cases were pending in his court. In addition, he took 3 million yuan in bribes from a contractor who supplied IT and interior furnishings for the new complex of the court.[6] Yan De, the president of the Maogang District basic-level court in the scandal-plagued city of the Maoming in Guangdong, was convicted of embezzlement, misappropriation of public funds, and bribery in 2012. His total corruption income exceeded 20 million yuan. But it consisted of 7.5 million yuan in embezzlement and 9.1 million yuan in misappropriated funds. Bribes, including those from a local mafia boss, junior colleagues seeking promotions, and litigants, totaled 3.8 million yuan, less than 20 percent of his total corruption income.[7]

By contrast, senior judges in charge of enforcement in intermediate and high courts have greater capacity for generating corruption income because, during the enforcement process, auction houses bribe these judges to get the coveted commissions to sell the property seized by the court. Typically, these companies pay the judges in charge of enforcement a share of their profits. Since claims of commercial disputes adjudicated in high and intermediate courts often exceed tens or hundreds of millions of yuan, even a small percentage of the fees paid to auction companies can mean millions of yuan for these corrupt judges. In the case of Wu Zhenhan, the president of the Hunan High Court, a firm that, during 1999–2000, tried to gain part of the commission for auctioning off a shopping plaza worth 400 million yuan offered Wu's son half of the fees (equal to 4 percent of the judgment). Wu gave the firm the commission.[8] Pei Hongquan, a vice president in charge of enforcement at the Shenzhen Intermediate Court, received 1.5 million yuan and 200,000 Hong Kong dollars (HKD) in bribes from an auction firm that had been awarded many commissions from the court in the late 1990s.[9] Fan Xin, a senior judge in the enforcement department of the Guangdong High Court, received 1.4 million yuan as his share of the profits from an enforcement action in 2005 that netted 3.1 million yuan for the middleman, a lawyer whose firm gained the authorization to execute a court judgment. This scandal implicated Yang Xiancai, the chief of enforcement of the court, and Huang Songyou, a vice president of the Supreme People's Court and a Guangdong native.[10] Zhang Tao, a vice president of the Chongqing High Court responsible for enforcement, took 2.17 million yuan in bribes during 1999–2002 from one private businessman, who used Zhang's influence to obtain properties auctioned off by the court at steep discounts.[11]

The punishment of judges prosecuted for corruption is relatively severe (Table A.5). Senior judges who reaped millions of yuan in corruption income typically drew suspended death or life sentences.

Judges who took less in bribes were also punished harshly. The average sentence for those whose punishment is known was 9.7 years (the median was 10 years). Compared with law enforcement and local officials prosecuted for protecting organized crime, the punishment for corrupt judges in the sample is roughly 25 percent more severe (the median sentence for law enforcement and local officials involved in protecting organized crime is eight years). A likely explanation is that crooked judges gain more corruption income than officials involved with organized crime. The average amount of corruption income for the chief protector of organized crime is 2.15 million yuan and the median is 0.66 million yuan, both lower than the amounts for corrupt judges (Tables A.4 and A.5). Adjusted for corruption income, the main criterion for deciding punishment, corrupt judges also receive slightly more severe punishment than county-level officials charged with selling government positions. The median corruption income for county-level officials is 2.4 million yuan, about three times more than the median corruption income of judges, but their median sentence is thirteen years, only three years longer (Table 3.2).

The Institutional Setting of Collusion

The spread of collusive corruption in the Chinese judiciary is no accident. Trial procedures and administrative hierarchies provide an institutional environment conducive to collusion among judges. A study conducted by two prosecutors in the Hubei Provincial Procuratorate and released in 2004 reported that 40 percent of the cases of judicial corruption in Hubei were crimes of collusion or were connected with each other.[12] In the Chinese judiciary, collusion is necessitated by two institutional features: the role of the "collegial panel" (*heyiting*) and the trial committees, and the administrative hierarchy that grants enormous power to those who head tribunals and courts. In Chinese courts, a collegial panel of three judges presides over a trial, and decisions are reached by a majority vote if there is no consensus. In theory, this system is supposed to minimize abuse and corruption by an individual judge, but in fact it creates incentives for litigants to bribe or influence judges who are assigned to their case. In reality, in most trial proceedings involving simple cases, a single judge is put in charge, and his decisions are vetted by the chief of the tribunal or the vice president responsible for his area of specialty (such as civil or criminal law). This arrangement also incentivizes collusion because litigants need to bribe or influence both the presiding judge and his superiors. Another unique institutional feature of Chinese courts—the trial committee—similarly encourages collusion among judges. Trial committees, formed by the president, vice presidents, chiefs of tribunals, and senior judges, decide on major cases or cases over which collegial panels have significant differences. Needless to say, litigants attempting to influence decisions made by trial committees must bribe multiple judges, as was the case with the scandal at the Wuhan Intermediate Court in 2003. One judge was bribed by litigants twenty-three times. On twelve occasions, she was bribed together with her colleagues, including a vice president, three deputy tribunal chiefs, and two judges. On seven occasions, she and the chief of her tribunal received bribes together. Her case was not exceptional. Other crooked judges at the Wuhan Intermediate Court often shared bribes with other judges, tribunal chiefs, and vice presidents.[13]

Unlike conventional courts of law, the Chinese judiciary functions as an instrument of rule for the CCP and is governed by a strict administrative hierarchy in which political status and administrative rank allow senior officials to exercise excessive influence over judicial proceedings and decisions. According to a lengthy report on judicial corruption published in 2013 in *Caijing,* judges in many courts must report to tribunal chiefs the acceptance, filing, and deliberations of their cases. Decisions on important and difficult cases must be vetted and approved by the presidents of their courts.[14] The outsized power wielded by senior judges appointed to leadership positions in Chinese courts makes them prime targets for bribery. In the study on judicial corruption in Hubei, half of the corrupt judges were presidents, vice presidents, tribunal chiefs, or deputy chiefs while they committed their crimes. Even though most of them were not directly responsible for trying cases, they controlled or influenced court judgments or enforcements.[15] Of the 200 corrupt judges included in the 2013 *Caijing* report, eighty-four were presidents or vice presidents and seventy-two were chiefs or deputy chiefs of tribunals and enforcement departments.[16] Of the thirty cases included in this study, all but two lead perpetrators were presidents, vice presidents, chiefs, or deputy chiefs of tribunals or enforcement departments. This evidence shows that collusive corruption in China is primarily a phenomenon involving senior judicial officials who often act as ringleaders.

The Market for Judicial Corruption

The growth of judicial corruption reflects an expanding illicit market in which bribes are traded for favorable legal outcomes. There are three participants in this market: litigants and intermediaries (lawyers and auction-house owners) on the demand side and judges on the supply side. In this section, we explore the strategies and tactics employed by those seeking favorable treatment from the Chinese judiciary.

In the post-Tiananmen era, stakes for businessmen embroiled in commercial litigation have grown considerably, mainly because many of these disputes threaten their property—commercial real estate, land and mining rights, and ownership of other valuable assets. Greater stakes create more powerful incentives for litigants to seek favorable legal outcomes. For these litigants, typically private businessmen, bribing judges is no different from bribing other government officials. As long as they believe that their bribes will yield positive returns, they will be tempted to try. To be sure, influencing judicial proceedings presents a daunting challenge, especially in cases involving significant monetary claims, because they are tried in intermediate courts and multiple judges are involved in the proceedings. However, enterprising businessmen can utilize personal contacts, Chinese cultural customs, and social rituals to influence judges and, when necessary, play the role of the central coordinator in facilitating collusion among judges who do not deal directly with each other. In the case that led to the arrest of thirteen judges at the Wuhan Intermediate Court in 2003, a private businessman, through his lawyer, bribed three deputy chiefs of tribunals and several other judges. In return, these judges ruled in favor of the private businessman's firm in a contract dispute with his joint-venture partner during 2004–2009.[17] In the scandal at the Foshan Intermediate Court in Guangdong, a private real estate developer entangled in an ownership dispute separately bribed three judges, including a vice president, to gain a favorable ruling.[18] A judge who shared his bribes with three colleagues at the Taijiang District Court in Fuzhou was initially approached in 2008 by the lawyer for a real estate developer who was the plaintiff in a contract dispute. In violation of the rules, the judge discussed the case with the lawyer privately several times and agreed to his demands to alter the claims and give them favorable consideration in his ruling. Such helpfulness earned the judge gifts worth nearly 30,000 yuan.[19]

In one of the earliest cases of collusive corruption in the judiciary, a Hebei businessman in Qiaoxi district in Zhangjiakou, who tried to prevail in a contract dispute in 1993, first approached the deputy secretary of the CCP's local politics and law committee, who in turn introduced him to the president of the district court, Cheng Guiqing. After receiving gifts and small bribes from the businessman, Cheng began a series of maneuvers, including replacing the judge who originally tried the case with a loyalist, to deliver a favorable ruling for the businessman. The businessmen entertained Cheng, the new judge overseeing his case, and the chief of the economic tribunal at a private banquet and gave them relatively small bribes. Such efforts produced a favorable decision for the businessman. During the appeal, the businessman managed to bribe a judge on the provincial high court and entertained him in a brothel. The judge duly ruled for the businessman.[20]

An equally egregious case in our sample occurred in the Shizuishan Intermediate Court, the Yinchuan Intermediate Court, and the Ningxia High Court. Ding Haiyu, an enterprising businessman, succeeded in bribing twenty-five judges on the three courts. Before he was arrested in 2006, he sued nearly all the companies that did business with him and "won" more than ten cases in the three courts. In one lawsuit, Ding and the president of the Shizuishan Intermediate Court faked evidence. Ding applied a proven formula to buy off the judges. He would first informally consult a judge to see if the lawsuit he was planning to file had any chance of success. Then he would take the judge out to dinner and give the judge instructions as to how to proceed. If the presiding judge was reluctant to help, Ding would approach the presidents of the courts and ask them to intervene. Sometimes Ding would demand that certain judges be assigned to his cases. In befriending the judges and officers of the Shizuishan

Intermediate Court, Ding turned his company into a virtual slush fund for them. Judges and officers of the court frequently came to his company to reimburse entertainment and cell phone expenses.[21]

A more disturbing variety of judicial corruption involves organized crime. Our sample contains three such cases. Liu Yong, a crime boss in Shenyang during 1995–2000, bribed the president and vice president of the Shenyang Intermediate Court, though the press did not report what kind of favors Liu received in return.[22] He Mingjie, chief of the civil tribunal at the Maogang District Court, helped a local mafia boss forge legal documents so that the court could help him collect on his high-interest loans in 2008.[23] Four senior judges in the Jilin High Court, including the chief and deputy chief of the criminal tribunal, were arrested in 2007 for taking bribes from the lawyer for a crime boss in exchange for reducing his sentence (from fifteen to five years) during the appeal.[24]

Obtaining a favorable judgment through bribery may seem an impressive accomplishment for private businessmen. But there is an even more desirable outcome they eagerly seek—favorable enforcement action. Given the difficulty in enforcing court judgments in China, litigants have a strong interest in ensuring either the effective enforcement of favorable judgments or the prevention of enforcement of adverse judgments.[25] They can achieve this objective by bribing the judges in charge of enforcement.

One example in our sample is Jia Yongxiang, president of the Shenyang Intermediate Court (who had headed the city's bureau of state security). After a local private businessman faced bankruptcy if an unfavorable judgment was enforced, he approached Jia for help in 1999. Jia called the court's chief of enforcement and instructed him to "provide assistance if it does not violate major principles." The chief of enforcement got the message and stopped the enforcement action, saving the private businessman, who later gave Jia a bribe of 20,000 yuan in appreciation.[26] Another example is Judge Lin at the Taijiang District Court in Fuzhou in 2009. At the request of a plaintiff who was willing to pay a bribe to ensure speedy enforcement of the judgment, Lin asked a colleague to find a "connection" in the enforcement department of the court. His colleague, who was promised a share of the bribe by Lin, managed to secure the help of Judge Liu in the enforcement department, promising an unspecified "reward." After Judge Liu quickly completed the enforcement action, Lin, who had already received a bribe from the plaintiff, hosted a dinner for his colleague (the intermediary) and Liu. During the dinner, Lin paid the intermediary an unspecified amount and gave Liu 50,000 yuan as his share of the bribe.[27] In the corruption scandal at the Zhanjiang Intermediate Court in Guangdong, the nine judges who had accepted bribes from litigants similarly sped up the trial and enforcement processes during 2002–2010.[28] Shang Jun, a president of the Fuyang Intermediate Court, also helped a defendant who lost a case evade enforcement action during 1994–1995.[29]

Behavioral Patterns in Judicial Collusion

The practice of paying bribes to secure judicial appointments and promotions is widespread inside the Chinese court system and has become the principal means of vertical collusion in the judiciary. In addition to subverting the process of judicial appointment based on qualifications and integrity, this practice also reinforces incentives for judicial corruption and facilitates collusive corruption among judges. Obviously, those who have obtained their judicial appointments or promotions through bribery need to recover their investments by extracting bribes from the litigants. Senior judges in administrative positions who have "sold" judicial appointments and promotions to their underlings can rely on them to cooperate in corrupt activities in the judiciary.

Among the cases in the sample, President Yan De of the Maogang District Court in Maoming City is an illustrative example. Besides protecting a local mafia boss and taking kickbacks from contractors who built the court's complex, before his arrest in 2009 Yan also engaged in appointing and promoting junior judges who paid him bribes.[30] In a scandal that implicated more than ten chiefs of tribunals and judges in the Hunan High Court in 2004, a vice president of the Changsha Intermediate Court who wanted a promotion paid 100,000 yuan to the wife of Wu Zhenhan, the president of the Hunan High Court.[31] In 1997, Liu Shi, the former president of the Shenyang Intermediate Court, received about 50,000 yuan in bribes from Chen Changlin, a subordinate seeking promotion and other favors. Chen also used 20,000 yuan in public funds to pay an artist for a painting as a gift to Tian Fengqi, the president of the Liaoning High Court (who was later arrested for corruption). Liang Fuquan, a vice president of the Shenyang Intermediate Court, asked Chen to deliver a bribe of 10,000 yuan to Liu Shi after Liu nominated him for the position in 1998. Chen not only survived the investigations following the notorious Shenyang scandal, which sent many of its senior leaders to jail in 1999–2000, but also continued to receive promotions. By the time Chen was detained for corruption in 2014, he had risen to be vice president in charge of enforcement at the Liaoning High Court.[32]

A particularly shocking instance of corruption in judicial appointments and promotions was the scandal at the Fuyang Intermediate Court, where three successive presidents were arrested on a variety of misconduct charges. Shang Jun, the president of the court, took bribes totaling 900,000 yuan from her subordinates seeking promotions and other favors. In 1996, she pocketed 30,000 yuan from a vice president of a county court and appointed him to the presidency of an urban district court; she appointed another underling to the presidency of a county court after receiving a bribe. Liu Jiayi, who succeeded Shang in 1997 and was reassigned in 2004, took bribes totaling 452,000 yuan from twelve subordinates in the court in return for promotions and appointments. Zhang Zimin, who took over Liu's post, secured his appointment after he asked Shang Jun to deliver his bribe to Wang Zhaoyao, a deputy provincial party chief in charge of law enforcement.[33]

Horizontal collusion among judges is facilitated by the bonds of personal trust forged through socialization and joint participation in illegal activities. Among the various social activities used as means of trust-building, judges and those seeking to bribe them prefer dinners and sleazy entertainment. The rationale behind involving multiple judges in such activities is self-evident: Since those who participate will have violated official rules against accepting meals, money, and gifts from litigants, they can be counted on to keep each other's secrets.[34]

One representative case in our sample was Judge Lin in the Taijiang District Court in Fuzhou. After Lin helped a litigant obtain speedy execution of the judgment in his case in 2009, he hosted a dinner for two of his colleagues, including the judge who had delivered the favorable enforcement. During the dinner, Lin shared the bribe from the litigant with his colleagues.[35] In the corruption scandal at the Shiyan Intermediate Court in Hubei in 2003, the owner of an auction house who brazenly attempted to use fraudulent means to seize 1,904 tons of steel belonging to a state-owned firm also wined and dined several judges together. During the meal, they played a card game and the businessman intentionally lost money to the judges.[36] A businessman embroiled in a lawsuit in the Qiaoxi District Court in Hebei in the early 1990s also entertained several judges of the district court and the provincial high court together (in one instance, the businessman hosted a dinner for several judges in a special private room where *sanpei* girls were available).[37] Another salacious case of judges engaging in sleazy entertainment was the scandal that led to the dismissal of four senior judges of the Shanghai High Court in 2013. They were entertained by a senior SOE executive, who later paid prostitutes to sleep with them. The judges were caught on video camera when they entered and exited the hotel. After the video was posted online and ignited a public uproar, the judges were expelled from the party and fired from their positions.[38]

Another factor reinforcing bonding and trust is shared financial interests. One method used by private businessmen eager to seek protection from officials (including judicial officials) is to give them direct financial stakes, often for free or at steep discounts, in their businesses. Usually these stakes take the form of "dry shares" (*gangu*), which allow officials to receive dividends but exercise no voting rights. Several judges at the Shiyan Intermediate Court in Hubei, including the vice president responsible for enforcement, who tried to help the owner of an auction house illegally seize 1,904 tons of steel in 2001, owned *gangu* in the auction house that generated regular dividend payments.[39] Similarly, the president of the Yichuan County Court in Henan, along with six of his colleagues (including a vice president, the chief of the civil tribunal, and the chief of the criminal tribunal), also owned *gangu* in a private local mining company whose owner received a favorable order from the court in 2009 that allowed him to operate his mines even though the owner was serving a suspended sentence and should not have been allowed to run his mining business. (Later one of his mines had an explosion that killed forty-four people.)[40]

A more blatant act of collusion that cements trust among crooked judges is the open acceptance, sharing, and distribution of bribes, a practice found in some of our sample cases. In probing the scandal at the Wuhan Intermediate Court in 2004, investigators found that one judge had accepted bribes twenty-three times; on twelve occasions, she collected her bribes together with her fellow judges, including a vice president, three deputy tribunal chiefs, and two other judges involved in the cases for which she was responsible. She was not alone in accepting or sharing the spoils with her colleagues. Other senior judges, including tribunal chiefs and vice presidents, routinely shared their bribes with their colleagues before their crimes were uncovered in 2004.[41] The same phenomenon was also found at the Fuyang Intermediate Court, where judges who had been bribed by litigants would divide up their bribes with other judges so that the latter would help their bribers. According to Xue Yi, a deputy chief of a civil tribunal of the court who drew a life sentence in 2005, eight fellow judges had approached him and given him envelopes filled with cash, along with case files, and asked him to "take care of them." He also claimed that judges would jointly attend dinners hosted by litigants, introducing each other to would-be bribers."[42]

Collusive Corruption in Regulatory Enforcement Agencies

The spread of collusive corruption to state agencies responsible for enforcing regulations in environmental protection, workplace safety, and food and drug safety should be considered another symptom of the decay of the Chinese party-state. In this section, we analyze corruption involving multiple individuals in three key state agencies: environmental protection bureaus, work safety bureaus (including coal mine safety bureaus), and food and drug administration.

Based on the data in Table A.6 on corruption involving multiple individuals in environmental protection bureaus (EPB), work safety bureaus (WSB), and food and drug administration (FDA), the duration of corruption for the chief perpetrators in the thirty selected cases is about six months longer than that for those in our selected cases of judicial corruption. The average and median duration is 6.3 and 5 years, respectively. The number of people implicated in each case is roughly the same as in the selected cases of judicial corruption. The average number is eight and the median is six, although the standard deviation is twice that of the selected cases of judicial corruption. One likely explanation is that collusion in these agencies does not require a very large number of individuals. Economically, given the limited income they can generate from their corrupt activities, regulatory officials may not want to involve more colleagues and dilute their earnings. Conversely, businessmen who bribe them also prefer not to waste money bribing too many officials. The median amount of corruption income of the lead perpetrators in these cases is 510,000 yuan, only slightly less than that in the selected cases of judicial corruption. One explanation is that most perpetrators have relatively low status and administrative authority. Half of the chief perpetrators in our sample are *ke*, or section-level, officials, one full notch below *chu* or division level, the rank of a county party chief. In addition, corruption purchased from these officials has limited value. Those engaging in corruption in regulatory enforcement deliver only "services" (such as protection in cases of regulatory enforcement), which are not as valuable as government posts or deeply discounted state-owned assets.

Despite the modest corruption income gained by officials in regulatory agencies, they received, by comparison, harsh punishment. The average length of a term sentence in our sample is 9.6 years and the median is ten years, similar to those in the selected cases of judicial corruption. Like crooked judges, corrupt regulatory and enforcement officials are given more severe punishment, adjusted for the amount of their corruption income, than local party chiefs, probably for two reasons. For all its tough rhetoric about punishing senior officials caught for corruption, the CCP actually gives them more lenient sentences in practice, as we have seen. Additionally, the discrepancy in sentencing according to the amount of corruption income is the result of both the lack of progressivity and the vagueness in China's legal system for determining punishment for corrupt officials. The penalties for those who have received bribes are only vaguely specified.[43]

Although their corruption income is not high, officials in regulatory enforcement agencies such as EPBs and WSBs nevertheless wield considerable power in granting approvals and levying penalties on businesses that have violated government regulations. Possession of such power gives these officials the ability to demand and extract bribes from businesses that seek to evade government regulations and sanctions. The corrupt relationship between regulatory enforcement officials and the businesses they are supposed to monitor is maintained through exchanges of regulatory favors and bribes. To date, corruption in Chinese regulatory agencies such as EPBs and WSBs has received widespread press coverage in China, but little scholarly attention. The brief analysis of the patterns of corruption in this section aims to shed some light on how such activities are carried out.

Corruption in Licensing and Enforcement Actions

The power to grant licenses can easily be converted into means of extracting bribes for regulatory officials. In the selected cases here, such behavior was widespread. In the scandal in the Wenzhou WSB in 2008 that implicated seventeen officials who pocketed bribes worth 1.87 million yuan, Chen Caixing, director of the Wenzhou Municipal WSB, received 97,000 yuan from a private businessman to help him obtain licenses to sell firecrackers and perform safety evaluation services.[44] Ye Liangang, the director of the Wenzhou Municipal EPB, took bribes from a businessman running an environmental service firm in exchange for helping the firm pass an inspection during 2006–2008. He also helped another businessman who owned a chemical plant to pass an environmental inspection.[45] In a scandal that roiled the Guangzhou Municipal EPB in 2004, the owner of a private environmental assessment firm bribed five senior officials of the municipal EPB, including its director, to gain enough favor so that his firm could help other businesses obtain approvals from the EPB for a fee.[46] In the scandal at Shanxi's Jiexiu Municipal EPB that implicated its three deputy directors in 2012, one of the deputy directors demanded bribes from fifty-nine firms with environmental assessment impact reports pending for his approval.[47] In the Cixi City EPB in Zhejiang, three successive directors were arrested for corruption. One director, Xu Hongjun, who headed the agency from 2002 to 2008, accepted bribes totaling 613,000 yuan on twelve occasions. In 2003, he took 300,000 yuan from a businessman to help his firm get a higher allocation of the pollution allowance. (Xu's predecessor was involved in a scandal that implicated seven officials in his bureau.) One businessman running a plating business separately bribed two officials to seek lax enforcement on the wastewater discharged by his firm.[48]

In the corruption case that brought down nine officials at the State Food and Drug Administration (SFDA) in 2006, Wei Wei, owner of a private drug company based in Jilin, bribed multiple officials at the SFDA to obtain about 200 licenses from the agency during three years (2002–2005). Through bribes, Wei first secured the collaboration of two senior officials at the Jilin FDA (a deputy director of the Jilin FDA and a deputy chief of the department licensing drugs) to obtain fraudulent approval for his firm's products. He then bribed Liu Yuhui, an official in the China Pharmaceutical Association (a government-affiliated industry group), who subsequently became his intermediary. With funds supplied by Wei, Liu bribed Cao Wenzhuang, chief of the licensing department at the SFDA (and a protégé of the director of the SFDA, Zheng Xiaoyu, who was later executed for taking millions of yuan in bribes). Also through Liu's contact, Wei established ties with a junior official, Mao Teng, who was in charge of "queuing up" drug applications for approval. (Drug companies must first receive a number for their product, and the number determines when it will be reviewed.) Mao received 300,000 yuan in bribes from Wei. Mao also helped Wei because he knew Wei was a close friend of his superior, Cao, and could help him be promoted.[49]

We can gain a deeper appreciation of the process of bribery and collusion from a separate incident also involving Wei. When he needed to have three drugs approved in 2004, Wei first used his contacts with Liu and Cao to secure a meeting with a junior official, Li Zhiyong, whose approval was required to start the review process. Wei then went to a more senior official, Wang Guorong, whose support was indispensable for final approval, but Wang initially refused to act on Wei's application. Undeterred, Wei gave 150,000 HKD to Li, who was Wang's protégé, and also paid 100,000 HKD to Wang. But Wang still refused to help Wei. Li told Wei that he "gave too little to

Wang" and suggested he "do a bit more to show his appreciation." Subsequently, Wei took $60,000 in cash and gave Li $10,000 and Wang $50,000. Even after paying a significant bribe, approval was not guaranteed. On the eve of the approval, Li told Wei to "show more appreciation to Wang." Wei reluctantly gathered another $80,000 in cash, and gave $30,000 to Li and $50,000 to Wang. Five days later, Wei received the coveted approval for the three drugs.[50]

Zheng Xiaoyu, the director of the SFDA, pocketed 6.4 million yuan in bribes directly from eight companies in return for approving twelve drugs before his arrest in 2006. One private drug company called Double Pigeon Co. paid him 2.9 million yuan. Zheng's wife served as an adviser to this company, while his son was given shares in the same company. When Double Pigeon needed approval for one of its products, Zheng directed his executive assistant to take the owner of the firm to meet Hao Heping, the division chief for medical equipment. After the meeting, approval was granted. (Hao was implicated in the SFDA scandal as well.) In another instance, Zheng took 1 million HKD from another private businessman whose company was applying for approval of one of its products at the SFDA. In return, Zheng instructed two subordinates to grant approval even though this violated the normal approval procedure.[51] Zheng was able to carry out his corrupt activities not only because of the powerful post he held, but also because of a network of loyalists whom he had placed in the SFDA. Shortly after he became the director of the agency, he appointed his allies to key positions. One protégé, who was also involved in the scandal, became the head of the personnel department of the agency. Another loyalist, Hao Heping, became the chief of the medical equipment division.[52]

The acceptance of bribes in exchange for lax enforcement actions is a widespread practice as well. Wu Shutian, director of the municipal WSB in Bengbu, Anhui, and his deputy each took about 50,000 yuan in bribes from the owner of a private firm where a major accident had killed three workers in 2007. They reduced the amount of the fine on the firm from 200,000 yuan to 70,000 yuan and cut the personal fine on the businessman from 40 percent of his prior-year income to only 2,000 yuan.[53] In the corruption case that brought down three deputy directors of the Jiexiu City EPB in Shanxi in 2012, one of them received bribes from firms that discharged industrial waste. His typical method of extracting bribes was to order his staff to first issue "notifications of fines" to these firms and then waive the fines if the notified firms paid him off.[54] Wang Guojun, deputy director of the Jilin Provincial Coal Mine Safety Bureau, pocketed over 2 million yuan in bribes during 1997–2007. One of his coconspirators was the deputy director of the provincial coal bureau in charge of mine safety. The duo often headed the provincial team that investigated coal mining accidents. They received bribes from coal mine owners in return for reducing fines or allowing them to retain their mining licenses.[55] In the case implicating more than thirty officials in the Nantong Municipal EPB in Jiangsu in 2012, the head of the agency and his deputy accepted bribes from businessmen whose firms processed hazardous waste without licenses.[56] At the Haiyan County EPB in Zhejiang during 2003–2013, its director, deputy director, and two other officials received bribes from businessmen in exchange for giving a stamp of approval to the equipment in their factories for discharging wastewater containing pollutants exceeding government standards.[57] Between 2007 and 2010, the deputy chief of the Hunan FDA and four other officials in the agency collectively protected a drug company that produced unsafe pharmaceuticals. They imposed light penalties for violations and allowed its products to be included in the province's official list of preferred drugs for public procurement. They took bribes totaling 1.86 million yuan.[58]

Collusion with Intermediaries

The Chinese government's regulations on work safety and environmental protection routinely require independent assessments of companies' qualifications or the environmental impact of their proposed activities and businesses. The cases selected in our sample reveal that this requirement has become a major source of bribe-extraction for Chinese regulators. Corruption involving collusion between a for-profit intermediary and regulatory officials is especially common in environmental protection agencies. Typically, many of these intermediaries are affiliated with the environmental protection agencies or other government entities. According to the Chinese Ministry of Environmental Protection, of the 1,162 environmental assessment firms in 2011, 333 were affiliated with local environmental protection agencies and 243 were classified as "nonprofit government agencies."[59] Those environmental assessment firms unaffiliated with local EPBs or other government entities are usually owned by former officials of the local EPBs. This arrangement not only causes conflicts of interest for local EPBs, but also induces collusion between officials in local EPBs and these intermediaries.

An illuminating case of corruption through government-affiliated intermediaries is the scandal that implicated more than ninety officials and private individuals, including five *chu*-level officials in the city's EPB and six directors of district or county EPBs, at the Hangzhou Municipal EPB in 2007. In this case, one enterprising official, Pan Jun, became the head of the research institute affiliated with the city's EPB, and he immediately approached the heads of the EPBs in the district and county of the city and promised them 30 percent kickbacks on the revenue generated from environmental assessment services they directed to his institute. Specifically, the EPBs would "recommend" the institute to the firms that needed such an assessment. Because the EPB had to approve the assessment, the firms had no choice but to retain Pan's institute. This deal increased the revenue for the institute tenfold within three years. The institute paid the EPBs 7.4 million yuan in "collaborative fees." Portions of these fees were illegally and privately shared by the officials in the EPBs. The director of the Tonglu County EPB split 455,000 yuan in such fees with two of his deputies between 2003 and 2006. Some of the fees went into slush funds in these EPBs that would be used to increase the income of their employees and reimburse the personal travel and entertainment expenses of the officials.[60]

In the corruption case at the Jiangmen Municipal EPB in Guangdong, three low-level officials were separately bribed by two private businessmen who established an "environmental assessment impact" firm in 2005, even though they lacked technical and financial qualifications. One of the officials they bought off approved the environmental impact reports the firm produced.[61] At the Liuyang County EPB in Hunan, six officials, including the director and the head of the agency's discipline inspection committee, were involved in a corruption case in 2004. Two of the disgraced officials pocketed kickbacks from companies that paid the EPB for finding qualified entities to perform "environmental impact assessment" reports. According to the prosecutors, officials in the EPB colluded with each other to embezzle the revenue generated by these "commissions" and divided up the spoils among themselves. This practice was an open secret in the Liuyang EPB, which asked entities qualified to perform environmental impact assessments to pay 35 percent in "collaborative fees." Such kickbacks were stashed in slush funds, which officials distributed among themselves before the plot unraveled in 2003.[62] At the Huzhou Municipal EPB, where twelve officials, including the director and two deputy directors, were arrested in 2005 for corruption, the case centered on the owner of a private firm specializing in environmental impact assessments. He bribed the key officials of the EPB to get the business. The head of the EPB confessed that he would recommend the company to firms seeking environmental impact assessments. Part of the income from the company, which had been an entity affiliated with the EPB before it was privatized, would be paid to the EPB off the books and would be used to increase the EPB's bonus pool.[63] Corruption through intermediaries was also found in the work safety agencies. For instance, Xie Guangxiang, director of the Hunan Provincial WSB and the Coal Mine Safety Bureau (CMSB), owned nonvoting, dividend-producing shares in a private company that provided safety assessment services. Such shares were merely another form of bribery paid by the firm to regulatory officials to gain business.[64]

Patterns of Collusion

Like other officials in the Chinese party-state, those working in regulatory agencies engage in patterns of collusion that have been documented in this study. In the cases selected here, we observe all three: vertical collusion through *maiguan maiguan*, horizontal collusion among insiders through joint participation in crime, and outsider–insider collusion aided by implicit knowledge of similar behavior by colleagues. As seen earlier, one of the critical bonds facilitating collusion among officials is *maiguan maiguan*. To be sure, officials in regulatory agencies possess, in comparison with local party chiefs, far less power to make personnel appointments. Nevertheless, the practice of paying bribes for appointments and promotions in these agencies is also found in some of the sample cases here. Xie Guangxiang, head of the Hunan Provincial WSB and CMSB who was arrested in 2008, not only protected a protégé, who had bribed him for promotion, from an antigraft investigation in 1999, but also elevated him to head a county WSB.[65] In the corruption case at the Guangzhou Municipal EPB, the head of the agency had taken bribes to fund his efforts to be promoted in 1999.[66] Cao Wenzhuang, who was given a suspended death sentence in 2007 for his involvement in the scandal at the SFDA, received 400,000 yuan from a junior official as funds to "compete" for the position as a deputy director of the agency.[67] The director of the Guangzhou FDA took bribes totaling 200,000 yuan from subordinates in return for appointments and promotions during 2000–2003.[68]

While *maiguan maiguan* can build mutually beneficial relations between a supervisor and a subordinate, sharing spoils is a routine form of horizontal collusion in these agencies. Direct participation in corrupt activities solidifies trust among its perpetrators. This dynamic is illustrated in the 2007 scandal at the Hangzhou Municipal EPB. The chief perpetrator, Pan Jun, privately shared his spoils with some of the officials in the EPBs. The director of the Tonglu County EPB split 455,000 yuan in such illicit income with two of his deputies. Some of the fees went into slush funds in these EPBs that were used to increase the income of their employees and reimburse the personal travel and entertainment expenses of the officials. The head of the department of pollution control in the Hangzhou Municipal EPB, the head of the general office of the Hangzhou EPB, and five or six of their colleagues formed a closely knit inner circle. They often socialized through gambling and shared bribes.[69] In the corruption case at the Hangzhou Municipal EPB, it was revealed that in 2005 the agency's officials illegally spent some of the funds allocated for environmental mitigation on bonuses and shared them among themselves, often using false documentation.[70] At the Haining Municipal WSB, one official who collected bribes from businessmen shared the bribes with three other officials in the same agency, including his direct superior.[71] At the Wuzhou FDA, between 2009 and 2011, seven officials split embezzled public funds among themselves.[72]

Unlike bribing superiors for promotions or sharing corruption income, outsider–insider collusion facilitated by implicit knowledge of similar acts committed by colleagues is more difficult to document. On the surface, such corruption, committed by individuals acting alone in a government agency in which multiple corrupt officials operate at the same time, might not qualify as collusion. However, this type of collusion, coordinated mainly by various businessmen, is implicit. Among the cases selected here, four examples offer tantalizing evidence. At the Jiexiu Municipal EPB in Shanxi province, all three deputy directors engaged in corruption, albeit individually, during 2008–2012. After they were arrested, all three officials tried to exonerate themselves by claiming, "I did this because I saw the others doing it."[73] When he was detained in 2006, Ren Weibin, director of the Shangcheng District EPB in Hangzhou, declared, "If we have to die, we all die together." He soon gave investigators information on the corrupt activities of another colleague, the head of the pollution control department, who had received bribes from a businessman. In 2004, Li Weiyu, the head of the Guangzhou Municipal EPB, turned himself in after learning that two of his colleagues had been detained, and he then provided information that led to the arrest of several other officials in the agency. These examples suggest that corrupt officials in such agencies most likely had implicit knowledge of their colleagues' misdeeds even if they did not collude directly.[74]

Collusion and the Local Mafia States

In this section, we shift our attention to provincial- and prefecture-level jurisdictions, where a very large number of top local officials have been implicated in *wo'an* or *chuan'an*. Although not all of these corrupt officials directly colluded with each other, investigations into the corrupt activities of some officials quickly uncovered the misdeeds of the others. The number of key local officials arrested for corruption is often so large that senior Chinese officials call these cases "collapse-style corruption" (*tafangshi fubai*).[75] Collapse-style corruption typically involves the most senior local officials (the party chief or the mayor) who collude with private businessmen, their subordinates, or even organized crime gangs. In some of the high-profile cases of collapse-style corruption, such as the ones we briefly describe below, successive party chiefs, mayors, and other key local officials all participated in corrupt activities. Theoretically, the phenomenon of collapse-style corruption is the logical outcome of collusion among local elites. In jurisdictions where collusive elites have gained dominant control over the local party-state, they transform the local party-state into local mafia states. Consequently, the collapse-style corruption that has subverted the authority of the CCP becomes all but inevitable.

Collapse-Style Corruption in Large Jurisdictions

Based on official press coverage, we assemble below a representative list of provinces and prefecture-level cities where a very large number of key local officials have been implicated in "collapse-style corruption" cases since the late 1990s. To be sure, this list is by no means exhaustive and excludes some of the jurisdictions where similar collapse-style corruption has occurred (such as Guangxi, Inner Mongolia, and Kaifeng).[76]

HEILONGJIANG. The scandal in this northeastern province was exposed during 2002–2005 and implicated 265 officials, including seven provincial-level cadres, more than thirty bureau-level officials, six prefecture party chiefs, and two prefecture mayors. Key provincial-level officials disgraced in the corruption case were Tian Fengshan, provincial governor (1995–2000); Han Guizhi, former provincial party organization chief (1996–1999); two deputy chiefs of the provincial organization department; the provincial propaganda chief; a deputy provincial governor; the president of the provincial high court; the head of the provincial procuratorate; the head of the provincial party secretariat; the director of the provincial justice department; a deputy secretary of the provincial politics and law committee; the director of the provincial personnel department; and the director of the provincial transportation department. Most of them engaged in buying and selling offices and accepting bribes from businessmen.[77]

SHANXI. This province, the power base of Ling Jihua, the former director of the CCP's General Office of the Central Committee (2007–2012) arrested in 2014 for alleged corruption, was hit hard by Xi Jinping's anticorruption drive in 2013–2014. Eight provincial-level officials were detained. While the total number of officials implicated in the scandal remains to be determined, key officials implicated include two sitting deputy governors; two former deputy governors; a former provincial propaganda chief; a deputy provincial party chief who headed the provincial discipline inspection committee and his chief deputy; the head of the provincial party secretariat; Ling's elder brother, who headed the provincial development and reform commission; three successive party chiefs and police chiefs of Taiyuan City, the provincial capital; and fifteen bureau-level officials in the provincial government, including the heads of the departments of land resources, transportation, and environmental protection.[78]

JIANGXI. The corruption case in this province came to light in 2014 when the former provincial party chief, Su Rong, was arrested. Following Su's fall, several of his close associates in the provincial government were also arrested. They included a deputy provincial governor, the head of the provincial party secretariat, a deputy chairman of the provincial people's congress, the director of the provincial tax bureau, two successive directors of the provincial development and reform committee, and more than forty prefecture-level officials.[79]

YUNNAN. The former party chief of the province, Gao Yan, fled China with his mistress in 2002. A former governor, Li Jiating, received a suspended death sentence in 2003 for accepting more than 18 million yuan in bribes and sharing a mistress with a local mafia boss. In 2014 and 2015, a series of arrests decimated the provincial leadership. Bai Enpei, a former provincial party chief, was arrested in 2014 for corruption. Several other senior provincial officials, including a former deputy provincial party secretary and a deputy governor, were also arrested. A former deputy governor committed suicide. Three successive party chiefs of Kunming, the provincial capital, were detained for corruption. In 2014, thirty-seven prefecture- and bureau-level officials, including the former head of the provincial transportation department, were arrested.[80]

FUZHOU, FUJIAN. In this case, which rocked Fujian's provincial capital (population 7.2 million), a crime boss, Chen Kai, once the city's richest man, whose crimes included international drug trafficking, gambling, and prostitution, paid about 10 million yuan to dozens of local officials between the mid-1990s and 2003. After Chen was arrested in 2003, investigations into his case implicated ninety-one officials, including fifty above the level of county and *chu*. Among the key city officials who protected Chen's criminal enterprise were two successive deputy party chiefs in charge of law enforcement, a deputy mayor, Fuzhou's two successive police chiefs, two deputy police chiefs, the head of the city's cultural bureau, a vice president of the city's intermediate court, the head of the Fuzhou party secretariat, the deputy chief of Fujian's department of state security, and the head of the Fuzhou branch of the Bank of China.[81]

SHENYANG, LIAONING. This scandal unfolded in this city of 8.2 million during 1999–2001, implicating 122 individuals and resulting in sixty-two criminal prosecutions. Among the key officials involved in the case were the city's mayor, Mu Suixin; the executive deputy mayor; two officials with deputy-mayor rank; eleven bureau-level officials, including the directors of the finance bureau, development commission, state asset supervision bureau, and tobacco bureau; and seven deputy bureau-level officials. In addition, the president and two vice presidents of the city's intermediate court and the city's chief prosecutor were arrested. A local crime boss, Liu Yong, bribed many city officials.[82]

FUYANG, ANHUI. Between 2000 and 2006, successive corruption scandals were exposed in this agrarian prefecture-level jurisdiction (population 9.3 million). In 2000, the city's mayor, Xiao Zuoxin, was arrested for corruption and later sentenced to life imprisonment. His case implicated sixty individuals. In 2002, a deputy governor of Anhui and former party chief of the prefecture, Wang Huaizhong, was arrested and later sentenced to death. More than 160 individuals were involved in his case. In 2005, Wang Zhaoyao, the head of the provincial politics and law committee and Wang Huaizhong's predecessor, was arrested for corruption. Among the officials arrested for corruption during this period were Xiao's successor, Mayor Li Hezhong, a deputy mayor, the chief of the party organization department, three successive presidents and two vice presidents of the city's intermediate court, the director of the city's bureau of state security, three successive police chiefs, the head of propaganda, and the head of the city's party secretariat.[83]

CHENZHOU, HUNAN. In 2006, Li Dalun, the party chief of this city of 4.6 million, was arrested for taking bribes exceeding 32 million yuan. Investigations into his case resulted in the arrest of 110 officials, including twenty officials at the prefecture level and sixty officials at the county level. The city's former mayor was also arrested. The head of the city's CCP discipline inspection committee was executed. Other key local officials brought down by the scandal included the chiefs of the CCP organization and propaganda departments, a deputy mayor, the party chief of the city's land and resources bureau, and two senior prosecutors. They engaged in selling offices, extortion, bribe-taking, and theft of public funds.[84]

MAOMING, GUANGDONG. In Maoming, a prefecture of 6.8 million in Guangdong, investigations into corruption by the city's leading officials between 2009 and 2015 brought down over 200 officials, including twenty-four prefecture-level officials and 218 county-level officials. The city's three successive party chiefs, two mayors, four deputy mayors, the head of the party's discipline inspection committee, and the city's police chief were all arrested. They engaged in selling offices, bribe-taking, and protecting organized crime.[85]

Notable Features of Local Mafia States

Despite the diversity in terms of the size, geography, and income levels of the jurisdictions, and the number, rank, and type of officials involved in collapse-style corruption cases, local mafia states in China share several noteworthy—and now familiar—characteristics: the prevalence of *maiguan maiguan,* collusion between officials and private businessmen, and collusion between officials and organized crime.

The practice of *maiguan maiguan* is the principal means of vertical collusion and the driver behind the formation of local corruption networks. The logic of "bad money driving out good money" means that jurisdictions in which a large number of officials engage in this illicit trade will likely degenerate into local mafia states. In the above list of representative cases of local mafia states, this practice is found in all of them. Wang Zhaoyao, Fuyang's party chief from 1989 to 1993, took bribes from thirty subordinates seeking appointments and promotions between 1991 and 2005. Xiao Zuoxin, Fuyang's mayor (1998–1999), sold offices to twenty-six officials. During the tenure of Wang Huaizhong, the prefecture's party chief from 1995 to 1999, nearly all the prefecture's key leaders, including Li Hezhong (the mayor from 1996 to 1998), two vice mayors, and the head of the party's organization department, were involved in selling offices. *Maiguan maiguan* was also widespread in the county governments in Fuyang. Zhang Huaqi, a county party chief and a prodigious seller of offices, took bribes from one hundred local officials seeking office.[86] In the mega scandal that implicated more than 200 local officials in Maoming in Guangdong, selling offices was the principal instrument for both self-enrichment and collusion. Zhou Zhenhong, the city's party chief from 2002 to 2007, took bribes from twenty-three individuals seeking offices and promotions, including the city's executive vice mayor, two other vice mayors, and a deputy party secretary. Luo Yingguo, who succeeded Zhou in 2007, accepted bribes of more than 23 million yuan (he also had unexplained wealth exceeding 50 million yuan) from sixty-four officials and businessmen. The city's police chief, Ni Junxiong, not only paid bribes to secure his own position but also extracted bribes from thirty-one police officers, including seven county and district police chiefs in the city, in exchange for appointments and promotions. Zhu Yuying, a county party chief, paid 200,000 HKD to Luo Yingguo to secure a promotion; he also collected bribes of over 17 million yuan from fifty-seven subordinates seeking office.[87] Even in the cases on this list in which the lead perpetrators specialized in other types of corruption, they also relied on *maiguan maiguan* to build their networks of loyalists. For example, Su Rong, the former party chief of Jiangxi, was accused of selling offices for bribes during his tenure (2008–2012). Li Dalun, the long-serving party chief of Chenzhou, pocketed large sums of bribes from his subordinates in return for appointments and promotions. In the Shanxi scandal, at least two provincial-level officials, deputy governor Du Shanxue and a member of the provincial party standing committee, Chen Chuanping, were accused of selling offices.[88]

Since the bulk of corruption income for local officials is derived from bribes paid by businessmen, collusion coordinated by outsiders (businessmen) plays a critical role in causing collapse-style corruption. A closer examination of the transactions between these officials and their cronies in the private sector further shows that businessmen were willing to pay huge bribes, mainly because local officials allowed them to gain control of state-owned property cheaply. Su Rong, the former party chief of Jiangxi, helped a business tycoon, Fang Wei, acquire mining rights and SOE assets in Gansu (where Su had previously served as provincial party chief) and Jiangxi. Su's wife also pressured a local mayor in 2009 to end an ongoing auction and sell the use rights to a prime plot of land to a favored private developer at only 20 percent of the market value.[89] In the mega scandal in Yunnan, a province rich in mineral resources, the disgraced party chief, Bai Enpei, a deputy provincial governor, and a former party boss of Kunming, were all involved in giving away mineral rights or mining assets of SOEs to private businessmen who had befriended them. Zhang Tianxin, one of the three disgraced former party chiefs of Kunming, reportedly helped a real estate developer acquire, for 19 million yuan, a state-owned tin mine worth several hundred million yuan in 2003 when the SOE was restructured. Qiu He, Zhang's predecessor, also helped a longtime friend and real estate developer, Liu Weigao, obtain several real estate development projects in Kunming.[90] During his tenure as the party chief of Fuyang, Wang Huaizhong helped his business cronies purchase land at deep discounts and avoid paying various taxes and fees. In one case, he pocketed a bribe of half a million yuan for helping a private businessman buy a hotel owned by the local government. Altogether, the government lost 136 million yuan through corrupt transactions involving state-owned assets.[91] The case of Li Dalun, Chenzhou's party chief from 1999 to 2006, involved more than twenty private businessmen. One of them, Xing Lixin, a real estate developer, used his friendship with Li to accumulate a fortune worth 100 million yuan. In return, he gave Li's wife a nearly 10 percent equity stake in one of his subsidiaries.[92]

Involvement with organized crime is the third characteristic of many jurisdictions hit by collapse-style corruption. The penetration of organized crime into the power center of the local party-state may be disturbing, but it is not surprising. Apart from their tools of trade, intimidation and violence, crime bosses are primarily profiteers. If close ties with local officials can help increase their profits, crime bosses will cultivate and invest in these relationships. In many instances, they also use their legitimate cover as successful businessmen to facilitate the building of personal ties with senior local officials. Liu Yong, Shenyang's onetime crime boss, was the chairman of Jiayang Group, a conglomerate that owned restaurants, shopping malls, retail stores, and entertainment outlets. Liu Han, a billionaire mining tycoon from Sichuan and reportedly a crony of disgraced former security chief Zhou Yongkang, was the chairman of Hanlong Group, a giant conglomerate that owned power stations and mines. Chen Kai, a drug kingpin and once Fuzhou's richest man, controlled an entertainment empire called Kaixuan Group. With the help of their friends in the government, these crime bosses were also covered with an additional gloss of prestige as members of the local people's congresses and the people's political consultative conferences. Liu Yong was a member of the Shenyang Municipal People's Congress and a recipient of awards such as "Outstanding Private Entrepreneur" and "Model Individual in Providing Assistance to the Poor." Liu Han, who was executed for murder in 2015, was a three-term member of the standing committee of the Sichuan People's Political Consultative Conference.

Under such legitimate covers, these crime bosses were able to use money and prostitutes to curry favor with local political leaders. Liu Yong paid large bribes to many senior local officials, including Mayor Mu Suixin; Ma Xiangdong, the executive vice mayor; Liu

Shi, the city's top prosecutor; and a vice president of the municipal intermediate court.[93] Chen Kai doled out nearly 10 million yuan to ninety-one officials and government workers, including two successive local police chiefs.[94] Liu Han, according to *Caijing,* a leading investigative publication, paid 20 million yuan in 2003 to Zhou Bin, Zhou Yongkang's son, for assets that were worth less than 6 million yuan. After he met Bai Enpei in 2000 (the party boss of Yunnan), Liu started giving him expensive jewelry and deliberately lost 100,000 yuan to Bai in each game of *mahjong.*[95] In return, these criminals not only received protection, but also acquired state-owned assets at very low prices or at no cost. Liu Yong, for example, was able to gain the use of 24,000 square meters of prime land in Shenyang's city center free of charge, due to $40,000 in bribes he paid to the executive vice mayor. The market price for the land was reportedly 350 million yuan. Intervention by Bai Enpei allowed Liu Han to pay 153 million yuan for a 60 percent share in a giant lead and zinc mine in Yunnan in 2003, reportedly worth tens of billions of yuan.[96]

Local Mafia States: Causes and Effects

The chief characteristics of the local mafia states sampled here suggest that two principal factors help a gang of criminals seize control of local governments and turn them into instruments for looting and petty despotism. The first and most important factor is the role played by a domineering top local leader, typically the party chief, who intimidates his colleagues and monopolizes most of the important personnel and economic decisions. This unchallenged power allows the party chief to act like a mafia boss, especially if he stays in the same jurisdiction for an extended period of time. Li Dalun, for example, served as the party chief of Chenzhou for eight years and brooked no opposition to his decisions. His authority was so absolute that, according to his interview with anticorruption investigators, the local CCP organization chief would not dare to appoint someone without checking with him first. Even the mayor, officially the number two executive in charge of economic affairs, had to seek approval from Li for key decisions. In Chenzhou, as Li boasted, "Only my word counts."[97]

Su Rong, the former Jiangxi party chief, also treated the province as his personal fiefdom. He promoted his loyalists and purged those who dared to defy him. In one case, after a local official told inspectors from Beijing about a shady land deal involving Su's wife, Su accused the whistle-blower of corruption and managed to get him convicted on charges of corruption and given a suspended death sentence in 2012.[98] Like Su Rong, Wang Huaizhong enjoyed a near monopoly of power as Fuyang's party chief. He would dictate a list of the officials he wanted promoted or appointed to the deputy party chief in charge of personnel matters and the head of the CCP organization department. Wang also directly interfered in the sale of the city's land, over which he had no formal authority. For a long time, he had final say over the sale of land in the most desirable parts of the city center.[99] Mu Suixin, the former mayor of Shenyang, was a bully, according to CCDI investigators. Called "*dage*" ("big brother," a term often used to refer to mafia bosses) by his loyalists, Mu asserted his strong personality and effectively sidelined the city's party chief, a rare feat for a mayor. Without Mu's approval, the city's CCP standing committee could not make key personnel decisions.[100]

Unlike the local party chiefs who behave like mafia bosses, real-world gangsters actually have far less capacity to create a local mafia state. When they do, they must rely on extraordinary entrepreneurship and abundant financial resources to buy off local officials. This combination is the second key factor responsible for the emergence of local mafia states in large jurisdictions. To be sure, while sensational collapse-style corruption cases attributed to a single crime boss such as Shenyang's Liu Yong or Fuzhou's Chen Kai tend to grab the headlines, such cases are rarer than similar cases featuring local party chiefs as the real supreme local gangsters. To succeed in sustaining and expanding their criminal enterprises, crime bosses need to have highly profitable businesses, legitimate covers, political status, and protection provided by crooked cops and their political masters. Liu Yong exemplified such criminal entrepreneurship. He had built a fortune worth hundreds of millions of yuan through violence and crime, acquired legitimate covers and status as a rich businessman and a delegate to the municipal people's congress, and used bribes to develop close personal friendships with key officials, including the mayor, executive deputy mayor, and the city's chief prosecutor.[101] Chen Kai in Fuzhou applied similar tactics to become the city's richest man and turned Fuzhou's key officials— deputy mayors, deputy party chiefs, police chiefs, prosecutors, and judges—into his accomplices.[102]

Of the two subtypes of local mafia states, those headed by real-world crime bosses are less destructive than those run by tyrannical party chiefs. Corrupt local party chiefs routinely appoint their cronies, usually those who have paid bribes to secure their appointments, to key positions, thus enabling the cronies to prey on society as well. Additionally, the shady activities of a corrupt local party chief produce externalities, one of which is the reduced risks of detection for corrupt officials in his jurisdiction. Obviously, those closely allied with the party chief will have little to worry about because of the protection they expect from him. But a corrupt party chief also has less of an incentive to crack down on corruption in his jurisdiction out of fear that anticorruption investigations may accidentally expose crimes committed by his own followers or himself. Another externality is the copycat effect. Corrupt party chiefs often inspire corruption among their underlings who feel they are just as entitled to bribery as their superiors. It is logical to conclude that, as corruption begets corruption, the market for corruption is significantly larger in local mafia states than it is in jurisdictions where local party chiefs are not directly involved in collusive corruption.

Conclusion

If we fail to govern our party effectively or strictly . . .
sooner or later it will lose its standing for ruling the country
and will be cast aside by history.

— Xi Jinping, June 28, 2013

THE WORRIES expressed by Xi that corruption could be the undoing of the CCP are understandable. Yet senior party leaders like him might need a better understanding of the roots of corruption in post-Tiananmen China to appreciate the difficulties they face in fighting this scourge and defending the party's rule. Our analysis of the cases of collusion among elites in this study shows that the roots of crony capitalism in general, and collusive corruption in particular, run much deeper. Mitigation of the pathologies of crony capitalism is unthinkable without severing its close link with public property that can be stolen with relative ease by the ruling elites. Beneath the unsightly surface of corruption hides a story of the looting of nominally state-owned property by elites who either have direct control over the disposal of such property or can seize such property through bribery or violence. Phrased differently, had public property not been made available for looting, the type of rapacious crony capitalism that has replaced Maoism would have been inconceivable. This statement does not imply that China's economic reform is to blame for the emergence of crony capitalism. Such reform, in and of itself, does not necessarily lead to crony capitalism, as the cases of Poland, the Czech Republic, the Baltic states, and, to a lesser extent, Hungary, show.[1] The critical determinant is the nature of the regime in control of the disposal of state-owned assets. Of course, the privatization of such assets in Eastern Europe was deeply flawed, largely due to the lack of basic institutions, such as capital markets and a functioning regulatory framework. The adverse macroeconomic environment, marked by a transitional recession, trade disruptions, and fiscal distress, further hampered the reform process.[2] Yet, despite all the turmoil and setbacks most Eastern European countries experienced during transition, they largely avoided the fate of the former Soviet Union, where a kleptocracy emerged from the ruins of communism.

The most likely explanation lies in the divergent political paths of these postcommunist societies. In the most successful Eastern European and Baltic states, democratic transitions and consolidations were accomplished quickly, thus constraining the ruling elites and preventing large-scale looting.[3] The experience of Eastern Europe provides a counterexample as well as an important clue about the linkage between the nature of the regime and the origins of crony capitalism in postcommunist states. Unlike Eastern Europe, post-Mao China has been ruled by a Leninist regime that, except for a brief period in the 1980s, has shown no inclination to liberalize its political system, let alone give up its monopoly of power. And unlike post-Soviet Russia, where the rapid collapse of the old regime allowed a tiny group of entrepreneurs to amass huge private fortunes but deprived most of the elites of the opportunity to loot, Chinese ruling elites have maintained political control and enjoyed boundless opportunities to convert the riches of the state into their personal wealth.

Thus, we need to incorporate insights from the literature on the predatory state to understand the origins of China's crony capitalism.[4] As Douglass North argues, the state defines and enforces property rights, and a predatory state always defines these rights to maximize its income and privileges.[5] In this light, the real rationale behind the CCP's post-Tiananmen approach to the restructuring of the rights of state-owned property—decentralization of control rights without clarification of ownership rights—becomes obvious. Such a change of the rights in the nominally state-owned property provides the ruling elites maximum advantage to extract wealth from society. If we follow the dismal reasoning of institutionalists, crony capitalism is the only logical and inevitable outcome of economic transition under a Leninist regime.

Identifying the critical linkage between property rights and the origins of crony capitalism enriches the institutionalist literature with a contemporary example of elite predation through a redefinition of property rights. By introducing the analytical concept of elite collusion, this study also advances our understanding of the micro-level dynamics of crony capitalism. In our theoretical formulation, collusion among elites is a predictable and rational micro-level response to substantive but incremental changes in the rights to public property. The interaction of institutional changes in property rights and the adaptive response by elites gives rise to crony capitalism. To fully understand China's crony capitalism, we must retrace these institutional changes, connect them to the resultant behavioral responses by the elites, and explore its manifestations in real life.

An important finding of this study of China's crony capitalism is its decentralized characteristics. The decentralization of administrative power, the fragmentation of political authority, a diverse manufacturing-based economy, and the close connection between the value of assets and macroeconomic performance ensure that looting must be decentralized and accomplished through collusion, which in turn allows lower-level elites to share some of the spoils. Our study indicates that China's crony capitalism may have produced a unique multilayered oligarchy, based largely on geographical jurisdictions in which a small group of elites connected with local party chiefs control an inordinate amount of power and have a capacity to loot that is disproportionate to their relatively modest status inside the Chinese party-state. While this observation explains why local elites in China have benefited immeasurably from the emergence of crony capitalism, we should also note the indispensable role played by private entrepreneurs. Another noteworthy feature of China's crony capitalism is that political elites, such as the princelings and family members of the elites, have not managed to loot all the wealth. It is true that they have gained enormous wealth, but the bulk of the benefits from the looting of the state appears to have flowed toward private entrepreneurs from ordinary or even humble backgrounds, people like Lou Zhongfu and Wang Chuncheng, whose stories we briefly tell in Introduction, as well as countless others who forged lucrative alliances with the local officials featured in our study. In addition to showing that China's crony capitalism, at least in its early phase, provides more open access and allows private entrepreneurs to bribe their way into an exclusive circle of power and wealth, our story merely reconfirms the well-established fact that private entrepreneurs possess far greater capabilities than political elites in making state-owned assets more productive and making them appreciate in value. The problem is, of course, that the gains from the conversion of unproductive state-owned assets to more productive private assets accrue to a small number of well-connected businessmen, not to the rightful owners of these assets: ordinary Chinese citizens.

It would be a mistake, however, to assume that these private entrepreneurs, once they have gained both economic wealth and political power, will prefer liberal capitalism to crony capitalism. Although the Chinese private sector has made tremendous progress since the 1990s, it has been hobbled by government restrictions and, as this study shows, incestuous ties with the political elites.[6] Research on the political values of Chinese private entrepreneurs also shows that they are highly sympathetic to those championed by the CCP.[7] The reason is not hard to fathom. Those already inside this select circle have every incentive to preserve their privileges and the institutions that make them possible.[8] But lucrative private returns from privileges granted under crony capitalism come at the expense of the social benefits of liberal capitalism. In pursuing collusion with government officials, private entrepreneurs not only waste precious resources that could have been invested more productively, but also divert their energy and talents into rent-rich sectors that are unlikely to be the growth engines needed to upgrade the Chinese economy. It is no coincidence that nearly all the biggest private fortunes in China are concentrated in real estate and mining, sectors most plagued by collusion. According to estimates, one-quarter of China's dollar billionaires in 2015 are in the real estate business.[9] China's dynamic information technology sector is one of the very few exceptions. The close ties between rent-seeking private entrepreneurs and political elites bode ill for the development of liberal capitalism. This alliance has exclusivist instincts because maintaining high barriers to entry protects the rich rents that accrue to its members and ensures its hereditary nature. The result is not competitive liberal capitalism, but oligarchical cronyism.

Collusion and Regime Decay

The emergence and entrenchment of crony capitalism in China's political economy, in retrospect, is the logical outcome of Deng Xiaoping's authoritarian model of economic modernization because elites in control of unconstrained power cannot resist using it to loot the wealth generated by economic growth. More than a quarter century after the Tiananmen crackdown, the limitations of this model have become plainly visible. Economically, the deceleration of growth exposes the underlying structural and institutional flaws of the Chinese economy.[10] Politically, endemic corruption raises the specter, as Xi Jinping warns, that the CCP could lose its grip on power. The logic of crony capitalism in general, and that of collusive corruption in particular, suggests that the top leaders of the party has good reason to worry. Ostensibly, they fear that corruption will destroy the legitimacy of the party by undermining economic growth and alienating the masses. While such conventional wisdom is not necessarily wrong, our study demonstrates that collusion among elites produces a self-destructive dynamic inside the Leninist regime that will almost certainly accelerate its demise through various mechanisms.

Although collusion among elites initially emerged in sectors where decentralized control of poorly defined property rights and lucrative infrastructure contracts attracted officials and businessmen, this behavior has spread throughout the Chinese state and public sector. Predictably, collusion has also invaded the agencies the CCP depends on to police its own members and to defend its security. For instance, more than a dozen senior officials on the CCP's commissions for discipline inspection, the agencies charged with monitoring and policing party officials, have been implicated in cases of collusive corruption.[11] The Ministry of State Security (MSS), China's equivalent of the Soviet

KGB, is also apparently riddled with corruption. Ma Jian, a vice minister in the MSS responsible for counterintelligence, was arrested in early 2015 in a mega corruption scandal. According to *Caixin*'s investigation, Ma not only used the power and spying capabilities of the MSS to help a real estate tycoon, but also amassed a personal fortune, maintained six mistresses (two of them MSS officers), and fathered two illegitimate children.[12] Le Dake, who served as the director of the MSS in Tibet between 2004 and 2013, was arrested for corruption in June 2015.[13] Among the cases collected for this study, three senior MSS officers, all directors of the agency in large municipalities (Shenyang, Fuzhou, and Fuyang), were involved in collusive corruption. (Two other senior MSS bureau directors, of Beijing and Qingdao, respectively, have also been arrested for corruption.)

Collusive corruption inside the People's Liberation Army (PLA), the ultimate guarantor of the CCP's survival, has reached similarly epidemic proportions. During Xi's anticorruption campaign, more than three dozen generals have been arrested. According to the PLA, 90 percent of the corruption cases occurred in military construction projects, logistics, real estate development, health care, finance, and personnel management. Collusive corruption—*wo'an* and *chuan'an*—is a prominent feature.[14] The rot has even spread to the highest level of the Chinese military command. The two most senior PLA commanders, former Politburo members and vice chairmen of the Central Military Affairs Commission, Guo Boxiong and Xu Caihou, were both arrested in 2014–2015 for accepting huge bribes in return for promoting subordinates.

The inexorable spread of collusion may be shocking, but it is not hard to explain theoretically. The prevalence of collusion in the Chinese regime can be attributed to the intrinsic attractiveness of collusion—higher potential returns from corruption and reduced risks of detection. Additionally, our study demonstrates that collusion begets collusion due to the dynamic of bad money driving out good money. Since collusive elites acquire competitive advantages vis-à-vis noncollusive elites, those who engage in *maiguan maiguan* are destined to rise faster and higher than their less unscrupulous comrades. Finally, collusion results in the progressive degeneration of the organizational norms of the party-state due to the behavioral requirements of collusion and its externalities. As we see in our case studies, colluders perform rituals such as joint participation in criminal activities or other degenerate acts to establish mutual trust. In organizations where collusion is rife, knowledge of corrupt acts perpetrated by colleagues often inspires similar acts. Corrupt leaders in these organizations predictably condone corruption by subordinates.

Taken together, these dynamics of regime decay destroy the institutional integrity of the Chinese party-state through three possible mechanisms. First, as collusive networks form and colonize all corners of the party-state, they subvert its political authority. These networks transform the authority of the regime into their private instruments of power. Instead of advancing the regime's interests, they primarily seek private benefits. While proclaiming loyalty to the party-state, they are beholden only to their local patrons, either the party chiefs or the wealthy businessmen. Second, corruption networks inevitably compete with each other for power and rents, thus weakening the CCP's internal unity and increasing the risk of purges that endanger the personal security of its top elites. As demonstrated by Xi Jinping's high-profile anticorruption campaign that felled hundreds of senior officials, many of them belonging to rival factions, power struggles, an inevitable product of the rise of collusive networks, have severely damaged the unity of leadership essential to the party's survival. Third, when collusive corruption pervades the security apparatus of the party-state, it is almost certain to undermine the effectiveness and loyalty of the pillar institutions upon which the party-state's survival rests.

Endemic collusion also challenges the theory of "authoritarian resilience."[15] Instead of evidence of institutional resilience, which ultimately rests on the political loyalty, integrity, and capabilities of the regime's core elites, this study finds pervasive institutional decay—degeneration of norms, disloyalty to the regime, and subordination of the regime's corporate interests to the private interests of members of corruption networks. The CCP has seen its power of personnel appointment, a key instrument in maintaining its institutional cohesion and integrity, appropriated by local party chiefs through the pervasive practice of *maiguan maiguan*. The patronage networks thus created have dubious loyalty to the party as an institution. Institutional decay has also spread to another key component of the CCP—SOEs, the economic pillar of the party-state. Our study of collusive corruption in SOEs offers evidence that the party's control over this vital sector is also slipping as the agents it has appointed to run these firms are engaged in systemic looting and self-enrichment. The rot of collusive corruption has also seeped into the key institutions of the Chinese party-state, such as the CDIs, police, the judiciary, and other regulatory agencies.

The practical effect of the decay of the critical institutions of the Chinese party-state leads not only to deteriorating governance, but also to elite disunity and power struggles. The disunity of elites is created by struggles for power and economic spoils. Collusion does not equal unity. In fact, collusive alliances compete with each other. The outcomes of this competition are unavoidably perceived as unfair by the losing side because the winners of such competitions simply have more power. The resentment of the losers thus constitutes a key source of elite disunity. Another political consequence, perhaps lethal to the CCP, is the opportunity created by a decaying regime for an opportunistic strongman who can vanquish his political opponents through tactics disguised as anticorruption efforts. Because of the widespread nature of corruption and its collusive characteristics, a strongman enjoys huge tactical advantages to destroy his political rivals. It is relatively easy to connect them with corrupt acts and, because their supporters and cronies are all tied together through collusion, the downfall of one patron typically claims all of his clients. Given the popular resentment against corruption, a strongman employing this strategy is sure to gain, at least initially, an immense boost in his political capital. Indeed, Bo Xilai, the former party chief of Chongqing who ironically was himself purged on charges of corruption, used this strategy with remarkable initial success in his quest for political visibility. His archrival, Xi Jinping, launched a ferocious anticorruption drive immediately after his rise to power and, in short order, dismantled the patronage networks of his political rivals. While conventional wisdom is inclined to see such an anticorruption drive as a positive for the CCP, the actual effects are likely to be the opposite. If anything, politically motivated anticorruption efforts will more likely increase insecurity and rivalry among elites, thus degrading the political cohesiveness of the autocratic regime and making it even more brittle.

Economic and Political Implications

In the literature on extractive institutions and economic development popularized by Daron Acemoglu and James Robinson, social, economic, and political arrangements that determine the allocation of property rights and access to wealth-creating opportunities are seen as key to the prosperity of nations. Societies where a small elite monopolizes such rights and opportunities are unlikely to produce lasting prosperity.[16] While this influential theory may be a prescient warning that China's autocratic development model is likely to end in failure, it does not pinpoint the mechanisms and processes through which the elite perpetrates extraction. Institutions themselves cannot extract wealth; only individuals in control of them can. The empirical evidence gathered for this study provides a useful contribution to the theory of extractive institutions by uncovering the underlying political alliances—collusive networks connecting political, business, and criminal elites—that create, manipulate, and operate these institutions. These alliances, both exclusive and oligarchical, are the inevitable outcomes of economic modernization under autocratic rule. Of course, similar alliances may also exist in democratic societies, and the existence of such alliances both undermines democracy and hampers economic development. In other words, democracy may not be a sufficient condition for ensuring inclusive institutions and political alliances. However, under autocratic rule, there can be no necessary, let alone sufficient, conditions for the formation of inclusive alliances and institutions. The autocratic ruling elites in control of the coercive capacity of the state are inherently hostile to inclusive political alliances because they threaten the survival of the autocracy itself. Theoretically, inclusive institutions under autocratic systems are similarly impossible because the essence of autocracy is the exclusion of the majority by a small minority of elites who rule through fear and violence.

If crony capitalism results in long-term economic stagnation, which in turn imperils the survival of the CCP, the question is whether the party itself can undertake the necessary reforms to address the pathologies of crony capitalism. As shown by Xi Jinping's sense of crisis and his anticorruption campaign, apparently he and his supporters believe they must—and can. Yet we must distinguish such campaign-style corrective actions from the self-corrective capacity of a Leninist regime. Corrective actions are effective only in a narrow, technical, and temporary sense. Individuals targeted in a crackdown are removed and punished. Looting is temporarily curbed. But a self-corrective capacity entails more: A regime possessing such a capacity is capable of both destroying the individual collusive networks and changing the underlying environments in which such networks breed, survive, and prosper. The evidence in this study shows that it is inconceivable that the CCP can reform the political and economic institutions of crony capitalism because these are the very foundations of the regime's monopoly of power.

Since the inevitable outcome of elite collusion is the enrichment of a small minority and high levels of inequality, socioeconomic conditions in a predatory autocratic regime are certain to be unfavorable to the consolidation of democracy or the establishment of liberal democratic institutions, even in the event of a collapse of the corrupt autocratic regime. If members of these collusive alliances survive the fall of autocracy physically, they will be well positioned to gain disproportionate influence in the postauthoritarian political order and to eviscerate the newly established democratic institutions. The unsuccessful experience of democratic consolidation in Russia and Ukraine during the last two decades could be repeated in China as well.[17]

One sobering conclusion is that the path to democracy in China is unlikely to be a linear or smooth one. If the rise of liberal capitalism facilitates the emergence of democracy, the entrenchment of crony capitalism in the Chinese case will make the transition both more difficult and more disorderly. A scenario of regime change initiated by elites becomes highly unlikely under crony capitalism. The capitalist class itself will be divided between well-connected cronies and excluded and frustrated entrepreneurs. The ruling elites will be less inclined to introduce political reform because such a step would threaten their economic interests. The fragility of the institutions of the party-state also raises fears that even modest reform efforts could unleash a revolution. The prospect of genuine market-oriented economic reform is equally unpromising because such a change would eliminate the source of rents for the ruling autocratic elites. If a regime transition should come, the initiating event is more likely to be a breakdown of the decaying autocracy, possibly induced by a split among the elites inside the party-state, a devastating economic shock, an Arab Spring–style mass revolt that the authorities fail to crush quickly, a disastrous external adventure, or a combination of such events. Unfortunately, even a revolutionary overthrow of the old order may not usher in the dawn of a liberal democracy. The legacies of crony capitalism—great inequality of wealth, local mafia states, and the entrenchment of privileged tycoons—will enable those who have acquired enormous illicit wealth under the old regime to wield outsized political influence in a struggling new democracy that will have poor odds of survival.

Appendix

Table A.1. Key characteristics of fifty cases of *maiguan maiguan*

Name	Position of perpetrator[a]	Number of positions sold	Duration of corruption	Promotion during the period	Total corruption income (million yuan)	Bribes from private businesses	Sentence[b]
Zheng Yuansheng	PC, Jiangxi (C)	40	1992–1995	no	0.13	no	13
Liu Xiutian	PC, Hebei (C)	14	1996–2000	no	0.17	no	11
Zhang Shujun	Land Bureau Director, Henan (C)	10	2005–2008	no	0.21	yes	12
Ye Dongxiong	SAIC Director, Hainan (C)	31	1995–2002	yes	0.22	no	16
Zhou Baofa	PC, Zhejiang (C)	7	1987–1996	yes	0.26	yes	life
Zhang Guiyi	PC, Anhui (C)	11	1999–2004	yes	0.28	yes	8
Qi Qingnian	Township PC, Henan	30	2003–2010	yes	0.36	yes	12
Hu Jianxue	PC, Shandong (PE)	42	1990–1995	no	0.61	yes	SD
Lu Xiaoyu	PC, Shandong (C)	70	1993–1998	yes	0.67	no	life
Zhang Erjiang	PC, Hubei (PE)	8	1992–2001	yes	0.8	yes	18
Mao Zhaode	Director of Hainan SAIC, Hainan (PE)	11	1998–2002	yes	0.92	yes	11
Ding Weibin	PC, Guangdong (C)	16	1996–2000	yes	1.0	yes	6
Zhang Gaiping	PC, Shaanxi (C)	28	2000–2005	yes	1.1	yes	13
Zhang Ruhua	Director, EPB, Jiangsu (C)	17	2003–2013	no	1.2	yes	7.5
Zhou Yinxiao	PC, Liaoning (PE)	5	1997–2005	yes	1.2	yes	14
Li Yulin	PC, Liaoning (C)	33	Unclear–2005	unclear	1.3	yes	13
Li Tiecheng	PC, Jilin (C)	162	1991–2000	yes	1.4	yes	15

(continued)

Table A.1 (continued)

Name	Position of perpetrator[a]	Number of positions sold	Duration of corruption	Promotion during the period	Total corruption income (million yuan)	Bribes from private businesses	Sentence[b]
Wu Miao	DO, Hainan (PE)	9	2004–2009	no	2.1	yes	13
Li Gang	PC, Heilongjiang (C)	131	1996–2002	yes	2.2	no	life
Liu Dexin	PC, Guangxi (C)	33	1996–2001	yes	2.6	yes	life
Cao Yongbao	DPC, Sichuan (PE)	32	1994–2004	yes	2.7	yes	13
Liang Bizhi	PC, Guangdong, (C)	13	2003–2012	yes	2.97	yes	13
Xu Shexin	PC, Anhui (C)	59	2002–2008	yes	3.2	yes	14
Zhang Zhi'an	PC, Anhui (C)	14	1994–2007	yes	3.6	yes	life
Yang Jianguo	PC, Anhui (C)	87	1998–2004	yes	3.8	yes	life
Yu Fanglin	PC, Guangxi (PE)	10	1989–1998	yes	3.83	yes	life
Shao Jianwei	Police Chief, Shanxi (PE)	41	1995–2004	yes	4.8	yes	9
Wang Xingbao	PC, Jiangxi (PE)	5	1994–1999	no	4.9	yes	life
Long Guohua	PC, Hunan (C)	35	1998–2007	yes	5.02	yes	life
Ni Junxiong	Police Chief, Guangdong (PE)	41	2001–2010	yes	5.1	yes	15
Zhang Huaqi	PC, Anhui, (C)	90	1997–2001	yes	5.3	no	life
Yang Songquan	PC, Henan (C)	20	2000–2005	no	5.5	yes	16
Li Guowei	Director of Highways, Jiangxi (PE)	23	1999–2004	yes	5.73	yes	life
Yang Yupei	PC, Chongqing (C)	60	1999–2003	no	5.8	yes	17
Ma De	PC, Heilongjiang (PE)	12	1992–2002	yes	6.0	yes	SD

Han Guizhi	DO, Heilongjiang (P)	63	1993–2003	yes	7.0	no	SD
Li Tianfu	Deputy Police Chief, Guangdong (PE)	13	2002–2009	yes	7.95	yes	16
Chen Shaoyong	CCP MSC, Fujian (P)	9	1992–2008	yes	8.2	yes	life
Liu Zhuozhi^c	DG, Inner Mongolia (P)	15	2002–2010	yes	8.2	yes	life
Chen Zhaofeng	PC, Anhui (C)	110	1990–2003	yes	8.3	yes	life
He Mingxu^c	DG, Anhui (P)	10	1991–2006	yes	8.41	yes	SD
Liu Zhenjian	PC, Shandong (C)	41	2007–2012	yes	8.58	yes	life
Li Chenglong	PC, Guangxi (C)	11	1991–1996	yes	10.4	yes	D
Wang Guohua^c	DO, Henan (PE)	38	1995–2008	yes	12.6	yes	15
Ren Zenglu	PC, Gansu (C)	129	2005–2012	yes	13.02	yes	life
Wang Zhaoyao^c	DG, Anhui (P)	26	1991–2005	yes	13.5	yes	SD
Li Senlin^c	DO, Henan (PE)	238	2001–2011	yes	15.46	yes	life
Wu Baoliang	PC, Anhui (C)	65	2003–2012	yes	20.7	yes	life
Tian Zhong	DPC, Jilin (PE)	12	1996–2006	yes	23.0	yes	life
Luo Yinguo	PC, Guangdong (PE)	15	1998–2011	yes	70.0	yes	SD

a. PC = Party Secretary; DO = Director of the Organization Department; DG = Deputy Governor; DPC = Deputy Party Secretary; PSC = Party Standing Committee; SAIC = State Administration of Industry and Commerce; MSC = Member of Standing Committee; C = county- or district-level; PE = prefecture-level; P = provincial- or ministerial-level; EPB = Environmental Protection Bureau.

b. Number of years; SD = suspended death sentence; D = death; only term sentences are calculated.

c. These officials sold most of their offices while occupying positions one level below their finally achieved rank.

Table A.2. Key characteristics of fifty cases of corruption involving multiple officials and businessmen

Chief perpetrator	Position; province[a]	Number of officials involved[b]	Duration of crime; promotion	Selling office	Main areas of corruption	Total corruption income (million yuan)[c]	Sentence[d]
Xiang Hongzu	PC, Hubei (SC)	11	2007–2012; no	no	Infrastructure	0.10	3
Feng Shunqiao	PC, Zhejiang (PE)	14	1993–2006; yes	yes	Real estate; bank loans	0.80	12
Zhang Yushun	Mayor, Gansu (PE)	7	2000–2002; no	no	Real estate	0.83	10
Zhang Shengxing	PC, Fujian (SC)	6	2003–2006; yes	no	Real estate	0.94	13
Ye Jinyin	Director, Land Bureau, Jiangxi (SC)	13	2003–2011; no	no	Real estate, infrastructure	1.05	12.5
Li Qiliang	Prefecture Deputy Mayor, Jiangxi (PE)	5	2001–2009; yes	yes	Mining, land, infrastructure	1.08	11
Pei Yongchun	Director, Municipal Water Works, Jiangxi (C)	125	1998–2013; yes	no	Infrastructure	1.51	12.5
Jiang Zhenghua	County DPC, Anhui (C)	21	2001–2006; no	yes	Real estate	1.56	8
Zhu Junyi	Bureau Chief, Shanghai (PE)	23	1999–2006; no	no	Loans; infrastructure	1.60	18
Lei Yaxin	Prefecture DSG, Shaanxi (PE)	5	2007–2009; yes	no	SOE assets	1.80	12.5
Shen Qinghua	Prefecture SG, Hunan (PE)	10	2000–2007; yes	no	Infrastructure	2.21	14
Tang Fujin	PC, Sichuan (C)	10	1998–2004; yes	yes	Mining; SOE assets; power stations	2.48	life
Li Zhongjie	PC, Zhejiang (SC)	56	1996–2009; yes	no	Land, real estate; SOE assets; infrastructure	2.78	13.5
Li Bin	District PC, Sichuan (C)	21	1997–2003; yes	no	Real estate	2.89	11
Wan Ruizhong	PC, Guangxi (C)	7	1999–2001; no	no	Mining	3.21	death
Fan Xuekan	DPC, Zhejiang (C)	6	1992–2005; yes	yes	Real estate; SOE assets	3.39	life

Quan Junliang	Deputy Mayor, Anhui (PE)	24	2004–2012; yes	yes	Mining, land	3.6	14.5
Ai Shanjiang	Mayor, Xinjiang (C)	8	2004–2013; yes	no	Land and real estate	4.17	15
Xie Lianzhang	Deputy Mayor, Henan (PE)	41	2001–2013; yes	yes	Land and real estate	4.54	12
Wang Yan	Assistant Mayor, Shandong (PE)	3	1999–2003; yes	yes	Land and real estate	4.96	SD
Fu Chunrong	PC, Jiangxi (C)	16	2000–2014; yes	no	Land and real estate; infrastructure	5.16	13
Kuang Guanghua	PC, Jiangxi (C)	20	2005–2013; yes	no	Mining	6.97	17
Shan Zengde	Executive Vice Mayor, Shandong (PE)	6	2003–2012; yes	yes	Land and real estate; infrastructure	7.37	15
Liu Zhuozhi	VG, Inner Mongolia (P)	14	2002–2010; yes	yes	Mining; land	8.17	life
Zhou Yizhong	Mayor, Henan (PE)	13	2003–2011; yes	yes	Land and real estate	9.51	life
Huang Yao	DPC, Guizhou (P)	5	1993–2009	yes	Bank loans; mining; land and real estate	9.54	SD
Wang Huaizhong	VG, Anhui (P)	160	1994–2001; yes	yes	Land and real estate; infrastructure; SOE assets	9.97	death
Song Yong	PC, Liaoning (PE)	59	2000–2009; yes	yes	Mining; land	10.22	SD
Wang Suyi	Director of United Front, Inner Mongolia (P)	6	2005–2013; yes	yes	Real estate; minerals	10.73	SD
Mao Shaolie	Deputy Mayor, Guangxi (PE)	7	1996–2012; yes	yes	Land; infrastructure	11.38	17
Tan Dengyao	Mayor, Hainan (C)	37	2006–2009; yes	yes	Land; infrastructure	12.50	18
Wang Xianmin	PC, Gansu (C)	9	2006–2010; yes	yes	Infrastructure	14.02	SD
Ma Xiangdong	Executive Vice Mayor, Liaoning (PE)	35	1986–1999; yes	yes	Land and real estate; infrastructure	16.7	death
Wang Min	PC, Ji'nan, Shandong (P)	4	1992–2015; yes	yes	Land and real estate	20	SNA

(continued)

Chief perpetrator	Position; province[a]	Number of officials involved[b]	Duration of crime; promotion	Selling office	Main areas of corruption	Total corruption income (million yuan)[c]	Sentence[d]
Zhu Weiping	PC, Jiangsu (PE)	15	1998–2012; yes	yes	Infrastructure; SOE assets	20.54	15
Yang Yueguo	PC, Yunnan (C)	10	2003–2013; yes	yes	Land and real estate; infrastructure	21.2	life
Wang Huayuan	Secretary for Discipline, Zhejiang (P)	6	1998–2009; no	yes	SOE assets; infrastructure; protecting criminals	26.52	SD
Xie Mingzhong	PC, Hainan (PE)	3	1992–2007; yes	yes	Real estate; infrastructure	26.64	SD
Liu Jiakun	PC, Anhui (C)	4	2007–2012; yes	no	Real estate; infrastructure	29.29	life
Tian Yufei	PC, Sichuan (C)	18	1999–2004; yes	yes	SOE assets; infrastructure; bank loans	30.43	SD
Li Dalun	PC, Hunan (PE)	110	1999–2006; no	yes	Mining; land; real estate; bank loans; infrastructure	31.64	SD
Xu Zongheng	Mayor, Shenzhen, Guangdong (PE)	3	2001–2009; yes	yes	Land; infrastructure	33.18	SD
Feng Weilin	Director, Highway Bureau, Hunan (PE)	27	2000–2014; yes	yes	Infrastructure; SOE assets; contracts	34.05	life
Ye Shuyang	Police Chief, Guangdong (PE)	Over 100	2001–2008; yes	yes	Mining; infrastructure; protecting criminals	34.53	SD

Li Yunzhong	Organization Chief, Yunnan (PE)	10	2009–2004; yes	yes	Infrastructure	40.0	SNA
Hu Xing	Deputy Mayor, Yunnan (PE)	5	1995–2004; yes	yes	Real estate; infrastructure	40.30	life
Zeng Jinchun	Secretary for Discipline Inspection Hunan (PE)	11	1997–2006; yes	yes	Mining; infrastructure; extortion	40.71	death
Yang Guangliang	Executive Deputy Mayor, Guangdong (PE)	Over 100	1992–2009; yes	yes	Land and real estate; infrastructure	45.33	19
Zhou Zhenhong	Director of United Front, Guangdong (P)	23	2002–2011; yes	yes	Land and real estate; SOE assets	61.6	SD
Hong Jinzhou	Deputy Mayor, Guizhou (PE)	5	1997–2013; yes	no	Land and real estate; infrastructure	71.9	SNA
Mean		25	9.1			15.7	13
Median		11	8.0			9.5	13
Standard deviation		34	4.6			16.8	3.5

a. Position when the perpetrator is arrested. In cases when the chief perpetrator is promoted or transferred to a ceremonial position (such as the local political consultative conference), we use his prior executive position in which he committed his main corrupt acts. In most cases, perpetrators committed their corrupt acts when they served as the party chief or mayor at a lower level. PC = Party Secretary; DPC = Deputy Party Secretary; VG = Vice Governor. Membership on a provincial CCP standing committee qualifies as provincial-level status; SG = Secretary General (equivalent to chief of staff of the Mayor); DSG = Deputy Secretary General; DG = Deputy Governor; P = provincial-level rank; PE = prefecture-level; C = county-level.; SC = subcounty level.

b. In a few cases featuring involvement by a very large number of individuals, we suspect that press and official reports did not distinguish between officials and private businessmen.

c. Total corruption income includes embezzlement, bribery, and misappropriation of public funds.

d. Years; SD = suspended death sentence; SNA = sentence not announced. Only term sentences are calculated.

Table A.3. Key characteristics of fifty cases of collusive corruption in SOEs

Company name	Years (from initial commitment of crime to arrest) as lead culprit; duration of crime	Position of lead culprit	Total number of people involved	Total amount of money (million yuan)[a]	Amount attributed to lead culprit (yuan)[b]	Sentence (years)[c]
Fujian Long Steel Group (Fujian)	1994–2003	President	21	1.7	86,000	5.5
Xinwang Technology (Shanghai)	2005–2010	Chairman	3	0.72	86,000	5
Qinghai Energy Development Group (Qinghai)	2005–2013	President	17	127	90,000	dismissal
Unnamed SOE in Taizhou (Jiangsu)	2000–2008	Manager	6	7	150,000	4
Wenzhou Hongfeng Food and Oil Group (Zhejiang)	2007–2011	Chairman	4	8	200,000	13
Lan'a Coal (Gansu)	2007–2010	General Manager	16	6	250,000	6
China Ocean Shipping Group (COSCO)	2007–2011	Senior Vice President	7	unknown	308,000	10
Huazhong Electric Power Group (Hubei)	1998–2002	President	35	unknown	370,000	13
Pengshui Food Services (Chongqing)	1998–2009	General Manager	4	1.85	403,000	10
Nanjing Changta Coal Co. (Fujian)	1992–2001	General Manager	10	1	420,000	20
Lanzhou Wanxia Co. (Gansu)	1999–2008	General Manager	4	85	530,000	20
Sanming City Materials Group (Fujian)	1998–2010	General Manager	3	1.81	797,000	15
Yushui Electric Power (Jiangxi)	2007–2013	General Manager	3	unknown	820,000	6.6
Lanzhou Tansu Group (Gansu)	1999–2006	Chairman	31	Over 50	930,000	10
Pinghu City TV Station (Zhejiang)	2003–2011	Deputy Manager	4	3.5	1.3 million	16

Company	Period	Position			Amount	Sentence
Lanzhou Liancheng Aluminum Corp. (Gansu)	1992–1996	General Manager	11	270	1.4 million	death
Hengshan Iron Corp. (Zhejiang)	1994–2003	President	19	15	1.6 million	SNA
Zhongshan Huaqiao Real Estate Co. (Guangdong)	1999–2000	General Manager	5	6.15	2.15 million	life
Guangzhou Yangcheng Group (Guangdong)	1995–2000	Chairman	15	16	2.7 million	SD
Zhejiang Juhua (Zhejiang)	2002–2009	Chairman	18	10	3 million	15
Beijing Heavy Turbine (Beijing)	2004–2009	Director of Supplies	7	4	3.57 million	13
Shaanxi Yanchang Oil Corp. (Shaanxi)	2006–2012	Deputy Chief Engineer	4	6.6	5.3 million	15
Shandong Gold Corp. (Shandong)	1992–2002	Chairman	11	unknown	6.06 million	SD
Agricultural Development Bank of China	1996–2003	Vice President	7	25	6.35 million	life
Qilu PetroChemical Corp. (Sinopec)	1998–2002	Chairman	20	unknown	6.5 million	SNA
Nanping Mining Development Corp. (Fujian)	2004–2011	General Manager	4	9.05	7 million	9
Qingqi Group (Shandong)	1994–2006	Chairman	48	57.2	10.70 million	life
Shaanxi Electric Power Group (Shaanxi)	1998–2004	President	54	40	7.1 million	life
China Mobile	1994–2009	Party Secretary and Vice President	15	Over 200	7.5 million	SD
Chongqing Haikang Group (Chongqing)	2000–2005	Chairman	10	185	9.84 million	18
Gujing Group (Anhui)	1991–2007	Chairman	11	80	10 million	life

(continued)

Table A.3 (continued)

Company name	Years (from initial commitment of crime to arrest) as lead culprit; duration of crime	Position of lead culprit	Total number of people involved	Total amount of money (million yuan)[a]	Amount attributed to lead culprit (million yuan)[b]	Sentence (years)[c]
Capital Highway Development Corp. (Beijing)	1997–2004	Chairman	19	unknown	10.04	SD
Anhui Jungong Group (Anhui)	1999–2012	Chairman	9	unknown	11.66	19
Yili Dairy (Inner Mongolia)	Unknown to 2004	Chairman	5	31.5	16.5	6
Yunnan Copper Group (Yunnan)	2003–2007	Chairman	70	2,000	19	life
Yao Coal Group (Gansu)	2003–2009	Chairman	16	unknown	20.3	SD
Sinograin Corp. (Henan Branch)	2002–2012	President	81	700	23	life
China Postal Savings Bank	2002–2015	President	4	440	24.7	SNA
China National Petroleum Corp. (CNPC)	2004–2013	Chairman	45	unknown	28.8	SNA
Huishang Group (Anhui)	2001–2007	Chairman	34	88	34	SD
Gongxin Co. (Shanghai)	2004–2010	General Manager	6	46	42	life
Liuzhou Iron and Steel Group (Guangxi)	2006–2013	Chairman	7	118.83	62.36	SNA
Hebi Coal Group (Henan)	2003–2013	Chairman	12	unknown	76.2	life

	Tenure	Position				Penalty
Guangzhou Baiyun Co. (Guangdong)	1998–2013	President	19	384	100	death
Huangyan Real Estate Development Corp. (Zhejiang)	2001–2004	President	6	Over 500	Over 100	19
Wenzhou Cailanzi (Zhejiang)	2003–2010	Chairman	47	400	216	SD
Xinguang Int'l Group (Guangdong)	2006–2010	Chairman	27	unknown	247	life
Shanghai Electric Group (Shanghai)	2001–2006	Chairman	5	unknown	306	SD
Phoenix Corp. (Shanghai)	1994–2000	Chairman	14	5	unknown	unknown
China Resources	2009–2014	Chairman	8	unknown	unknown	SNA
Mean	7.4		17	156	29.9	12.5
Median	7.0		11	28	6.4	13
Standard deviation	3.4		17.5	345	63.7	5

a. The amount includes bribes, embezzlement, misappropriation, market value of illegally privatized SOE assets, and income derived from ill-gotten wealth.

b. Arranged in ascending order based on the amount stolen by the chief culprit.

c. Penalty: Years of imprisonment; SD = suspended death; SNA = sentence not announced. Only term sentences are calculated.

Table A.4. Key characteristics of fifty cases of collusion between law enforcement officials and organized crime (arranged according to the severity of the punishment for the chief protector, in descending order)

Name of crime boss (location)	Duration of crime	Major criminal activities[a]	Sentence[b]	Chief protector, rank, and corruption income[c] (million yuan)	Number of officials involved (no. of LEO)[d]	Sentence[b]
Tang Zonghu (Huaiyuan, Anhui)	1997–2001	P	life	Lu Xuefa, DPC (C); 0.04	8 (3)	3.5
Wang Yiqiang (Tuzhou, Anhui)	1997–2006	G	death	Wang Hongjun, DPC (C); n.a.	3 (3)	2
Xu Jie (Shunchang, Fujian)	1991–2001	G, LS, OB	death	Li Jian, SPLC (C); 0.67	8 (8)	life
Chen Kai (Fuzhou, Fujian)	1991–2003	G, P, RE, HT	death	Xu Congrong, PC (PE), n.a.	35 (8)	Fled abroad
Lin Qiuwen (Minhou, Fujian)	1996–2001	G, K, M, OB	death	Zhou Guozhen, County Magistrate; 2.0	12 (6)	15
Long Jiefeng (Sihui, Guangdong)	1999–2005	E, G, K, M	killed by rival gang	Chen Guoyang, DPC (C); n.a.	3 (3)	8.5
Li Zhengang (Maoming, Guangdong)	2001–2010	E, G, K, LS	20	Yang Qiang, PC (C); 14.19	5 (5)	life
Liao Fudong (Wuxuan, Guangxi)	1997–2010	A, G, OB, OM	20	Li Qilian, Party Chief (C); 1.08	5 (1)	11
Zhou Shounan (Baishe, Guangxi)	1995–1999	A, G, M, P	life	Li Hongzhuan, PC (PE); 0.15	22 (8)	13
Li Changyu (Beihai, Guangxi)	1993–1999	A, DT, E, G, M, R	death	He Jiatai; PC (C); 0.27	5 (5)	6
Cheng Xuede (Cenxi, Guangxi)	1992–2002	E, G, LS, OM	20	Su Zhuxian, Vice Mayor (C); n.a.	13 (5)	SNA
Gan Anyi (Wangmo, Guizhou)	2003–2008	G, OM, P	20	He Yaomin, PC (C); 0.03	3 (2)	5

Zhang Zhixin (Qiqihaer, Heilongjiang)	1993–2003	A, G, P, OB	death	Wang Rui, Police SDIC (PE); 0.9	11 (11)	SNA
Chen Jiaogui (Zhengzhou, Henan)	2012–2013	P	life	Zhou Tingxin, DPC (PE); 0.71	8 (8)	6
Yang Xinsheng (Linzhou, Henan)	1996–2005	A, M, OM	n.a.	Zai Yinchang, PC (C); n.a.	6 (3)	SNA
Yu Lin (Laohekou, Hubei)	1994–2006	A, E	death	Lei Xinyuan, DPC (C); n.a.	4 (2)	15
Jiang Qixin (Dongan, Hunan)	1993–2001	A, OB	20	Hu Dongchun, SPLC (C); 0.08	12 (2)	8
Tan Heping (Lianyuan, Hunan)	1995–2001	A, BF, E	life	Liao Hongri, Vice Police Pol. Commissar (C); n.a.	17 (4)	2
Tang Hong (Suining, Hunan)	1993–2000	E, P, R	life	Hou Wanhu, PC (C); n.a.	7 (6)	SNA
Yuan Xueming (Zixing, Hunan)	1997–2001	M, OM	n.a.	Xie Kongbin, Deputy SPLC (PE); n.a.	4 (2)	SNA
Ou Tao (Rucheng, Hunan)	1997–2002	G, OB	life	Huang Guoxiong, PC, (C); n.a.	4 (3)	SNA
Yao Zhihong (Shaoyang, Hunan)	1994–2002	E, G, LS, P	death	Li Yong, Deputy Chief Prosecutor (PE); n.a.	14 (12)	SNA
Ou Jian (Xiangtan, Hunan)	1989–2010	A, DT, G, LS, OB	20	Cai Yabin, DPC (PE); 8.44	4 (4)	12
Liu Junyong (Xinhua, Hunan)	1995–2005	G, M, OM	death	Wu Fuquan, DPC (C); n.a.	4 (4)	3
Xie Wensheng (Heyang, Hunan)	1997–2006	E, G, OM	20	Xiao Qiang, PC (C); 0.23	6 (4)	12
Shi Chuanhai (Huai'an, Jiangsu)	1992–2001	E, DT, P	20	Li Yang, DPC (C); 0.04	13 (n.a.)	3.5
Chen Shuguo (Pingxiang, Jiangxi)	1990–2001	A, DT, M, R	death	Zhou Xingeng, DPC (C); n.a.	5 (5)	8
Xiong Xinxin (Fuzhou, Jiangxi)	1996–2004	A, G, LF, RE	death	Xu Xiaogang, DPC (P); 5	6 (6)	life
Lan Linyan (Hengfeng, Jiangxi)	1998–2010	A, OM	20	Wu Xuance, Party Chief (C); 1.8	10 (1)	11

(continued)

Table A.4 (continued)

Name of crime boss (location)	Duration of crime	Major criminal activities[a]	Sentence[b]	Chief protector, rank, and corruption income[c] (million yuan)	Number of officials involved (no. of LEO)[d]	Sentence[b]
Zhu Family (Qianshan, Jiangxi)	1989–2001	A, G, M, OM	death (for one member)	Tu Fusheng, Party Chief (C); 0.14	23 (5)	3
Hao Weicheng (Changchun, Jilin)	1990–2010	E, K, OB, RE	20	Wang Zitong, DSPLC (P); 0.55	18 (6)	SNA
Tian Bo (Meihekou, Jilin)	1995–1999	OM	death	Zhang Deyi, Deputy Mayor (C); n.a.	14 (n.a.)	SNA
Wang Yufan (Tonghua, Jilin)	2002–2009	DT, E, OM	SD	Wang Yufang, DPC (PE); 18.1	6 (5)	SD
Wang Jun (Liaoyuan, Jilin)	1998–2009	LS, OB	death	Liu Changlin, PC (C); 0.25	5 (3)	13
Liu Yong (Shenyang, Liaoning)	1995–2000	A, RE	death	Liu Shi, Chief City Prosecutor (PE); 0.69	10 (n.a.)	20
Hao Wanchun (Shenyang, Liaoning)	2000–2006	A, LS, RE	SD	Zhang Jianming, DPC (PE); 0.66	3 (3)	SNA
Zhang Xiuwu (Lingyuan, Liaoning)	2001–2008	R, E, K, OM	SD	Zhang Lin, PC (C); 1.56	6 (5)	SNA
Song Pengfei (Shenyang, Liaoning)	1995–2006	DT, M, OB	death	Zhang Baohua, PC (C); n.a.	13 (13)	SNA
Dong Baojun (Jinzhou, Liaoning)	1995–2006	A, OM	20	Zhu Liang, DPC (PE); 0.18	6 (6)	6
Nie Lei (Qingdao, Shandong)	2000–2010	DT, G, P, RE	death	Wang Yanqiu, DPC (PE); 1.98	8 (8)	15
Li Erbao (Huangling, Shaanxi)	1992–2001	E, K, OM	death	Liu Faxue, PC (C); n.a.	4 (4)	3
Dong Tianyun (Weinan, Shaanxi)	1995–2001	A, OB	20	Ding Shuliang, PC (C); 0.03	8 (8)	7
Feng Yongqiang (Tongguan, Shaanxi)	1998–2007	A, M, OM	life	Tian Liping, DPC (C); n.a.	6 (6)	9

Guan Jianjun (Yangquan, Shanxi)	1990–2010	G, K, OM	15	Liang Huakui, DPC (PE); n.a.	3 (3)	SNA
Song Kuixiang (Gaoping, Shanxi)	1992–2001	A, E, K, OM	20	Zhang Xilai, Party Chief (C); 1.35	6 (3)	7
Li Manlin (Taiyuan, Shanxi)	1991–2001	A, G, K	death	Shao Jianwei, PC (PE); 4.8	4 (4)	9
Zeng Shaolin (Fushun, Sichuan)	1997–2001	A, E, G	20	Chen Xingliang, Head of Criminal Unit (C); n.a.	5 (3)	8
Zou Jiubao (Xishuangbanna, Yunnan)	2002–2006	A, G, S	18	Duan Kailin, DPC (PE); 0.12	4 (3)	5
Jia Jianjun (Yiwu, Zhejiang)	1993–2001	A, K, OB	death	Liu Zhiduo, PC (C); 0.45	5 (5)	life
Zhang Wei (Wenling, Zhejiang)	1995–2000	E, BF, M	death	Yang Weizhong, PC (PE); 0.26	66 (14)	14
Mean	8			2.15	10 (5)	8.5
Median	9			0.66	6 (5)	8.0
Standard Deviation	2.8			4.11	10 (3)	4.6

a. A = assault; BF = bank fraud; DT = drug trafficking; E = extortion; F = fraud; G = gambling; HT = human trafficking; K = kidnapping; LF = loan fraud; LS = loan sharking; M = murder; OB = other business; OM = own/operate coal, gold, and metal mines; P = prostitution; R = robbery; RE = real estate; S = smuggling.

b. Number of years; SD = suspended death; SNA = sentence not announced.

c. PC = Police Chief (Director of the Public Security Bureau in Chinese); PE = prefecture-level; PR = provincial-level; C = county-level (including district-level in urban areas); DSPLC = Deputy Secretary of Politics and Law Committee; SPLC = Secretary of Politics and Law Committee; SDIC = Secretary of the Discipline Inspection Committee; corruption income (million yuan) includes bribes, embezzlement, and misappropriated public funds.

d. LEO = Law enforcement officials, including the chief protector, involved; this category includes prosecutors, judges, and the CCP secretary of politics and law. The number is in parentheses.

Table A.5. Key characteristics of thirty cases of corruption involving multiple judges

Chief perpetrator, rank, location	Chief perpetrator's duration of corruption	Total number of judges implicated (including chief perpetrator)	Chief perpetrator's total corruption income (million yuan)	Chief perpetrator's sentence[a]
Liu Jiayi, president, Fuyang Intermediate Court, Anhui	1997–2004	12	0.90	13
Wang Jianmin, vice president, Fuyang Intermediate Court, Anhui	1993–2005	9	0.33	10
Gao Haiguang, chief of civil tribunal, Wuhu Intermediate Court, Anhui	2002–2008	6	0.18	10
Gong Dongsheng, vice president, Shunyi District Court, Beijing	2008–2010	5	n.a.	3
Guo Shenggui, president, Xicheng District Court, Beijing	1999–2007	3	7.97	SD
Chen Xueming, chief, civil tribunal, Shanghai High Court	n.a.–2013	4	(Patronizing prostitutes together)	Expulsion from the party
Zhang Tao, vice president, Chongqing High Court	1999–2009	14	9.02	SD
Judge Lin, Taijiang District Court, Fujian	2007–2012	4	0.19	3
Yan De, president, Maogang District Court, Guangdong	2001–2009	3	20.46	SD
Yang Xiancai, chief of enforcement, Guangdong High Court, Guangdong	1996–2008	14	11.8	life
Zeng Youhuan, vice president, Foshan Intermediate Court, Guangdong	2004–2007	3	0.37	SNA
Liu Kuan, deputy chief of enforcement, Zhanjiang Intermediate Court, Guangdong	2003–2007	9	0.86	SNA
Pei Hongquan, vice president, Shenzhen Intermediate Court, Shenzhen, Guangdong	1994–2006	5	11.42	life
Huang Aiquan, president, Pingnan County Court, Guangxi	1998–2005	8	0.09	6
Cheng Guiqing, president, Qiaoxi District Court, Hebei	1994–1997	9	0.01	3
Zhang Guoqing, president, Yichuan County Court, Henan	2008–2010	7	0.53	10

Li Xiaoyu, deputy chief, civil tribunal, Zhengzhou Intermediate Court, Henan	2005–2011	5	0.20	10
Li Xula, deputy chief of enforcement, Wuhan Intermediate Court, Hubei	2005–2009	6	0.18	10
Ke Changxin, executive vice president, Wuhan Intermediate Court, Hubei	1994–2003	13	0.77	13
Li Jingxue, vice president, Shiyan Intermediate Court, Hubei	2000–2002	3	n.a.	n.a.
Wu Zhenhan, president, Hunan High Court, Hunan	1998–2003	10	6.07	SD
Song Xiang, chief of criminal tribunal, Jilin High Court, Jilin	2003–2007	4	n.a.	SNA
Su Yingxu, deputy chief of civil tribunal, Jilin High Court, Jilin	n.a.–2007	8	over 0.20[c]	SNA
Zhang Yongyi, vice president, Qingyuan County Court, Liaoning	2009–2014	10	n.a.	SNA
Liu Shi, president, Shenyang Intermediate Court, Liaoning	1993–2000	5	0.76	20
Li Feng, chief of enforcement, Yinchuan Intermediate Court, Ningxia	2007	3	0.35	11
Wei Lanfeng, president, Shizuishan Intermediate Court, Ningxia	2001–2006	12	n.a.	Expulsion from the party[b]
Liu Qingfeng, vice president, Qingdao Intermediate Court, Shandong	2000–2009	4	3.64	14
Sun Weimin, deputy chief of the civil tribunal, Tianjin High Court	2006–2007	4	0.91	10
Yin Jianchu, judge, civil tribunal, Wenzhou Intermediate Court, Zhejiang	n.a.–2008	8	0.14	SNA
Mean	5.9	7	3.35	9.7
Median	5	6	0.76	10
Standard Deviation	3.3	3.5	5.34	4.6

a. Years; SD = suspended death sentence; SNA = sentence not announced.

b. Her coconspirators were sentenced to jail terms.

c. For all perpetrators.

Table A.6. Key characteristics of thirty cases of corruption involving multiple officials in regulatory enforcement agencies

Position of the chief perpetrator	Chief perpetrator's duration of corruption	Number of officials implicated (including chief perpetrator)	Chief perpetrator's corruption income (million yuan)	Chief perpetrator's sentence[b]
(1) Environmental Protection Bureau (EPB)				
Li Longbing, Director, Jiaocheng District EPB, Haozhou, Anhui	2010–2012	21	0.23	SNA
Li Weiyu, Director, Guangzhou EPB, Guangdong	n.a.–2004	11	0.68	7
Yuan Shaodong, Director, Dongguan City EPB, Guangdong	2007–2012	3	8.70	14
Ouyang Jie, Director, Guangning County EPB, Guangdong	n.a.–2013	3	n.a.	SNA
Xie Xudong, Deputy Department Chief, Jiangmen City EPB, Guangdong	2006–2009	3	0.85	10
Zheng Zhigui, Director, Shijiazhuang EPB, Hebei	1998–2001	5	0.11	SNA
Yuan Nianshou, Director, Liuyang City EPB, Hunan	1995–2003	11	0.32	10
Wen Bada, Director, Chenzhou City EPB, Hunan	2000–2001	5	0.37[a]	10
Lu Boxin, Director, Nantong City EPB, Jiangsu	2008–2012	30	1.33	12
Ma Yuankun, Deputy Director, Feng County EPB, Jiangsu	2007–2010	6	0.03	3
Gao Rensheng, Deputy Director, Jiexiu City EPB, Shanxi	1993–2012	3	3.18	8
Xu Hongjun, Director, Cixi City EPB, Zhejiang	2002–2008	7	0.61	11
Pan Jun, Director, Institute of Environmental Science, part of the EPB in Hangzhou, Zhejiang	2002–2007	over 90	0.58	15
Ye Liangang, Director, Wenzhou City EPB, Zhejiang	2005–2008	20	0.27	10.5
Wang Anjian, Director, Huzhou City EPB, Zhejiang	1999–2005	12	0.17	7
Zhu Xiaofang, Director, Haiyan County EPB, Zhejiang	2004–2014	6	0.40	SNA
(2) Work Safety Bureau (WSB) and Coal Mine Safety Bureau (CMSB)				
Wu Shutian, Director, Bengbu City WSB, Anhui	2002–2012	3	1.43	18

Wang Xiping, Deputy Director, Chongqing CMSB, Chongqing	2000–2009	7	8.9	life
Director, Liangping County WSB, Chongqing	2005–2009	3	0.07	3
Director, Dongguan WSB, Guangdong	n.a.–2012	3	0.40	13
Xie Guangxiang, Director, Hunan WSB, Hunan	1996–2008	3	2.0	14
Wang Guojun, Deputy Director, Jilin CMSB, Jilin	1997–2007	3	2.34	14
Ao Jianrong, Director, Xinghualing District WSB, Taiyuan, Shanxi	2002–2006	9	0.40	7
Chen Caixing, Director, Wenzhou WSB, Zhejiang	2005–2008	23	0.10	5
Lu Zhuping, Deputy Director, Haining City WSB, Zhejiang	2010–2013	6	0.13	6.75
(3) Food and Drug Administration (FDA)				
Yang Weidong, Director, Guangzhou FDA, Guangdong	1998–2003	4	0.44	6.5
Wu Fu, Director, Wuzhou FDA, Guangxi	2008–2013	7	0.08	5.5
Liu Guisheng, Deputy Director, Hunan FDA, Hunan	2005–2011	5	0.82	SNA
Zheng Xiaoyu, Director, State FDA	1998–2005	9	6.49	death
Wei Liang, Section Chief, State FDA	2006–2010	6	1.47	SNA
Mean	6.3	8	1.52	9.6
Median	5.0	6	0.51	10
Standard deviation	4.0	7	2.40	4

a. The amount was for all five officials involved in this case.

b. SNA = sentence not announced.

Abbreviations

Newspapers

BN	新京报	(Beijing News)
BYD	北京青年报	(Beijing Youth Daily)
CDID	中国纪检监察报	(China Discipline Inspection Daily)
CEH	21 世纪经济报道	(21st Century Economic Herald)
CYD	中国青年报	(China Youth Daily)
JT	京华时报	(Beijing Times)
LD	法制日报	(Legal Daily)
OMN	东方早报	(Oriental Morning News)
PD	检察日报	(Prosecutorial Daily)
PSD	人民日报	(People's Daily)
SD	南方日报	(Southern Daily)
SW	南方周末	(Southern Weekend)

Magazines

ACH	反腐败导刊	(Anticorruption Herald)
CGO	廉政瞭望	(Clean Government Outlook)
CI	中国监察	(China Inspection)
CNW	中国新闻周刊	(China Newsweek)
DAL	民主与法制	(Democracy and Legal System)
ERR	经济研究参考	(Economic Research Reference)
OL	瞭望	(Outlook)

OO   *瞭望东方* (Oriental Outlook)

PV   *检察风云* (Prosecutorial View)

RIR   *改革内参* (Reform Internal Reference)

News Websites

CJN   *财经网* (Caijing Net)

CNN   *中国新闻网* (China News Net)

CXN   *财新网* (Caixin Net)

JN   *正义网* (Justice Net)

PN   *人民网* (People Net)

XHN   *新华网* (Xinhua Net)

Notes

Introduction

Epigraph: 习近平关于党风廉政建设和反腐败斗争论述摘编 [Selected speeches by Xi Jinping on building party norms and integrity and on fighting corruption] (Beijing: 中央文献出版社, 2015): 24. All translations from the Chinese are mine.

1. Xi targeted Zhou mainly because of his close association with Bo Xilai, Xi's political rival who was purged in 2012 and sentenced to life in 2013.

2. These officials were all arrested shortly after Zhou retired from the PSC. "周永康系列落马官员" [Fallen officials in Zhou Yongkang's network], *CXN*, http://china.caixin.com/2014-12-07/100760100.html; in July 2015, the party chief of Hebei, Zhou's one-time chief of staff, was arrested.

3. "周永康的红与黑" [Zhou Yongkang's red and black], *CXN*, July 2014, http://chinadigitaltimes.net/chinese/2014/07/ 财新网-周永康的红与黑/.

4. Because the arrest of Zhou was not yet announced, the news story referred to him obliquely. "刘汉兄弟涉黑敛财轨迹" [The Liu brothers' record of organized crime and wealth accumulation], *BN*, February 21, 2014.

5. "周永康一审被判处无期徒刑" [Zhou Yongkang sentenced to life], *XHN*, June 11, 2015, http://news.xinhuanet.com/legal/2015-06/11/c_1115590 304.htm; "周永康的红与黑" [Zhou Yongkang's red and black].

6. "令氏兄弟" [The Ling brothers], *Caixin* (December 26, 2014).

7. "楼忠福广夏往事" [Lou Zhongfu's past at Guangxia Corp.], 时代在线, January 6, 2015, http://www.time-weekly.com/html/20150106/27939_1.html; "楼忠福政治献金被查" [Lou Zhongfu investigated for making political

donations], 无界新闻, July 14, 2015, http://finance.sina.com.cn/chanjing/sdbd /20150714/203822684481.shtml.

8. "起底铁路大亨王春成" [Exposing railway tycoon Wang Chuncheng], 中国经营报, August 12, 2014; "王春成沉浮" [Wang Chuncheng's rise and fall], *Caijing* (July 28, 2014); "中共中央决定给予徐才厚开除党籍处分" [The CCP Central Committee decides to expel Xu Caihou from the party], *XHN*, June 30, 2014, http://news.xinhuanet.com/politics/2014-06/30/c_1111388235.htm; "国贼徐才厚查抄内幕" [Inside story of the search of the house of Xu Caihou, thief of the nation], 凤凰周刊, http://chinadigitaltimes.net/chinese/2014/11 /凤凰周刊｜国贼徐才厚查抄内幕/.

9. "The new age of crony capitalism," *The Economist* (March 15, 2014).

10. Karen Dawisha, *Putin's Kleptocracy: Who Owns Russia?* (New York: Simon and Schuster, 2014).

11. The official definition of *wo'an* is the discovery of three or more cases of corruption in one government institution or agency within a relatively short period of time. *Chuan'an* refers to the discovery of three or more cases of corruption originating from a single lead. Based on the information provided by the Shanghai procuratorate, *wo'an* and *chuan'an* are classified and counted separately. When multiple cases of corruption occur in a "unit," this occurrence is classified as a group (*zhu*), but implicated individuals are prosecuted separately (*jian*); the same method of classification and accounting applies to *chuan'an* as well. In 2000, there were nine groups of *chuan'an* consisting of thirty-four cases and twenty groups of *wo'an* consisting of eighty-eight cases (averaging four individuals per group). This is evidence that individuals involved in collusive corruption are prosecuted separately, so the data for *wo'an* and *chuan'an* are not reflected in the aggregate annual data on prosecution published by the Chinese procuratorate. This classification of *wo'an* and *chuan'an* is confirmed in a separate report by the Shenzhen procuratorate in 2013. "上海贪污受贿串窝案近八成在国企" [Nearly 80 percent of collusive embezzlement and bribery cases in Shanghai occur in SOEs], 解放日报, October 20, 2000; "深圳检察院: 窝案串案占70%以上" [The Shenzhen procuratorate reports *wo'an* and *chuan'an* account for more than 70 percent of all corruption cases], 第一财经日报, January 23, 2013.

In today's sea of information *The Economist*'s insightful, independent coverage of world events is more valuable than ever. Why not consider giving a gift subscription to *The Economist*?

Enjoy preferential rates on our gift subscriptions, plus your own free gift: an Economist black notebook.

▶ Give a gift online:
<u>economist.com/gifting19</u> and enter code 1OLIW

◯ Give a gift by phone:
Call toll free 1-800-456-6086 and quote code 1OLIW

(Mon to Fri 8.30am–8pm, Sat 10am–7pm)

12. For a survey of corruption in China, see Yan Sun, *Corruption and Market in Contemporary China* (Ithaca: Cornell University Press, 2004).

13. A representative collection of corruption cases is 当前经济领域违法违纪典型案例评析 [Analysis of representative contemporary cases of illegal activities in the economy] (Beijing: 中国工商联合出版社, 1996). 中国法律年鉴 also contains a small collection of major corruption cases in its annual issue. A possible exception was the sensational corruption ring headed by a low-level official, Wang Shouxing, in Heilongjiang in the early 1980s. The investigative journalist Liu Binyan exposed the ring in his long article, "人妖之间" [Between man and monster]. In comparison with the corruption networks uncovered since the 1990s, the Wang case was relatively minor in both scope and the size of the theft.

14. There was no reference to *wo'an* (窝案) prior to 1992; all four pre-1992 references to *chuan'an* (串案) were made in the context of criminal acts unrelated to official corruption; the database is available at www.cnki.net.

15. Two researchers have studied collusive corruption in China. See Ting Gong, "Dangerous collusion: Corruption as a collective venture in contemporary China," *Communist and Post-Communist Studies* 35 (2002): 85–103; Shawn Shieh, "The rise of collective corruption in China: The Xiamen smuggling case," *Journal of Contemporary China* 14 (2005): 67–91.

16. "我在中纪委 24 年" [My twenty-four years in the CCDI], 新民周刊 (March 9, 2003).

17. See He Qinglian's ground-breaking study on local mafia states, 何清涟, 中国政府行为的黑社会化 [Mafia-style behavior of the Chinese government], http://heqinglian.net/3782-2/.

18. Bruce Dickson, *Red Capitalists in China: The Party, Private Entrepreneurs, and Prospects for Political Change* (Cambridge, UK: Cambridge University Press, 2003).

19. Sun, *Corruption and Market in Contemporary China*; Andrew Wedeman, *Double Paradox: Rapid Growth and Rising Corruption in China* (Ithaca, NY: Cornell University Press, 2012); Tak-Wing Ngo and Yongping Wu, eds., *Rent-Seeking in China* (London: Routledge, 2009); Melanie Manion, *Corruption by Design: Building Clean Government in Mainland China and*

Hong Kong (Cambridge, MA: Harvard University Press, 2009); Yongshun Cai, *State and Agents in China: Disciplining Government Officials* (Stanford, CA: Stanford University Press, 2015).

20. Shawn Shieh, "The rise of collective corruption in China"; Jiangnan Zhu, "Why are offices for sale in China?" *Asian Survey* 48 (2008): 558–579; Ko-lin Chin and Roy Godson, "Organized crime and the political-criminal nexus in China," *Trends in Organized Crime* 9 (2006): 5–44.

21. Ting Gong, "Dangerous collusion"; Minxin Pei also briefly discusses collusive corruption in *China's Trapped Transition: The Limits of Developmental Autocracy* (Cambridge, MA: Harvard University Press, 2006): 159–166.

22. "Planet plutocrat," *Economist* (March 15, 2014).

23. Thane Gustafson, *Capitalism Russian-Style* (Cambridge, UK: Cambridge University Press, 1999); Louise Shelley, "Crime and corruption," in Stephen White, Alex Pravda, and Zvi Gitelman, eds., *Developments in Russian Politics* (Durham, NC: Duke University Press, 2001): 239–253; Rasma Karklins, "Typology of post-communist corruption," *Problems of Post-Communism* 49 (2002): 22–32; Federico Varese, "The transition to the market and corruption in post-socialist Russia," *Political Studies* 45 (1997): 579–596.

24. Lawrence King, "Postcommunist divergence: A comparative analysis of the transition to capitalism in Poland and Russia," *Studies in Comparative International Development* 37 (2002): 3–34; Roman Frydman, Andrzej Rapaczynski, and Joel Turkewitz, "Transition to a private property regime in the Czech Republic and Hungary," in Wing Thye Woo, Stephen Parker, and Jeffrey D. Sachs, eds., *Economies in Transition: Comparing Asia and Europe* (Cambridge, MA: MIT Press, 1997): 41–102; David Lane, "What kind of capitalism for Russia? A comparative analysis," *Communist and Post-Communist Studies* 33 (2000): 485–504.

25. Sergei Guriev and Andrei Rachinsky, "The role of oligarchs in Russian capitalism," *Journal of Economic Perspectives* 19 (2005): 131–150; Michael McFaul, "State power, institutional change, and the politics of privatization in Russia," *World Politics* 47 (1995): 210–243; Joseph Blasi et al., *Kremlin Capitalism: The Privatization of the Russian Economy* (Ithaca, NY: Cornell University Press, 1997); Andrew Barnes, *Owning Russia: The Struggle over Factories, Farms, and Power* (Ithaca, NY: Cornell University Press, 2006).

26. Andrei Shleifer and Robert Vishny, "Corruption," *Quarterly Journal of Economics* 108 (August 1993): 599–617.

27. J. S. Hellman, G. Jones, and D. Kaufmann, "Seize the state, seize the day: State capture and influence in transition economies," *Journal of Comparative Economics* 31 (2003): 751–773.

28. Kathryn Stoner-Weiss, "Central weakness and provincial autonomy: Observations on the devolution process in Russia," *Post-Soviet Affairs* 15 (1999): 87–106.

29. Odd-Helge Fjeldstad, "Decentralization and corruption: A review of the literature" (University of Bergen, mimeo, 2003); Paul Seabright, "Accountability and decentralisation in government: An incomplete contracts model," *European Economic Review* 40 (1996): 61–75. He argues decentralization will control corruption, assuming strong monitoring by civil society and an independent judiciary. Prateek Goorha makes the same argument in "Corruption: Theory and evidence through economies in transition," *International Journal of Social Economies* 27 (2000): 1180–1204.

30. Ichiro Iwasaki and Taku Suzuki, "Transition strategy, corporate exploitation, and state capture: An empirical analysis of the former Soviet states," *Communist and Post-Communist Studies* 40 (2007): 393–422.

31. Andras Sajo, "From corruption to extortion: Conceptualization of post-communist corruption," *Crime, Law & Social Change* 40 (2003): 171–194.

32. Tanya Frisby, "The rise of organised crime in Russia: Its roots and social significance," *Europe-Asia Studies* 50 (1998): 27–49.

33. Steven Solnick, *Stealing the State: Control and Collapse in Soviet Institutions* (Cambridge, MA: Harvard University Press, 1998); Gustafson, *Capitalism Russian-Style.*

34. Kathleen Collins, "The logic of clan politics: Evidence from the Central Asian trajectories," *World Politics* 56 (January): 224–261.

35. Federico Varese, *The Russian Mafia: Private Protection in a New Market Economy* (Oxford: Oxford University Press, 2001); Vadim Volkov, *Violent Entrepreneurs: The Use of Force in the Making of Russian Capitalism* (Ithaca, NY: Cornell University Press, 2002); Leslie Holmes, "Corruption and organised crime in Putin's Russia," *Europe-Asia Studies* 60 (2008): 1011–1031;

Maria Los, "Crime in transition: The post-communist state, markets and crime," *Crime, Law & Social Change* 40 (2003): 145–169.

36. Stephen Haber, *Crony Capitalism and Economic Growth in Latin America: Theory and Evidence* (Stanford: Hoover Press, 2002).

37. Raymond Fisman, "Estimating the value of political connections," *American Economic Review* 91 (2001): 1095–1102.

38. Mara Faccio, "Politically connected firms," *American Economic Review* 96 (2006): 369–386.

39. Paul Hutchcroft, "Oligarchs and cronies in the Philippine state: The politics of patrimonial plunder," *World Politics* 43 (1991): 414–450.

40. Oliver Schlumberger, "Structural reform, economic order, and development: Patrimonial capitalism," *Review of International Political Economy* 15 (2008): 622–649; David C. Kang, *Crony Capitalism: Corruption and Development in South Korea and the Philippines* (New York: Cambridge University Press, 2002); Gulnaz Sharafutdinova, *Political Consequences of Crony Capitalism Inside Russia* (Notre Dame, IN: University of Notre Dame Press, 2010).

41. Marshall Goldman, *The Piratization of Russia: Russian Reform Goes Awry* (New York: Routledge, 2003).

42. Putin reversed this process in some key industries, chiefly energy and the media.

43. "中国 '国家账本' 出炉" [Unveiling the balance sheet of the Chinese state], *CJN*, http://economy.caijing.com.cn/20150727/3934030.shtml.

1. The Origins of Crony Capitalism

Epigraph: 习近平关于党风廉政建设和反腐败斗争论述摘编 [Selected speeches by Xi Jinping] (Beijing: 中央文献出版社, 2015): 112.

1. Peter Murrell and Mancur Olson, "The devolution of centrally planned economies," *Journal of Comparative Economics* 15 (1991): 239–265.

2. See Robert Masson and Joseph Shaanan, "Social costs of oligopoly and the value of competition," *Economic Journal* 94 (1984): 520–535.

3. George Stigler, "A theory of oligopoly," *Journal of Political Economy* 72 (1964): 44–61; Susan Rose-Ackerman, *Corruption and Government: Causes,*

Consequences, and Reform (New York: Cambridge University Press, 1999): 66; Margaret Levenstein and Valerie Y. Suslow, "What determines cartel success?" *Journal of Economic Literature* 44 (2006): 43–95.

4. Jean Tirole, "Hierarchies and bureaucracies: On the role of collusion in organizations," *Journal of Law, Economics, and Organization* 2 (1986): 181–214; Jean-Jacques Laffont and Jean-Charles Rochet, "Collusion in organizations," *Scandinavian Journal of Economics* 99 (1997): 485–495; Fred Kofman and Jacques Lawarree, "Collusion in hierarchical agency," *Econometrica: Journal of the Econometric Society* 61 (1993): 629–656.

5. Jean-Jacques Laffont, "Collusion and delegation," *RAND Journal of Economics* 29 (1998): 280–305; Nahum Melumad, Dilip Mookherjee, and Stefan Reichelstein, "Hierarchical decentralization of incentive contracts," *RAND Journal of Economics* 26 (1995): 654–672.

6. Xueguang Zhou, "The institutional logic of collusion among local governments in China," *Modern China* 36 (2010): 47–78.

7. Ting Gong, "Dangerous collusion: Corruption as a collective venture in contemporary China," *Communist and Post-Communist Studies* 35 (2002): 85–103.

8. Federico Varese, "Pervasive corruption," in A. Ledeneva and M. Kurkchiyan, eds., *Economic Crime in Russia* (London: Kluwer Law International, 2000): 99–111; Francis Lui, "A dynamic model of corruption deterrence," *Journal of Public Economics* 31 (1986): 215–236.

9. In a study of 526 corruption cases involving officials at or above the level of *chu* (division) and county between 1978 and 2004, the duration of corruption averaged 2.19 years during 1980–1988, 2.13 years during 1989–1992, 2.67 years during 1993–1997, and 5 years during 1998–2004. The amount of corruption income also rose significantly during the post-1992 period. Before 1990, not a single corruption case involved more than 1 million yuan. During the period of 1991–2000, bribes exceeded 1 million yuan in 31 percent of the cases; during 2001–2004, bribes exceeded 1 million yuan in 79 percent of the cases. Yong Guo, "Corruption in transitional China: An empirical analysis," *China Quarterly* 194 (2008): 349–364.

10. Andrei Shleifer and Robert Vishny, "Corruption," *Quarterly Journal of Economics* 108 (1993): 599–617.

11. Another suspect in the origins of crony capitalism is China's investment-driven development strategy, which created abundant opportunities for graft and theft. However, the profit potential in infrastructure projects and other types of fixed-asset investments, while large, is less than that from the acquisition of state-owned assets at steep discounts or at no cost. One piece of evidence is the dominance of real estate developers in the ranks of China's wealthy businessmen. While we do not exclude the role of the investment-driven growth strategy in the rise of crony capitalism, we believe that our theory of collusion can be applied to the story of how this strategy contributed to crony capitalism because the same factors—decentralized control, unclear ownership, and competition for spoils—also drive collusive corruption in the sector of fixed-asset investments.

12. See George Tsebelis, *Veto Players: How Political Institutions Work* (Princeton, NJ: Princeton University Press, 2002).

13. As we note later, local party chiefs can usually impose their will due to their near monopoly of personnel power within their jurisdictions.

14. Kenneth Lieberthal and David Lampton, eds., *Bureaucracy, Politics, and Decision Making in Post-Mao China* (Berkeley: University of California Press, 1992); Tony Saich, *Governance and Politics of China* (London: Palgrave Macmillan, 2010).

15. John Burns, "China's administrative reforms for a market economy," *Public Administration and Development* 13 (1993): 345–360.

16. The reform of the cadre management system was announced in 1984 and implemented shortly after, but the rules governing the new system, "政领导干部选拔任用工作暂行条例" [Interim rules on selecting and promoting party and government officials], were not promulgated by the CCP until February 1995. http://cpc.people.com.cn/GB/64162/71380/71387/71591/4855103.html.

17. 中央办公厅, "关于对违反党政领导干部选拔任用工作暂行条例行为的处理规定" [Rules on dealing with violations of the interim rules on selecting and promoting party and government officials], May 16, 1997, http://cpc.people.com.cn/GB/64162/71380/71382/71384/4857746.html.

18. Chinese scholars and journalists use *yibashou* (no. 1 official) to refer to party chiefs, local mayors, and heads of government agencies and SOEs.

In reality, despite his equal rank as the party chief, the mayor is politically subordinate to the party chief. Most heads of government agencies and SOEs are simultaneously party chiefs.

19. The same practice has been observed in Kyrgyzstan. Johan Engvall, "Why are public offices sold in Kyrgyzstan?" *Post-Soviet Affairs* 30 (2014): 67–85.

20. A 2015 survey of 3,671 individuals, including 395 county party chiefs, 511 prefecture-level officials, and 912 county-level officials, reports that 64 percent of the respondents agreed that the most important criterion used by a county party chief for selecting an official is his "political loyalty." 冯志峰, "县委书记的权力运行现状" [Status of the use of power by county party chiefs], *CXN*, March 3, 2015, http://opinion.caixin.com/2015-03-25/100794533.html.

21. Ben Hillman's study illuminates how factions in a county engage in competition for power and spoils. Hillman, "Factions and spoils: Examining political behavior within the local state in China," *China Journal* 64 (2010): 1–18.

22. 乔德福, "改革开放以来市'一把手' 腐败案例研究报告" [Research report on cases of corruption among top officials in cities since the reform and opening], *理论与改革* 5 (2013).

23. Vertical collusion can also occur in SOEs, especially large ones when their *yibashou* officials have total control over personnel matters and can coerce subordinates into compliance.

24. Diego Gambetta, ed., *Trust: Making and Breaking Cooperative Relations* (Cambridge: Blackwell, 1988); Roderick Kramerk, "Trust and distrust in organizations: Emerging perspectives, enduring questions," *Annual Review of Psychology* 50 (1999): 569–598.

25. Arthur Frass, and Douglas Greer, "Market structure and price collusion: An empirical analysis," *Journal of Industrial Economics* 26 (1977): 21–44; Levenstein and Suslow, "What determines cartel success?"

26. Levenstein and Suslow, "What determines cartel success?" 44.

27. Stigler, "A theory of oligopoly."

28. Clan ties are the basis of factions among county officials. Hillman, "Factions and spoils: Examining political behavior within the local state in China."

29. That is why, as part of Xi Jinping's anticorruption campaign, the Central Organization Department in 2013 issued a directive banning the formation of "small circles" in cadre training programs. "关于在干部教育培训中进一步加强学员管理的规定" [Rules on strengthening the supervision of trainees during cadre education], *PSD,* March 19, 2013. The idea that party schools help forge personal networks harmful to the party challenges the view that these schools have helped make party officials more professional and better educated. See David Shambaugh, "Training China's political elite: The party school system," *China Quarterly* 196 (2008): 827–844.

30. One such example occurred in Pingxiang in Jiangxi. "江西萍乡落马书记陈安众坦白罪行" [Fallen party chief of Pingxiang in Jiangxi confesses crimes], *中国经济周刊* (December 23, 2014). See Raub Werner and Gideon Keren, "Hostages as a commitment device: A game-theoretic model and an empirical test of some scenarios," *Journal of Economic Behavior & Organization* 21 (1993): 43–67.

31. In Sicily, one ritual of initiation required the novice to shoot at a picture of Christ to prove his commitment. See Diego Gambetta, *The Sicilian Mafia: The Business of Private Protection* (Cambridge, MA: Harvard University Press, 1993): 263; Paolo Campana and Federico Varese, "Cooperation in criminal organizations: Kinship and violence as credible commitments," *Rationality and Society* 25 (2013): 263–289; Klaus Von Lampe and Per Ole Johansen, "Organized crime and trust: On the conceptualization and empirical relevance of trust in the context of criminal networks," *Global Crime* 6 (2004): 159–184.

32. One study shows that of the 142 prefecture-level *yibashou* officials caught for corruption between 1983 and 2012, only one official (out of six) caught before 1989 was accused of "moral degeneration"—a code phrase for sexual promiscuity. But 11 of the 47 caught between 1990 and 2002, and 40 out of the 89 caught between 2003 and 2012, were accused of "moral degeneration." 乔德福, "改革开放以来市一把手腐败案例研究报告" [Research report on cases of corruption among top officials in cities since the reform and opening].

33. The deputy director of the research office of the discipline inspection committee (CDI), Liu Chunjin, revealed in a lecture that 90 percent of the officials caught for corruption maintained mistresses. "中纪委研究室原副主任: 九成落马贪官包养情人" [Former deputy director of research of the CCDI claims 90 percent of corrupt officials maintain mistresses], *环球时报*, No-

vember 12, 2008. "A Renmin University study of 367 *ting* or *ju*-level officials caught for corruption between 2000 and 2014 finds that 47 percent of them had mistresses. 人民大学国家发展与战略研究院, *中国创新报告 2014* [China innovation report 2014] (Beijing: Renmin University, 2014).

34. Intriguingly, except for one case, all corrupt officials included in the 260 sample cases delivered on their promises.

35. In this study, we have two such cases of bitter rivalry between the party chief and the mayor, Ma De and Wang Shenyi in Suihua City (Heilongjiang) and Wang Jun and Zhang Yushun in Lanzhou (Gansu). Ma knew of Wang's corruption but did not denounce him until after his own arrest; Zhang did the same to Wang. Another well-known case is the rivalry between Yang Weize and Ji Jianye, respectively Nanjing's party chief and mayor. They disliked each other intensely. After Ji's arrest in 2014, his father-in-law denounced Yang to the investigators and Yang was arrested. "市长不服市委书记" [Mayors defy party chiefs], *BN*, July 19, 2015.

36. Albert Wohlstetter, *The Delicate Balance of Terror* (Santa Monica: RAND Corporation, 1958).

37. The criminal code rewards those who provide leads on other criminals. "中华人民共和国刑法" [Criminal code of the PRC], http://www.npc.gov.cn/wxzl/wxzl/2000-12/17/content_4680.htm.

38. "深挖窝案串案三法" [Three approaches to digging up *wo'an* and *chuan'an*], 人民检察, July 8, 2004; "职务犯罪窝案串案深挖若干策略" [Several strategies for digging up *wo'an* and *chuan'an* committed by officials], *中国检察官* 7 (2009).

39. "江苏: 反贪大案率连年全国第一" [Jiangsu tops nation for years in prosecuting major corruption cases], *PD*, June 1, 2015.

2. The Soil of Crony Capitalism

Epigraph: *习近平关于党风廉政建设和反腐败斗争论述摘编* [Selected speeches by Xi Jinping] (Beijing: 中央文献出版社, 2015): 17.

1. For studies on property rights reform in the 1990s, see Gary Jefferson and Thomas Rawski, *How Industrial Reform Worked in China: The Role of Innovation, Competition, and Property Rights* (Washington, DC: World

Bank, 1994); Jean C. Oi and Andrew G. Walder, eds., *Property Rights and Economic Reform in China* (Stanford, CA: Stanford University Press, 1999).

2. 龚婷, 吴木銮, "我国 2000–2009 年腐败案例研究报告" [Research report on cases of corruption in China during 2000–2009], 社会学研究 4 (2012): 204–220.

3. 张元瑞, "我国房地产市场要放开" [Open up China's real estate market], *ERR* 73 (1992): 21.

4. 曹华, "在当前条件下发展我国房地产业的对策" [Policies addressing China's real estate sector under the current conditions], *ERR* 148 (1993): 24.

5. 中国土地年鉴 1994–1995 [China land yearbook 1994–1995] (Beijing: 中国大地出版社, 1996): 29.

6. Ibid.

7. 黄燕芬等, "走出土地财政难在哪里?" [Where lies the difficulty in moving away from land-based finance?], *RIR* 5 (2007): 13.

8. 满燕云, "土地财政求解" [Seeking solutions to land-based finance], 中国改革 (August 2010): 17–18; Ministry of Finance Report to the National People's Congress, 2011, http://www.mof.gov.cn/zhengwuxinxi/caizhengshuju /201207/t20120711_665583.html.

9. Data on local land revenue are from the Ministry of Finance reports to the National People's Congress on the implementation of the central and local budgets, 2009, 2010, and 2011.

10. In 1993, the central government's share of fiscal revenue was only 22 percent; in 1994, the year of implementation of the new fiscal system, its share rose to 55.7 percent. Between 1995 and 2009, the central government's share averaged 52.3 percent. Calculated from 中国统计年鉴 2010 [Statistical yearbook of China 2010] (Beijing: 中国统计出版社, 2010): 288.

11. 温铁军, "三十年来的三次圈地运动" [Three land enclosure movements in three decades], *RIR* 3 (2009): 5–7.

12. 景明, "万亿土地出让金" [A trillion yuan in land lease payments], 半月谈 10 (2008): 5.

13. 林炎, "土地财政的形成" [The emergence of land-based finance], 中国国土资源经济 2 (2010): 17.

14. Peter Ho, "Who owns China's land? Policies, property rights and deliberate institutional ambiguity," *China Quarterly* 166 (2001): 394–421.

15. 张琦, "关于中国土地市场化的思考" [Thoughts on the marketization of land in China], *ERR* 83 (2006): 33.

16. 满燕云, "土地财政求解" [Seeking solutions to land-based finance], 16.

17. Ministry of Finance reports to the National People's Congress on the implementation of the central and local budgets, 2009, 2010, and 2011.

18. 黄燕芬等, "走出土地财政难在哪里?" [Where lies the difficulty in moving away from land-based finance], 13.

19. 林双林, "赤字连年不止" [Deficits keep rising for years], *RIR* 30 (2010): 26.

20. 廖明, "三架马车拉动高房价" [Three forces drive up housing prices], *RIR* 17 (2010): 5.

21. These agencies are: the Office of Land Acquisition (征地办), Office of Removal (拆迁办), Office of Housing Reform (房改办), Bureau of Land Resources (国土资源局), Bureau of Housing Administration (房管局), Bureau of Zoning and Planning (规划局), Bureau of Construction (建设局), Committee of Land Administration (土地管理委员会), Committee of Construction (建设委员会), and Committee of Urban Redevelopment (城市改造委员会).

22. "城市土地之秘" [The secret of urban land], *Caijing* (January 20, 2003): 34.

23. Shen and Gunson claim that "China has more small-scale miners mining a larger diversity of ores than anywhere else in the world." Lei Shen and Aaron James Gunson, "The role of artisanal and small-scale mining in China's economy," *Journal of Cleaner Production* 14 (2006): 429.

24. Ibid., 431.

25. Shen and Gunson note that China's small mines have very small proven reserves they can legally mine. They estimate that, in 1995, the percentages of proven reserves available for such mines in China were 9.2 percent of coal, 3.3 percent of iron ore, 5 percent of nonferrous metals, and 10 percent of gold. Ibid.

26. 矿产资源资产化课题组, "当前我国矿产资源的基本形势" [Current status of China's mineral resources], *ERR* 38 (March 8, 1993): 31–35.

27. 王保喜, "云南省矿产资源资产化管理调研" [Research report on the management of Yunnan's mineral resources], *ERR* (January 11, 1993): 44–45.

28. Township and village coal mines emerged as a response to China's energy shortages. The Chinese government has encouraged them since the

1970s, even though it did not establish a legal or regulatory framework for such mines. Philip Andrews-Speed et al., "A framework for policy formulation for small-scale mines: The case of coal in China," *Natural Resources Forum* 26 (2002): 45–54.

29. 刘永平, "改革开放以来我国煤炭工业投资情况分析" [Analysis of investment in China's coal industry since the reform and opening], *煤炭经济研究* 30 (July 2010): 19.

30. Lei Shen and Philip Andrews-Speed, "Economic analysis of reform policies for small coal mines in China," *Resources Policy* 27 (2001): 250.

31. The State Council's rule explicitly bans the transfer of exploration rights for profit. 刘生辉, "对矿产资源管理进一步法制化规范化的思考" [Thoughts on the further legalization and normalization of the management of mineral resources], *中国自然资源经济* (August 2010): 15.

32. In 1995, a large share of township and village coal mines (TVCMs) were actually private coal mines; they accounted for 10 percent of the TVCMs in Shanxi, 16 percent in Hebei, 27 percent in Sichuan, 80 percent in Yunnan, 79 percent in Guizhou, and 80 percent in Jiangxi. Andrews-Speed et al., "A framework for policy formulation for small-scale mines," 46.

33. During a crackdown on illegal mining in Shanxi in 2005, the authorities shut down 4,876 mining locations. Nine hundred fifty-two government officials and SOE executives were found to have invested 156 million yuan in these coal mines. *RIR* 7 (2006): 48.

34. Feng Chen, "Privatization and its discontents in Chinese factories," *China Quarterly* 185 (March 2006): 42–60.

35. 周玉, "关于辽宁省国有企业股份制改革的调研报告" [Research report on the reform of shareholding in state-owned enterprises in Liaoning], *ERR* 126 (1993): 3; 姚树人, "关于股份有限公司试点的有关问题" [On several issues concerning pilot projects on limited stock companies], *ERR* 126 (1993): 13.

36. 中国企业家调查系统, "股份制: 改革中国企业体制的一条道路" [The shareholding system: A path to reforming China's corporate system], *ERR* 96 (1994): 7.

37. Jilin issued its own regulations on selling the assets of small and medium-sized SOEs and restructuring their management in March 1995; Hunan announced rules on restructuring small SOEs in July 1997.

38. Yuanzheng Cao, Yingyi Qian, and Barry R. Weingast argue that hard budget constraints forced local governments to privatize. See Cao et al., "From federalism, Chinese style to privatization, Chinese style," *Economics of Transition* 7 (1999): 103–131.

39. W. K. Lau, "The 15th Congress of the Chinese Communist Party: Milestone in China's privatization," *Capital and Class* 22 (1999): 51–87. 秦晖, "有疑问的国资退出" [A questionable exit of state capital], *RIR* 28 (2004): 3.

40. 秦晖, "有疑问的国资退出" [Questionable exit of state capital], 3.

41. Nicholas Lardy, *Markets over Mao: The Rise of Private Business in China* (Washington, DC: The Peterson Institute for International Economics, 2014).

42. For descriptions and analyses of these changes, see Melanie Manion, "The cadre management system, post-Mao: The appointment, promotion, transfer and removal of party and state leaders," *China Quarterly* 102 (1985): 203–233; Xueguang Zhou, "Partial reform and the Chinese bureaucracy in the post-Mao era," *Comparative Political Studies* 28 (1995): 440–468; John P. Burns, "Strengthening central CCP control of leadership selection: The 1990s *nomenklatura*," *China Quarterly* 138 (1994): 458–491.

43. The rules are spelled out in "党政领导干部选拔任用工作条例" [Rules on selecting and promoting party and government officials]. The document has been updated since it first came out in 1995. The 2014 version was printed in 人民日报, January 16, 2014.

44. For an excellent account of decentralization, see Dwight Perkins, "Reforming China's economic system," *Journal of Economic Literature* 26 (1988): 601–645.

45. For a descriptive account of the decentralization of management authority in SOEs, see Justin Yifu Lin, ed., *State-Owned Enterprise Reform in China* (Hong Kong: Chinese University Press, 2002).

46. In a 2015 survey of 3,671 individuals (including 395 county party chiefs, 511 prefecture-level cadres, and 912 county-level cadres), 62 percent agreed that a county party chief has enormous power in personnel and budgetary matters. For the appointment and promotion of officials, 53.2 percent report that only the decision of the county party chief counts. 冯志峰, "县委书记的权力运行现状" [Status of the exercise of power by county party chiefs], *CXN*, http://opinion.caixin.com/2015-03-25/100794533.html. *Yibashou* officials account

for a disproportionate share of the disgraced officials. One study conducted by Renmin University shows that, of the 367 prefecture- or *ting*-level officials arrested between 2000 and March 2014, 219 of them (60 percent) were *yibashou* officials; of the 440 individuals whose cases were published on the website of the Central Commission for Discipline Inspection (CCDI) as of August 2014, 166 (38 percent) were *yibashou* officials at or above the county level. "今年落马官员三成是一把手" [Thirty percent of fallen officials this year were top officials], *CNN,* http://www.chinanews.com/gn/2014/08-19/6505124.shtml. Of the 115 senior SOE executives arrested for corruption between 2014 and May 2015, 65 were *yibashou* officials. "1 年半内至少 115 名国企高管落马" [At least 115 senior executives in state-owned enterprises have fallen during the last year and a half], *JD,* May 17, 2015.

47. Yasheng Huang, "Managing Chinese bureaucrats: An institutional economics perspective," *Political Studies* 50 (2002): 61–79.

48. Pierre Landry details how the CCP tried to solve this dilemma in *Decentralized Authoritarianism in China* (New York: Cambridge University Press, 2008).

49. For the evolution of corruption in the early years of reform, see Yan Sun, *Corruption and Market in Contemporary China* (Ithaca, NY: Cornell University Press, 2004).

50. One indication that the new system became mature and fully functional in the mid-1990s is the first set of interim regulations on cadre appointment and promotion, "党政领导干部选拔任用工作暂行条例" [Interim rules on selecting and promoting party and government officials], which were not promulgated by the CCP until February 1995, http://cpc.people.com.cn/GB/64162/71380/71387/71591/4855103.html.

51. Since 2003 the CCDI and the Central Organization Department have also sent ad hoc inspection teams to conduct inspection tours of provinces and ministerial-level SOEs. But these tours are focused on provincial-level leaders and are infrequent.

52. Melanie Manion, *Corruption by Design: Building Clean Government in Mainland China and Hong Kong* (Cambridge, MA: Harvard University Press, 2009): 119–154; Yongshun Cai, *State and Agents in China: Disciplining Government Officials* (Stanford, CA: Stanford University Press, 2015): 49–70;

Ting Gong, "The party discipline inspection in China: Its evolving trajectory and embedded dilemmas," *Crime, Law and Social Change* 49 (2008): 139–152.

53. 福建省情资料库, http://www.fjsq.gov.cn/ShowText.asp?ToBook=207 &index=272&; "纪委办案人," *CGO*, November 1, 2014; "中纪委增加百余名 办案人员" [The CCDI adds more than one hundred case officers], *OMN*, March 20, 2014.

54. "一把手腐败是最大难题" [The most difficult issue is corruption by top officials], *SW*, November 14, 2013.

55. 习近平关于党风廉政建设和反腐败斗争论述摘编 [Selected speeches by Xi Jinping]: 59.

56. "查办腐败案件体制机制改革" [Reforming the system of investigating corruption cases], *XHN*, August 29, 2014, http://news.xinhuanet.com/politics /2014-08/29/c_1112285898.htm.

3. Public Offices for Sale

Epigraph: *习近平关于党风廉政建设和反腐败斗争论述摘编* [Selected speeches by Xi Jinping] (Beijing: 中央文献出版社, 2015): 102.

1. 乔德福, "改革开放以来市, '一把手' 腐败案例研究报告" [Research report on cases of corruption among top officials in cities since the reform and opening], *理论与改革* 5 (2013): 68.

2. 龚婷, 吴木銮, "我国 2000–2009 年腐败案例研究报告" [Research report on cases of corruption in China during 2000–2009], *社会学研究* 4 (2012): 215.

3. Only one study has examined a particularly egregious case of *maiguan maiguan*. See Jiangnan Zhu, "Why are offices for sale in China? A case study of the office-selling chain in Heilongjiang province," *Asian Survey* 48 (2008): 558–579; Yongshun Cai briefly notes the prevalence of this practice. See Cai, *State and Agents in China* (Stanford: Stanford University Press, 2015): 44–47.

4. The hard data collected in Table A.1 come from official media reports, published indictments, and court sentencing documents. Whenever available, we treat sentencing documents as the most authoritative accounts of acts of corruption committed by disgraced officials.

5. See the discussion of this change in Chapter 2.

6. For example, Guo Boxiong and Xu Caihou, both vice chairmen of the Central Military Affairs Commission and Politburo members, allegedly engaged in the taking of large bribes from military officers in exchange for promotions.

7. Most provincial officials engaged in *maiguan* while they were prefecture party secretaries, but we do not count them as prefecture party secretaries here.

8. For a survey of the power enjoyed by county party chiefs, see 冯志峰, "县委书记的权力运行现状" [Status of the exercise of power by county party chiefs], *CXN*, http://opinion.caixin.com/2015-03-25/100794533.html.

9. The small differences in the number of positions sold between provincial and prefecture officials are largely due to the fact that provincial officials included in this sample, except for Han Guizhi, sold offices while they were prefecture party chiefs.

10. Ministry (*bu*) and province (*sheng*) levels are above bureau (*ju* or *ting*) and prefecture (*di*) levels, which are above county (*xian*), district (*qu*), and department (*chu*) levels. Subcounty positions are section-level (*ke*).

11. Tian Zhong was a deputy party chief in charge of personnel matters.

12. One transaction worth 380,000 yuan involving Zhang Gaiping is excluded because it is an obvious outlier.

13. One plausible alternative explanation for the greater price differentials in the positions sold by prefecture party chiefs is the greater heterogeneity in the desirable positions available for purchase in a prefecture, which often have large economic disparities among its counties.

14. The duration in this sample is longer than that found in Yong Guo, "Corruption in transitional China: An empirical analysis," *China Quarterly* 194 (2008): 349–364; another study of more than 3,000 corrupt officials and government employees in the mid-2000s reports that the duration of crime exceeded five years for 26 percent of the perpetrators. "当前职务犯罪呈十大特点" [Contemporary committing of crimes using public office shows ten major characteristics], *PD*, March 27, 2007.

15. Even during 2014, the height of Xi Jinping's anticorruption drive, only 5.2 percent of the 232,000 party members disciplined by the CCP were criminally prosecuted. "十八届中央纪委第五次全会工作报告" [Work report to

the fifth plenum of the eighteenth CCDI], *XHN,* January 29, 2015, http://news.xinhuanet.com/politics/2015-01/29/c_1114183996.htm. Manion finds that, during 1987–1996, officials were eight times less likely to be prosecuted for property crimes than ordinary people. Melanie Manion, *Corruption by Design: Building Clean Government in Mainland China and Hong Kong* (Cambridge, MA: Harvard University Press, 2009): 151.

16. Courts also weigh other factors in deciding penalties. In addition to the amount of corruption income, they consider whether a perpetrator confessed his crime, provided useful tips to prosecutors, showed contrition for his crime, and returned the stolen money to the state.

17. Cai, *State and Agents in China,* 75.

18. A typical example is Hu Jianxue. He was given a suspended death sentence in 1996 but later had it reduced five times, to fifteen years and six months. In 2006, he received medical parole. But he was sent back to jail in 2014 during a crackdown on leniency toward convicted corrupt officials. "76 名原厅官监外执行被建议收监" [Seventy-six former bureau-level officials serving sentences outside of prisons are recommended to be returned to jail], *PN,* http://politics.people.com.cn/n/2014/0826/c1001-25539880.html.

19. "立功减刑 谁打开纵恶之门" [Earning merit to reduce sentences: Who opens the door to condoning evil], *CDID,* February 28, 2014; 汪华, "职务犯罪为何减免刑过半," *南风窗* 4 (2006): 20.

20. "贫困县富书记的生财之道" [The path to wealth for a rich party chief in an impoverished county], *西安日报,* March 3, 2004.

21. "原抚顺书记受贿内幕" [The inside story of the bribery of the former party chief of Fushun], *CNN,* January 4, 2005, http://www.chinanews.com.cn/gn/news/2007/01-04/848479.shtml#.

22. "绥化马德卖官案侦查终结 透视绥化畸 官场生态" [End of the investigation into Ma De's selling of public offices in Suihua], *CYD,* August 25, 2004.

23. 北京市高级人民法院刑事裁定书, "马德受贿案" [Ma De's bribery case] (2005): 高刑复字第 564 号.

24. "安徽省第一巨贪县令陈兆丰 110 顶官帽卖出 150 万" [Anhui's most corrupt county party chief, Chen Zhaofeng, sold 110 official positions for 1.5 million yuan], *XHN,* October 16, 2006, news.xinhuanet.com/legal/2006-10/16/content_5206943.htm.

25. "张治安、汪成受贿、报复陷害案" [Case of bribery, retaliation, and framing by Zhang Zhi'an and Wang Cheng], *中华人民共和国最高人民检察院公报* 5 (2010).

26. 江西赣州中级人民法院刑事判决书, "李国蔚受贿巨额财产来源不明案" [Li Guowei's case of bribery and his large amount of unexplained wealth], (2005): 赣中刑初字第 4 号.

27. "陈少勇受贿案" [Chen Shaoyong's bribery case], *中华人民共和国最高人民检察院公报* 2 (2010).

28. "原广西钦州市委书记俞芳林受贿案侦破纪实" [The true story of the investigation into the bribery of case of Yu Fanglin, former party chief of Qinzhou in Guangxi], *PD*, December 1, 2000.

29. "马德受贿案" [Ma De's bribery case].

30. "现行法律下认定卖官有四难点" [Four sticking points in determining the sale of public office under current law], *CNN*, http://www.chinanews.com/other/news/2006/10-01/799055.shtml.

31. "揭开用人提名权黑幕" [Lifting the dark curtain to reveal the power to nominate officials], *半月谈内部版* 12 (2006).

32. "浙江纪检监察机关去年立案 8915 件 处分 8907 人" [Zhejiang's discipline inspection agencies filed 8,915 cases and disciplined 8,907 individuals last year], *中央纪委监察部网站*, http://news.163.com/14/0215/06/9L3TDHIT00014JB5.html; *湖南省志* [Provincial gazetteer of Hunan] (北京: 五洲传播出版社, 2006): 376. In 2007, the CCDI revealed that it had a staff of 700 people (roughly 40 percent of whom were involved in investigations). "中纪委编制" [Establishment of the CCDI], *BN*, December 11, 2014.

33. "九起实名举报事件回顾" [Recalling nine instances of using real identities to expose corruption], *Caixin*, November 29, 2012, http://economy.caixin.com/2012-11-29/100466286.html.

34. "李铁成受贿案侦破纪实" [The true story of the investigation into the bribery case of Li Tiecheng], *CNN*, February 19, 2003, http://www.chinanews.com/n/2003-02-19/26/274088.html.

35. "黑色日历: 黑龙江近年官场腐败编年史" [Dark calendar: A chronicle of recent cases of official corruption in Heilongjiang], *Caijing* (May 2, 2005): 36.

36. "安徽省第一巨贪县令陈兆丰 110 顶官帽卖出 150 万" [Anhui's most corrupt county party chief, Chen Zhaofeng, sold 110 official positions for 1.5 million yuan].

37. "白宫书记买官卖官被公诉 买官者仍在任" [White House party chief indicted for buying and selling offices; purchasers remain in power], 大江网, July 19, 2009, http://news.163.com/09/0719/06/5EIJL0100001124J.html.

38. "黑色日历: 黑龙江近年官场腐败编年史" [Dark calendar: A chronicle of recent cases of official corruption in Heilongjiang], 36–37.

39. "李铁成受贿案侦破纪实" [The true story of the investigation into the bribery case of Li Tiecheng].

40. "90 人向他行贿买官" [Ninety people bribed him for office], 中国新闻网, May 22, 2004, http://news.sina.com.cn/c/2004-05-22/10442598067s.shtml; "贫困县书记敛财" [Party chief of an impoverished county amassed wealth], *ACH* 2 (2005): 30–32.

41. Xu succeeded Zhang Huaiqi as the party chief of Yingshang County, but is not included in the sample. "安徽颍上县两任县委书记腐败之路" [Corrupt path of two county party chiefs in Anhui's Yingshang County], *PN*, February 20, 2006, http://politics.people.com.cn/GB/1026/4122368.html.

42. This practice has become so widespread that the CCDI routinely issues circulars warning against it during holidays. "中央纪委监察部通知要求两节期间改进工作作风加强廉洁自律" [CCDI and supervisory agency urge improvement of work style and strengthening of integrity and self-discipline during the two festivals], *XHN*, December 27, 2012, http://news.xinhuanet.com/politics/2012-12/27/c_114184193.htm.

43. "陕西省商洛市卖官书记张改萍" [Zhang Gaiping, office-selling party chief of Shangluo City in Shaanxi], *PN*, July 20, 2006, http://politics.people.com.cn/GB/1026/4609043.html.

44. "一个市委副书记的敛财人生" [A municipal deputy party chief's life devoted to amassing wealth], *PV* 4 (2011): 23–25.

45. "陈少勇受贿案" [Chen Shaoyong's bribery case].

46. "拆解黑龙江卖官链" [Unraveling the chain of the selling of public offices in Heilongjiang], *Caijing* (May 2, 2005): 30.

47. "陕西省商洛市卖官书记张改萍" [Zhang Gaiping, office-selling party chief of Shangluo City in Shaanxi].

48. "拆解黑龙江卖官链" [Unraveling the chain of the selling of public offices in Heilongjiang], 30.

49. "再探茂名窝案" [Revisiting the Maoming *wo'an*], *CXN*, http://china.caixin.com/2015-01-27/100779039_all.html.

50. "原茂名公安局长贿赂案一审宣判" [Announcement of the verdict in the bribery trial of Maoming's former police chief], 广州日报, June 28, 2012; "茂港区原公安分局局长杨强大肆受贿" [Yang Qiang, former police chief of Maogang District, took bribes recklessly], *SD*, June 20, 2011.

51. "90 人向他行贿买官" [Ninety people bribed him for office]; "贫困县书记敛财" [Party chief of an impoverished county amassed wealth].

52. "安徽和县原县委书记杨建国的卖官经" [The craft of selling public office according to Yang Jianguo, party chief of He County in Anhui], 法制周报, July 9, 2006; 徐江善, "罕见的卖官案" [A case of selling public office rarely seen in the past], 四川监察 5 (1997).

53. This case is not included in the sample. The information is from Xie's sentencing document. 河南省驻马店中级人民法院刑事判决书, "谢连章受贿一审判决书" [Verdict in Xie Lianzhang's trial for bribery] (2014): 驻刑一初字第 27 号.

54. "菏泽买官卖官调查" [Investigation of the buying and selling of public office in Heze], *CNW* (July 6, 2015).

55. "绥化政界的生态危机" [Ecological crisis in Suihua's officialdom], *CNW* (April 11, 2005).

56. The person who borrowed from the private businessman used only 20,000 yuan of his own money (4 percent of the total cost) to fund the purchase. "绥化政界的生态危机" [Ecological crisis in Suihua's officialdom]; "马德受贿案" [Ma De's bribery case]; "一个贫困地区的官场投资交易" [Trading in the investment in the officialdom of a poor area], *PN*, July 19, 2006, http://politics.people.com.cn/GB/8198/4606311.html.

57. One of the party chiefs was Luo Yinguo, an official included in this sample. "再探茂名窝案" [Revisiting the Maoming *wo'an*]. Yang's case is selected in Chapter 5. "茂名巨贪杨光亮一审" [Yang Guangliang, Maoming's notorious corrupt official, stands trial], 羊城晚报, December 16, 2011.

58. "刘秀田受贿卖官案纪实" [Liu Xiutian's case of bribery and selling of public offices: The real story], *XHN*, www.he.xinhuanet.com/zt/zhuanti002.htm.

59. "一个贫困地区的官场投资交易" [Trading in the investment in the officialdom of a poor area].

60. 安徽蚌埠市禹会区人民法院刑事判决书，"张桂义挪用公款受贿案" [Zhang Guiyi's case of misappropriation of public funds and acceptance of bribes] (2005): 禹刑初字第 14 号.

4. Cronyism in Action

Epigraph: 习近平关于党风廉政建设和反腐败斗争论述摘编 [Selected speeches by Xi Jinping] (Beijing: 中央文献出版社, 2015): 38.

1. The most successful official-turned-entrepreneur is Ye Chenghai, who left the government in 1985 after he was demoted from his position as vice mayor of Shenzhen the previous year. Ye later became a billionaire by founding a pharmaceutical firm. "叶澄海: 从副省级高官连贬三级到亿万富翁" [Ye Chenghai, demoted from deputy-provincial rank, becomes a tycoon worth one hundred million yuan],中国周刊 (October 22, 2009).

2. Report by the Supreme Procuratorate to the National People's Congress, March 10, 2013, http://www.spp.gov.cn/gzbg/201303/t20130316_57131 .shtml. Because during the same five-year period 19,599 county-level officials were disciplined and 12,193 were prosecuted for committing crimes by using their office, we estimate that 72 percent of county-level officials punished by the CCP committed crimes by using their office.

3. Since 1999, embezzlement and bribery cases in which the amount of money exceeds 50,000 yuan have been designated "major." Supreme Procuratorate's Report to the National People's Congress, March 11, 2012, http://www .spp.gov.cn/gzbg/201208/t20120820_2499.shtml

4. 龚婷, 吴木銮, "我国 2000–2009 年腐败案例研究报告" [Research report on cases of corruption in China during 2000–2009], 社会学研究 4 (2012): 215.

5. 乔德福, "改革开放以来市一把手腐败案例研究报告" [Research report on cases of corruption among top officials in cities since the reform and opening], 理论与改革 5 (2013): 67.

6. Jiangnan Zhu, "The shadow of the skyscrapers: Real estate corruption in China," *Journal of Contemporary China* 21 (2012): 243–260.

7. Corrupt officials may simultaneously engage in corruption in several sectors.

8. However, a close examination of the history of the corruption of these individuals shows that most of them perpetrated their acts while they were party chiefs or mayors. For instance, Lei Yaxin, Li Qiliang, Liu Zhuozhi, Huang Yao, Wang Yan, Wang Huaizhong, and Mao Shaolie committed most of their crimes when they were local party chiefs.

9. According to Yang Guangliang, the executive deputy mayor of Maoming City in Guangdong, his corruption income rose with his promotions. When he was a deputy county magistrate, he took cash gifts wrapped inside "red envelopes" totaling 1 million yuan a year; when he served as the county magistrate and county party chief, his annual bribes were about 2 million yuan; when he was made a deputy mayor of Maoming City, his corruption income rose to 3 million yuan a year. After he became the executive deputy mayor, he collected 3.5 million yuan a year. "巨贪杨光亮的腐败样本" [A sample of the misdeeds of Yang Guangliang, an official with insatiable greed], *PV* 15 (2011): 24–26.

10. Both provincial- and prefecture-level officials are overrepresented among those who gained above-median corruption income, whereas county-level officials are underrepresented. In the above-median corruption income group, the shares of provincial-, prefecture-, and county-level officials are, respectively, 24, 56, and 20 percent, while their shares in the total sample are, respectively, 14, 50, and 28 percent.

11. 驻马店中级人民法院刑事判决书，"谢连章受贿一审判决书" [Verdict in the trial of Xie Lianzhang's bribery case] (2014): 驻刑一初字第 27 号.

12. 长沙中级人民法院，"李大伦受贿案" [Li Dalun's bribery case] (2007): 长中刑二初字第 19 号.

13. The projects for which Wang helped various businessmen to receive multiagency approvals in this manner typically were large real estate development projects. 济南中级人民法院刑事判决书，"王怀中受贿巨额财产来源不明案" [Wang Huaizhong's case of bribery and his large amount of unexplained wealth] (2003): 济刑初字第 32 号.

14. 宿州市中级人民法院刑事判决书，"刘家坤，赵晓莉受贿一审判决书" [Verdict in the bribery case of Liu Jiakun and Zhao Xiaoli] (2013): 宿中刑初字第 37 号.

15. "谭灯耀受贿案" [Tan Dengyao's case of bribery], *中国纪检监察报*, February 3, 2012; "东方土地腐败调查" [An investigation into the land scandal in Dongfang], *CNW* (April 14, 2011); "东方市土地腐败窝案" [The land *wo'an* in Dongfang City], *XHN*, February 14, 2011, http://news.xinhuanet.com/legal /2011-02/14/c_121074654.htm.

16. "刘卓志官市" [Liu Zhuozhi's marketing of public office], *Caijing* (July 31, 2012).

17. 宿州市中级人民法院刑事判决书, "权俊良滥用职权受贿案" [Quan Junliang's case of abuse of power and bribery] (2014): 宿中刑初字第 29 号.

18. "杨跃国案件剖析" [Anatomy of the case of Yang Yueguo], *CDID*, January 5, 2015; 昆明铁路运输中级法院刑事判决书, "杨跃国贪污受贿案" [Yang Yueguo's case of embezzlement and bribery] (2014): 昆铁中刑初字第 104 号; 云南省芒市人民法院刑事判决书, "王成钢受贿, 行贿案" [Wang Chenggang's case of accepting and paying bribes] (2014): 芒刑初字第 102 号.

19. Zhou's sentencing document was leaked and posted online: "周镇宏受贿巨额财产来源不明案" [Zhou Zhenhong's case of bribery and his large amount of unexplained wealth], http://www.zjms114.com/news/bencandy .php?fid=156&id=8552.

20. "犍为县原县长杨国友称为保官位不得不受贿" [Yang Guoyou, former Jianwei County magistrate, claims he had to take bribes to keep his position], *成都晚报*, November 5, 2005.

21. "广东韶关 8.14 腐败案揭秘" [Exposing the August 14 corruption scandal in Shaoguan in Guangdong], *SD*, August 12, 2010.

22. "利欲熏心后, 人伸罪恶手" [Greed and crime], *CI* 14 (2004): 42–45.

23. "王春成浮沉" [Wang Chuncheng's rise and fall], *Caijing* (July 28, 2014).

24. "南丹特大矿难" [Nandan's mega mining disaster], *PSD*, January 9, 2002; "南丹矿难的祸根" [The roots of Nandan's mining disaster], *浙江廉政在线*, http://jct.zj.gov.cn/fanfubai/detail.asp?id=505.

25. "雷副市长的堕落" [The fall of deputy mayor Lei], *PV* 7 (2006): 22.

26. "绍兴新版官场现形记" [The true character of officialdom in Shaoxing revealed], *法治与社会* (May 6, 2009).

27. 南京市中级人民法院刑事判决书, "马向东等贪污, 受贿, 挪用公款, 巨额财产来源不明判决" [Verdict in the trial of Ma Xiangdong and others for

embezzlement, bribery, misappropriation of public funds, and a large amount of unexplained wealth] (2001): 宁刑初字第 110 号.

28. "嘉兴 56 名落马官员的红黑江湖" [The double lives of fifty-six disgraced officials in Jiaxing], 法人 (September 2010): 43.

29. "触目惊心的塌方式腐败" [Shocking cases of collapse-style corruption], *CDID,* November 18, 2014.

30. "贪欲让明星深陷沼泽" [Greed sinks a star], *CDID,* March 10, 2014.

31. "傍官富豪" [A tycoon with an official pal], *DAL* 9 (May 2006): 7.

32. "东方土地腐败调查" [An investigation into the land scandal in Dongfang].

33. "毛绍烈受贿逾千万" [Mao Shaolie's bribes exceeded 10 million yuan], *CNN,* April 1, 2015, http://www.chinanews.com/fz/2015/04-01/7177164 .shtml.

34. "青岛土地窝案深层透视" [An in-depth look at Qingdao's land *wo'an*], 中国网, January 25, 2005, http://big5.china.com.cn/chinese/2005/Jan/767588 .htm; "绥化原市长王慎义案开庭, 马德因揭发立功" [Trial of Suihua's former mayor Wang Shenyi opens; Ma De earns credit for providing information] 法制晚报, March 23, 2005.

35. "广东韶关 8.14 腐败案揭秘" [Exposing the August 14 corruption scandal in Shaoguan in Guangdong].

36. "三任县委书记的前腐后继" [Three corrupt county party chiefs followed each other], *DAL* (May 31, 2011).

37. "刘卓志官市" [Liu Zhuozhi's market of public office]; "王素毅堕落轨迹" [Wang Suyi's journey of corruption], *XHN,* July 17, 2014, http://news .xinhuanet.com/lianzheng/2014-07/17/c_1111672855.htm; "贵州凯里市长洪金州涉刘铁男案落马" [Hong Jinzhou, mayor of Kaili City in Guizhou, arrested for involvement in the case of Liu Tienan], *OMN,* August 13, 2013; "一个能人腐败的标本" [A representative case of the corruption by a capable individual], *CDID,* November 4, 2014.

38. "被情人绊倒的明星干部" [A star official tripped by his mistress], *CDID,* December 15, 2014; "毛绍烈腐败案剖析" [Anatomy of Mao Shaolie's corruption], *CDID,* July 25, 2014; "巨贪杨光亮的腐败样本" [A sample of the misdeeds of Yang Guangliang, an official with insatiable greed].

39. "郴州落马纪委书记" [Chenzhou's disgraced anticorruption chief], *CNW* (April 30, 2008).

40. 九江国土系统腐败窝案" [The *wo'an* in Jiujiang's land management system], *CDID*, October 15, 2013.

41. "王敏案件警示录" [Lessons from the corruption case of Wang Min], *XHN*, March 31, 2015, http://news.xinhuanet.com/legal/2015-03/31/c _127639414.htm.

42. "周滨: 最著名的神秘富商" [Zhou Bin: The most famous mysterious rich businessman], *CXN*, July 29, 2014, http://china.caixin.com/2014-07-29 /100710373.html; "Billions in hidden riches for family of Chinese leader," *New York Times,* October 25, 2012; for information on Liu Lefei, see his bio at http://www.daonong.com/huiyuan/liulefei/.

43. "陈良宇案" [The case of Chen Liangyu], *Caijing* 79 (March 31, 2008): 78–86; "富商周滨" [Rich businessman Zhou Bin], *CXN*, March 3, 2014, http:// china.caixin.com/2014-03-03/100645962.html.

44. "周政坤的黑色愚人节" [Zhou Zhengkun's dark April Fool's day], *PV* 10 (2007).

45. "云南省交通厅原副厅长胡星归案" [Hu Xing, former deputy director of Yunnan's transportation department, is in custody], 人民监督网, April 29, 2007, http://www.rmjdw.com/yongguandangan/20060501/4509.html.

46. "触目惊心的塌方式腐败" [Shocking cases of collapse-style corruption].

47. "江西安远涉 20 余名官员稀土腐败案" [A rare-earth corruption scandal in Jiangxi's Anyuan implicates more than twenty officials], *XHN*, December 18, 2014, http://news.xinhuanet.com/legal/2014-12/17/c_1113681761 .htm; 赣州市中级人民法院刑事裁定书, "邝玉珍, 谢鸣等人非法采矿行贿案" [The case of illegal mining and bribery by Kuang Yuzhen, Xie Ming, and others] (2014): 赣中刑终字第 89 号.

48. "海南东方土地腐败调查" [An investigation into the land scandal in Dongfang in Hainan]; "海南东方市土地窝案" [The land *wo'an* in Dongfang City in Hainan], *BN*, February 15, 2011; "海南东方市原市长谭灯耀" [Tan Dengyao, former mayor of Dongfang City in Hainan], *PD*, May 24, 2011.

49. "绍兴新版官场现形记" [The true character of officialdom in Shaoxing revealed].

50. "刘卓志落马内情" [The inside story of the fall of Liu Zhuozhi], *CEH* (August 5, 2011).

51. "一个副省级高官的深度堕落" [The steep fall of a deputy provincial-level official], *清廉网*, July 7, 2011, http://www.jcj.dl.gov.cn/content.aspx?id=2011-7-7%2F20117785510.htm.

52. "权俊良滥用职权受贿案" [Quan Junliang's case of abuse of power and bribery].

53. "傍官富豪王德军" [Wang Dejun, a tycoon backed by officials], *DAL* 9 (2006): 7.

54. "还原张荣坤" [Revealing the real Zhang Rongkun], *Caijing* 202 (January 2008): 88–100.

55. "最高人民检察院关于反贪污贿赂工作情况的报告" [Report on the fight against embezzlement and bribery by the Supreme People's Procuratorate], *中国人大网*, http://www.npc.gov.cn/npc/xinwen/2013-10/22/content_1810629.htm.

56. A typical prefecture-level committee of discipline inspection has about twelve staff members. An average prefecture has six to ten counties or districts and has between two to four million people. The Central Discipline Inspection Commission, even after its expansion in 2013, has only 360 staff and officials. The entire Chinese procuratorate had 154,664 prosecutors and professional staff in 2012. "纪委办案人: 我们也需要心理辅导" [Investigators of discipline committees say they also need psychological guidance], *CGO*, November 17, 2014; "中央纪委增加百余名办案人员" [CCDI adds more than one hundred investigators], *OMN*, March 20, 2014; *中国法律年鉴 2013* [China law yearbook 2013] (Beijing: 中国法律年鉴出版社, 2013): 1213.

57. Zhou's case is described in the Introduction. During the purge of Ling Jihua, the former director of the Central General Office of the CCP, dozens of officials and businessmen in Shanxi who were closely associated with him were arrested. The fall of Su Rong, the former party chief of Jiangxi, also resulted in the arrests of many officials who worked with him there. "令氏兄弟" [The Ling brothers], *财新新世纪* 50 (December 29, 2014); "苏荣腐败案" [Su Rong's corruption case], *JT*, March 6, 2015.

58. "嘉兴李中杰案牵出 46 名官员" [Li Zhongjie of Jiaxing implicates forty-six officials in a corruption scandal], 浙江在线新闻网, December 5, 2009, http://zjnews.zjol.com.cn/05zjnews/system/2009/12/05/016127544.shtml.

59. "湖南娄底市政府办公楼搬迁引发窝案" [A *wo'an* triggered by the relocation of the office complex of the Loudi municipal government in Hunan], *CYD*, November 2, 2008.

60. "直击绍兴房地产官商勾结" [Crackdown on collusion between real estate businessmen and government officials in Shaoxing] 决策探索 (November 2008): 66–68.

61. "权力资本化" [The capitalization of power], *OL* 22 (2005): 10.

62. "南丹特大矿难" [Nandan's mega mining disaster].

63. "两任市长相继落马" [The fall of two successive mayors], *SW*, June 30, 2005.

64. "郴州巨贪曾锦春曾 10 万元悬赏举报者人头" [Zeng Jinchun, Chenzhou's insatiably greedy official, offered 100,000 yuan for the head of a whistle-blower], 广州日报, April 23, 2008.

65. "开发商遭报复反咬出省府高官" [Victim of retaliation, real estate developer exposes senior provincial official], *SW*, October 9, 2008.

66. "单增德受贿案剖析" [Anatomy of Shan Zengde's bribery case], *CDID*, December 12, 2014.

67. "许宗衡落马" [The fall of Xu Zongheng], *CNW* (June 22, 2009): 25; "许宗衡官市一角" [A corner in Xu Zongheng's market of public office], *Caijing* 20 (September 27, 2009).

68. "兰州掀起反腐风暴" [Lanzhou launches crackdown on corruption], *SW*, June 30, 2005.

69. These two cases are not in the sample. "媒体揭官员内斗" [Media reveals rivalry among officials], 廉政瞭望杂志 (October 16, 2015); "知情人披露季建业岳父举报杨卫泽原因" [Insider reveals why Ji Jianye's father-in-law exposed Yang Weize], 文汇网, January 15, 2015, http://news.wenweipo.com/2015/01/15/IN1501150093.htm.

70. "直击绍兴房地产官商勾结" [Crackdown on collusion between real estate businessmen and government officials in Shaoxing].

71. "行贿的受贿的都是被迫的" [Bribe-givers and bribe-takers were all coerced], *经济参考报*, October 24, 2008.

72. "广东韶关 8.14 腐败案揭秘" [Exposing the August 14 corruption scandal in Shaoguan in Guangdong].

73. 山东省滨州市人民检察院, "单增德起诉书" [The indictment of Shan Zengde] (2013): 滨检刑诉 47 号.

74. "矿难新闻灭火队长" [Official who suppressed news of mining disasters], *PV 1* (2008).

75. "黄光裕案细节" [Details of Huang Guangyu's case], *新世纪周刊* (May 24, 2010): 73–78.

76. 山东省高级人民法院刑事裁定书, "王华元受贿、 巨额财产来源不明案" [Wang Huayuan's case of bribery and his large amount of unexplained wealth] (October 12, 2010).

77. "三任县委书记的前腐后继" [Three corrupt county party chiefs followed each other].

78. "南丹特大矿难" [Nandan's mega mining disaster].

79. "王先民收受贿赂单" [List of bribes collected by Wang Xianmin], http://www.shijiahh.com/420887.html.

80. "王怀忠受贿, 巨额财产来源不明案" [Wang Huaizhong's case of bribery and his large amount of unexplained wealth].

81. "李大伦受贿案" [Li Dalun's bribery case].

82. 长沙市人民检察院, "曾锦春起诉书" [Indictment of Zeng Jinchun] (2008): 长检刑诉第 2 号.

83. "郴州落马纪委书记" [Chenzhou's disgraced anticorruption chief].

84. "前茂名书记落马案" [The fall of Maoming's former party chief], *OO* (February 20, 2011).

85. "王华元受贿、 巨额财产来源不明案" [Wang Huayuan's case of bribery and his large amount of unexplained wealth].

86. "广东韶关 8.14 腐败案揭秘" [Exposing the August 14 corruption scandal in Shaoguan in Guangdong].

87. "周镇宏受贿巨额财产来源不明案" [Zhou Zhenhong's case of bribery and his large amount of unexplained wealth].

88. "刘卓志官市" [Liu Zhuozhi's market of public office].

5. Stealing from the State

Epigraph: 习近平关于党风廉政建设和反腐败斗争论述摘编 [Selected speeches by Xi Jinping] (Beijing: 中央文献出版社, 2015): 129.

1. Zhejiang's provincial procuratorate reported that, between 2001 and 2013, 20 percent of the corruption cases in SOEs were *wo'an;* Shanghai's procuratorate reported that 52 percent of the corruption cases in SOEs were *wo'an.* "浙江检察机关三年查国企领域蛀虫" [Prosecutors in Zhejiang uncover thieves in SOEs during the last three years], *JN,* August 27, 2014, http://news.jcrb.com/jxsw/201408/t20140827_1426681.html; "上海上半年反贪污贿赂立案 187 件" [Shanghai files 187 cases of embezzlement and bribery in the first half of the year], *PN,* July 25, 2014, http://politics.people.com.cn/n/2014/0725/c1001-25345255.html.

2. Scholars have studied corruption, but not its collusive variant, in Chinese SOEs. See Linfen Jennifer Huang and Robin Stanley Snell, "Turnaround, corruption and mediocrity: Leadership and governance in three state owned enterprises in mainland China," *Journal of Business Ethics* 43 (2003): 111–124; Feng Chen, "Subsistence crises, managerial corruption and labour protests in China," *China Journal* 44 (2000): 41–63. Xueliang Ding examines illicit asset-stripping in X. L. Ding, "The illicit asset stripping of Chinese state firms," *China Journal* 43 (2000): 1–28. Melanie Manion also mentions similar behavior briefly in *Corruption by Design* (Cambridge, MA: Harvard University Press, 2004): 107–110. Ding's study is based on interviews conducted at six unidentified firms and does not contain detailed information on the individual characteristics of these firms or the main perpetrators. Neither Ding nor Manion study collusion in SOE corruption.

3. "上海贪污受贿串窝案近八成在国企" [Nearly 80 percent of collective embezzlement and bribery cases in Shanghai occur in SOEs], *解放日报,* October 20, 2000; "江苏今年职务犯罪案件中窝案串案占三成六" [*Wo'an* and *chuan'an* account for 36 percent of crimes committed using public office in Jiangsu this year], *CNN,* http://review.jcrb.com.cn/ournews/asp/readNews.asp?id=13942; "浙江检察机关三年查国企领域蛀虫" [Prosecutors in Zhejiang uncover thieves in SOEs during the last three years].

4. The share of corruption cases involving SOE executives included in the reports was 44 percent in 2011, 35 percent in 2012, and 24 percent in 2013. 中国企业家犯罪媒体案例分析报告 *2012* [Analysis of crimes of Chinese corporate executives reported in the media in 2012], 法人 (March 2013): 16–40; 中国企业家犯罪媒体案例分析报告 *2013* [Analysis of crimes of Chinese corporate executives reported in the media in 2013] 法人 (February 2014): 34–47; 中国企业家犯罪报告 *2011* [Report on crimes of corporate executives in 2011], *XHN,* http://news.xinhuanet.com/legal/2012-01/16/c_122590462.htm.

5. 中国企业家犯罪媒体案例分析报告 *2013* [Analysis of crimes of Chinese corporate executives reported in the media in 2013].

6. 中国企业家犯罪研究报告 *2014* [Research report on crimes of Chinese corporate executives in 2014], http://www.cclpp.com/article_show.jsp?f_article_id=9674.

7. 中国企业家犯罪报告 *2011* [Report on crimes of Chinese corporate executives in 2011].

8. 中国企业家犯罪媒体案例分析报告 *2012* [Analysis of crimes of Chinese corporate executives reported in the media in 2012].

· 9. 中国企业家犯罪研究报告*2014* [Report on crimes of Chinese corporate executives in 2014].

10. Ibid.

11. Ibid.

12. In this study, we rely on official information regarding the amounts stolen by the convicted perpetrators. When such information is not available, we rely on the amounts used in the charges filed against these officials. When such amounts are not officially disclosed, we rely on the amounts reported by the media.

13. In cases involving only three individuals, all of them were SOE executives.

14. One was dismissed because his corruption income consisted of unauthorized bonuses paid out of concealed profits. "国资损失八千万" [Loss of 80 million yuan in state-owned assets], *CDID,* April 21, 2014.

15. China implemented a major reform to "kill fewer and kill cautiously" in 2007, and the Supreme People's Court, not the provincial high courts, now has final approval authority. Stephen Noakes, "Kill fewer, kill carefully: State

pragmatism, political legitimacy, and the death penalty in China," *Problems of Post-Communism* 61 (2014): 18–30.

16. Since the 1990s, only three officials at or above the provincial rank have been executed. They were Cheng Kejie, former governor of Guangxi and a vice chairman of the standing committee of the National People's Congress; Hu Changqing, deputy governor of Jiangxi; and Wang Huaizhong, deputy governor of Anhui. Only one vice minister–level official, Zheng Xiaoyu, the former head of the Chinese Food and Drug Administration, was executed.

17. "明星国企垮塌的背后" [Behind the collapse of a star SOE], *CI* 12 (2009): 51–54.

18. "突破一人，抓住一串" [Break one person, catch a group], *PD*, http://www.jcrb.com/n1/jcrb515/ca273970.htm.

19. "'横铁' 是怎样被 '蛀' 空的" [How Heng Iron was looted], *PV* 7 (2005): 14–16.

20. "中移动窝案 14 名高管已落马" [Fourteen senior ChinaMobile executives have been arrested], *中国经营网*, November 20, 2013, http://www.cs.com.cn/ssgs/gsxw/201311/t20131120_4215134.html.

21. "一个大型国企沉浮的背后" [Behind the rise and fall of a large SOE], *CDID*, August 19, 2011.

22. "铁帚除硕鼠" [Iron fist hits thieves], *CI* 8 (2006): 43–47.

23. There was an earlier case of collusive corruption in the same SOE involving more than ten individuals. "陕西延长石油腐败窝案" [A case of *wo'an* in Yanchang Petroleum Corp. in Shaanxi], *OO* 47 (2012): 43–50.

24. There is a third category: private distribution of public assets (*sifen*). If stolen public funds are shared among several individuals in the SOE or the government, this is often classified as *sifen*. In this chapter we treat *sifen* as a form of collective embezzlement.

25. "徐敏杰为妻子违规报销" [Xu Minjie violated the rules by getting his wife's expenses reimbursed], *BN*, June 10, 2015.

26. "齐鲁石化公司腐败案" [Corruption in Sinopec Qilu Corp.], *XHN*, August 11, 2004, http://news.sina.com.cn/c/2004-08-12/10143380310s.shtml.

27. "中山端掉一个五人贪污窝案" [Zhongshan cracks a five-person embezzlement case], *JN*, April 2, 2001, http://review.jcrb.com.cn/ournews/asp/readNews.asp?id=29921.

28. 重庆市第四中级人民法院刑事裁定书，"彭水饮食公司窝案" [The wo'an in Pengshui Food and Beverage Co.] (2011): 渝四中法刑终字第52号.

29. "毕玉玺相关串案开审" [Trial of a corruption case related to Bi Yuxi opens], 北京晚报, September 13, 2005.

30. "国资损失八千万" [Loss of 80 million yuan in state-owned assets].

31. "盗矿经理的黄粱梦" [The sweet dream of a thieving mine manager], *CDID*, August 28, 2013.

32. 山东省济南中级人民法院刑事判决书，"薛玉泉受贿挪用公款案" [Xue Yuquan's case of bribery and misappropriation of public funds] (2001): 济刑二初字第2号.

33. "齐鲁石化窝案真相" [The truth behind the wo'an at Sinopec Qilu Corp.], *CEH*, November 23, 2005.

34. "温州菜篮子集团窝案" [The wo'an at Wenzhou Cailanzi Group], *CNN*, December 31, 2012, http://fanfu.people.com.cn/n/2012/1231/c64371-20062003.html.

35. "广西柳钢集团原董事长梁景理受审" [Liang Jingli, former chairman of Guangxi Liuzhou Iron and Steel Group, stands trial], 人民法院报, May 27, 2015.

36. "国资损失八千万" [Loss of 80 million yuan in state-owned assets].

37. "横铁是怎样被烛空的" [How Heng Iron was looted].

38. "引爆张春江案的两根导火线" [Two fuses that detonated the case of Zhang Chunjiang], *PV 17* (2011): 24–27.

39. "华中电力集团原总经理林孔兴受审" [Lin Kongxing, former general manager of Huazhong Electric Power Group, stands trial], 江淮晨报, November 3, 2004.

40. "解密农发行窝案" [Shine a spotlight on the wo'an in the Agricultural Development Bank], 法庭内外, 3 (2007): 4–13.

41. "传中海系茅士家被查因儿子儿媳倒油" [COSCO executive Mao Shijia allegedly investigated because son and daughter-in-law engaged in flipping oil], *JT*, November 27, 2013.

42. "广西柳钢集团原董事长梁景理受审" [Liang Jingli, former chairman of Guangxi Liuzhou Iron and Steel Group, stands trial].

43. "吴日晶受审" [Wu Rijing stands trial], 广州日报, October 12, 2011.

44. The Shaanxi Communist Party Provincial Discipline Inspection Committee, http://www.sxdaily.com.cn/data/dajs/20051126_8775072_0.htm.

45. "中原煤老虎李永新落马记" [The fall of Li Yongxin, central China's coal tiger], *CYD*, February 24, 2014.

46. "羊城集团何以成国资黑洞?" [How did Yangcheng Group become a black hole for state-owned assets?], *XHN*, July 28, 2003, http://www.southcn.com/news/gdnews/gdtodayimportant/200307280259.htm.

47. "兰州审判疯狂诈骗国有资产 1.9 亿元连铝案" [The court in Lanzhou tries brazen fraud case at Liancheng Aluminum Corp. that defrauded the state of 190 million yuan], *兰州晨报*, December 15, 2004; "魏光前窝案" [The case of Wei Guangqian], *党风通讯* 10 (2000): 24–34.

48. "泰州查处某国企窝案" [Taizhou investigates a *wo'an* in an SOE], *CDID*, September 30, 2011.

49. In addition to this shady deal, Xiang was also accused of embezzling 490,000 yuan, unauthorized use of 7.3 million yuan in public funds, theft of 6 million yuan of company funds, and unexplained wealth of 2 million yuan. "重庆企业老总骗取国家补偿款 2683 万" [Corporate chief defrauded the state of 26.83 million yuan in compensation funds], *重庆晨报*, May 28, 2006; "渝东第一贪 法庭上忏悔" [Courtroom remorse of eastern Chongqing's most corrupt person], *XHN*, May 25, 2006, http://news.xinhuanet.com/legal/2006-05/25/content_4598265.htm.

50. "王成明终审被判死缓" [Wang Chengming gets suspended death penalty at his final trial], *Caijing*, http://www.caijing.com.cn/2008-03-20/100053279.html.

51. "国企老总侵吞 2.84 亿" [SOE chief stole 284 million yuan], *CNN*, June 26, 2014, http://www.chinanews.com/fz/2014/06-26/6324703.shtml.

52. "温州国企腐败窝案" [A *wo'an* in a Wenzhou SOE], *经济参考报*, February 8, 2013; "温州应国权腐败窝案" [Ying Guoquan's case of collective corruption], *PN*, December 21, 2011, http://fanfu.people.com.cn/GB/16666065.html.

53. One study finds that the price discount of SOE assets is only 5–7 percent. This estimate is likely too low since such a thin profit may not even cover the cost of bribes, typically 10 percent of the transaction. Raymond Fishman and Yongxiang Wang, "Corruption in Chinese privatization," *Journal of Law, Economics and Organization* 31 (2015): 1–29.

54. "企业自卖自买国企暴露改制黑洞" [Sale and purchase of an SOE reveals the black hole in corporate restructuring], *XHN*, December 21, 2004, http://news.xinhuanet.com/newscenter/2004-12/21/content_2361966.htm; "黄岩区原区长蒋万明被起诉" [Jiang Wanming, former head of Huangyan District, is indicted], *PV*, http://www.jcrb.com/n1/jcrb752/ca354768.htm.

55. 重庆市第四中级人民法院刑事裁定书, "彭水饮食公司窝案" [The *wo'an* in Pengshui Food and Beverage Co.].

56. "万夏公司窝案" [The *wo'an* in Wanxia Corp.], 兰州晨报, August 25, 2012.

57. "国企女掌门贪腐" [The corruption of a female SOE chief], *经济参考报*, July 14, 2012.

58. "蒋洁敏被控受贿" [Jiang Jiemin charged with bribery], *XHN*, April 13, 2015, http://news.xinhuanet.com/legal/2015-04/13/c_1114954907.htm.

59. "周氏攫财录" [How the Zhou family amassed wealth], 财新网, July 29, 2014, http://china.caixin.com/2014-07-29/100710329.html; "红顶 灰顶 和 黑顶" [Red hat, gray hat, and black hat], *财新网*, http://china.caixin.com/2014-07-29/100710327.html.

60. "安徽军工原董事长黄小虎受审" [Huang Xiaohu, former chairman of Anhui Jungong Group, stands trial], *安徽商报*, May 30, 2014.

61. "张新明的华润百亿交易案" [The case of 10 billion yuan in trade Zhang Xinming conducted with China Resources], *BN*, June 3, 2014; "华润窝案中的利益 连环网" [The network of interests in the *wo'an* in China Resources], 环球人物周刊, September 26, 2014.

62. "解密农发行窝案" [Shine a spotlight on the *wo'an* in the Agricultural Development Bank].

63. "中储粮河南多个粮库骗 7 亿粮食资金" [Several storage sites in Sinograin (Henan) defrauded of 700 million yuan in grain funds], *OL* (August 17, 2013).

64. "李人志受贿案" [Li Renzhi's bribery case], 甘肃日报, December 24, 2011.

65. "三明市物资集团公司高管腐败案" [Corruption of senior managers of Sanming City Materials Group], *CDID*, March 18, 2014.

66. "福建南靖县长塔煤矿三任矿长落马" [Fall of three general managers of Changta Coal in Nanjing County in Fujian], *XHN*, July 16, 2002; http://www.people.com.cn/GB/shehui/44/20020716/777503.html.

67. "温州国企腐败窝案" [A *wo'an* in a Wenzhou SOE]; "国企老总侵吞 2.84 亿" [SOE chief stole 284 million yuan].

68. "军工集团原董事长举报前任立功" [Former chairman of Jungong Group exposes his predecessor, earning credit], *XHN*, May 29, 2014, http:// fanfu.people.com.cn/n/2014/0529/c64371-25082987.html; "检察官谈毕玉玺 落马经过" [Prosecutor recounts the fall of Bi Yuxi], *北京晨报*, March 23, 2005.

69. "中储粮河南多个粮库骗 7 亿粮食资金" [Several storage sites in Sinograin (Henan) defrauded of 700 million yuan in grain funds].

70. Many of the largest SOEs owned by the central government have vice-ministerial status. As such, their chief executives are equivalent to vice ministers and must be appointed by the CCP's organization department.

71. "横铁是怎样被烛空的" [How Heng Iron was looted]; "揭开一个老牌 国企的破产迷局" [Crack the riddle of the bankruptcy of a well-established SOE], *CDID*, June 24, 2011.

72. "中原煤老虎李永新落马记" [The fall of Li Yongxin, central China's coal tiger].

73. "徽商集团窝案" [The *wo'an* at Huishang Group], *法制与新闻* (April 2009): 27–29.

74. "中国轻骑集团原董事长张家岭判无期" [Zhang Jialing, former chairman of China Qingqi Group, gets life term], *XHN*, February 11, 2009, http://news.xinhuanet.com/legal/2009-02/11/content_10804781.htm.

75. "魏光前窝案" [The case of Wei Guangqian].

76. "徽商集团窝案" [The *wo'an* at Huishang Group].

77. "解密农发行窝案" [Shine a spotlight on the *wo'an* at the Agricultural Development Bank].

6. In Bed with the Mafia

Epigraph: *习近平关于党风廉政建设和反腐败斗争论述摘编* [Selected speeches by Xi Jinping] (Beijing: 中央文献出版社, 2015): 124.

1. The official definition of organized crime, called "*heishehui xingzhide zuzhi*," has evolved over the years. The most authoritative and updated definition is in item 294 of the Chinese Criminal Code, revised in 2011. Organized crime (1) has a tight organizational structure, relatively large membership,

clear organizers, leaders, regular key members, and strict organizational discipline; (2) gains economic benefits through illegal and other means and possesses considerable economic resources; (3) uses bribes and intimidation to entice or force state employees to participate in its activities; (4) deploys violence, intimidation, and harassment to extort, monopolize, and instigate fights and incidents in a defined geographic area and results in severe damage to economic and social order.

2. The list is available at http://blog.sina.com.cn/s/blog_425d3adf0100ve9m.html.

3. Ming Xia, "Organizational formations of organized crime in China: Perspectives from the state, markets, and networks," *Journal of Contemporary China* 17 (2008): 1–23; Andrew Wedeman, "The challenge of commercial bribery and organized crime in China," *Journal of Contemporary China* 22 (2013): 18–34; Sheldon X. Zhang and Ko-lin Chin, "Snakeheads, mules, and protective umbrellas: A review of current research on Chinese organized crime," *Crime, Law, and Social Change* 50 (2008): 177–195.

4. An earlier and informative study on this subject is Ko-lin Chin and Roy Godson, "Organized crime and the political nexus in China," *Trends in Organized Crime* 9(3) (Spring 2006): 5–44.

5. "陕西潼关公安局长参与黑社会" [Police chief in Tongguan in Shaanxi participated in organized crime], *OO* (April 22, 2008); "新化黑社会团伙调查" [An investigation into organized criminal groups in Xinhua], *新世纪周刊* (April 21, 2006); "江西铅山党政干部涉黑" [Party and government officials in Qianshan in Jiangxi involved in organized crime], *CNN*, October 16, 2001, http://www.chinanews.com/2001-10-16/26/130530.html; "锦州涉黑团伙" [Groups involved in organized crime in Jinzhou], http://news.xinhuanet.com/legal/2006-06/29/content_4765278.htm; "被黑老大腐蚀掉的官员" [Officials corrupted by a crime boss], *DAL* 30 (2012): 31–33; "横峰县涉黑组织大案" [A major case of organized crime in Hengfeng County], *江南都市报*, November 29, 2012; "禾阳谢文生兄弟涉黑案调查" [An investigation into the involvement of Xie Wensheng and his brother in organized crime in Heyang], *CYD*, September 19, 2008; "山西打黑第一案" [Shanxi's no. 1 case of fighting organized crime], *中广网*, January 4, 2002, http://www.cnr.cn/home/society/200201040099.html.

6. "沈阳打黑英雄涉黑受审" [Shenyang's mafia-fighting hero on trial for involvement in organized crime], *CJN,* June 30, 2008, http://www.caijing .com.cn/2008-06-30/100072176.html; "黑龙江第一涉黑案" [Heilongjiang's no. 1 case of organized crime], *SW,* September 2, 2004; "聂磊被执行死刑" [Nie Lei executed], *青岛新闻网,* September 17, 2013, http://qd.sohu.com /20130917/n386740645.shtml; "茂名涉黑案重审" [Maoming's organized crime case retried], *羊城晚报,* September 20, 2014; "宋鹏飞涉黑案" [The case of Song Pengfei's involvement in organized crime], *OO* (July 14, 2008); "福州高层大地震" [Major earthquake at the top of the Fuzhou government], *PV* 2 (2004): 14–17; "长春黑老大受审" [Changchun's crime boss on trial], *CNN,* October 20, 2010, http://www.chinanews.com/sh/2010/10-20 /2598451.shtml; "曾腐蚀干警称霸今待严惩" [In the past he has bribed police officers and bullied others; today he is awaiting severe punishment], *XHN,* April 15, 2002, http://news.xinhuanet.com/newscenter/2002-04/15 /content_359105.htm; "横行湘潭 20 多年非法获利过亿" [Gangster who dominated Xiangtan for more than two decades and gained illegal profits of over one hundred million yuan], *红网,* December 26, 2011, http://hn.rednet .cn/c/2011/12/26/2473681.htm.

7. "三涉黑团伙沈阳覆灭记" [The destruction of three criminal organizations in Shenyang], *BN,* July 16, 2008.

8. A study of organized crime in Jilin reveals a similar penetration by organized crime into mining and real estate. Of the fifty criminal groups dismantled in Jilin between 2006 and 2011, fifteen were involved in mining and seven had real estate business. 靳高风, "吉林省涉黑犯罪调查" [An investigation into organized crime in Jilin province], *山东警察学院学报* 121 (2012): 86.

9. "红与黑" [Black and red], *PV* 1 (2001): 2–5.

10. "沈阳公安局原副局长涉黑" [Former deputy police chief of Shenyang involved in organized crime], *BN,* July 16, 2008.

11. "一位高官的腐化生活" [The corrupt life of a senior official], *PV* 7 (2007): 8–9.

12. "义乌公安局长倒于石榴裙下" [Police chief of Yiwu fell for a woman], *JT,* April 20, 2002.

13. "一场官黑相傍的罪恶" [A symbiotic evil relationship between officials and organized crime], *ACH* 5 (2002): 36.

14. "黑龙江最大涉黑组织关系网曝光" [The organizational network of Heilongjiang's largest mafia exposed], *CYD*, August 16, 2004.

15. "充当黑社会保护伞, 淮安 13 名干警被起诉" [Thirteen police officers in Huai'an indicted for protecting organized crime], *PN*, April 25, 2002, http://www.people.com.cn/GB/shehui/44/20020424/716650.html.

16. "福建剿灭一黑社会组织" [Fujian destroys a criminal organization], *CNN*, July 22, 2002, http://www.chinanews.com/2002-07-21/26/204699.html.

17. "湘潭公安局原副局长涉黑" [Former deputy police chief of Xiangtan involved in organized crime], *法制网*, April 23, 2014, http://www.legaldaily.com.cn/index_article/content/2014-04/23/content_5474291.htm?node=5955.

18. "邵阳特大涉黑团伙覆灭记" [The destruction of a mega criminal organization in Shaoyang], *CNN*, December 4, 2003, http://www.chinanews.com/n/2003-12-04/26/376809.html.

19. "陕西潼关公安局长参与黑社会" [Police chief in Tongguan in Shaanxi participated in organized crime].

20. "新化黑社会团伙调查" [An investigation into organized criminal groups in Xinhua].

21. "福州首富陈凯的发家史" [The rise of Chen Kai, Fuzhou's richest individual], *三联生活周刊* (December 19, 2003).

22. "值得警惕的涉黑案" [A case of organized crime that deserves our vigilance], *南风窗* (January 16, 2004): 21.

23. "邵阳特大涉黑团伙覆灭记" [The destruction of a mega criminal organization in Shaoyang]; "一个政协常委的黑道人生" [The life of a dark mafia-boss, a member of the standing committee of the PPCC], *时代潮* 2–3 (2004).

24. "拿掉官方保护伞" [Take away official protection], *潇湘晨报*, August 3, 2002.

25. "郑州皇家一号被查" [Zhengzhou's Royal One raided], *CNW* (May 17, 2014).

26. "充当保护伞, 郴州多名政法干部被查" [Several law enforcement officials in Chenzhou investigated for protecting organized crime], *CYD*, November 5, 2001.

27. "山西阳泉警方多名官员因资产过亿巡警案被调查" [Several police officers in Yangquan in Shanxi investigated for owing assets of over one hun-

dred million yuan], 中国广播网, December 19, 2010, http://fanfu.people.com
.cn/GB/13521419.html.

28. "通化公安局原副局长王禹帆涉黑" [Former deputy police chief of
Tonghua Wang Yufan involved in organized crime], *XHN*, November 24,
2009, http://news.xinhuanet.com/legal/2009-11/24/content_12530921.htm.

29. "龙兴社覆灭" [Destruction of the Longxing Society], *OL* (November
27, 2005).

30. "揭开沈阳刘涌犯罪集团黑幕" [Raise the dark curtain on Liu Yong's
criminal organization in Shenyang], 北京新报, http://news.sina.com.cn/c
/2001-09-06/349390.html.

31. "邵阳摧毁以二汤为首的黑社会组织" [Shaoyang destroys a criminal
organization headed by the two Tang brothers], *PN*, January 15, 2002, http://www
.people.com.cn/GB/shehui/212/4250/6398/20020115/648185.html.

32. "黑市长是怎样发迹的" [The rise of an underworld mayor], 半月谈内
部版 1 (2002): 57–60.

33. "铅山党政干部涉黑" [Party and government officials in Qianshan in
Jiangxi involved in organized crime].

34. "横峰县涉黑组织大案一审宣判" [Verdict in the trial of a major case of
organized crime in Hengfeng County announced], 江南都市报, November 29,
2012.

35. "黑帮无恶不作近 10 年 湖南涟源 39 名官员被查" [A criminal organ-
ization committed every conceivable crime for nearly a decade; thirty-nine
officials in Lianyuan in Hunan are investigated], *CNN*, February 8, 2002,
http://www.chinanews.com/2002-02-08/26/161076.html.

36. "富顺县房管局原副局长获刑" [Former deputy chief of housing in
Fushun County sentenced], *PD*, http://www.jcrb.com/n1/jcrb345/ca194821
.htm

37. "茂港区原公安局长杨强受贿" [Yang Qiang, former police chief of
Maogang District, took bribes], *SD*, June 20, 2011.

38. "义乌公安局长到于石榴裙下" [Police chief of Yiwu fell for a
woman].

39. "郑州公安原副局长周廷欣被判" [Zhou Tingxin, former deputy po-
lice chief of Zhengzhou, is sentenced], *PN*, February 13, 2015, http://politics
.people.com.cn/n/2015/0213/c70731-26562304.html.

40. "顺昌黑帮保护伞被起诉" [Protectors of a criminal organization in Shunchang indicted], *CNN*, January 29, 2002, http://news.sina.com.cn/c/2002 -01-29/459171.html.

41. "吸毒局长蔡亚斌一审" [Cai Yabin, the drug-snorting police chief, stands trial], 潇湘晨报, August 24, 2012; "湖南公安厅原副厅级干部局长黄桂生受贿开庭" [Trial for bribery opens for Huang Guisheng, a bureau chief in the Hunan provincial police department], *CNN*, December 27, 2012, http://www.chinanews.com/fz/2012/12-27/4443907.shtml.

42. "福建剿灭一黑社会组织" [Fujian authorities destroy a criminal organization]; "淮安市淮阴公安局原副局长李杨被判徒刑" [Li Yang, former deputy police chief of Huaiyin in Huai'an City, is sentenced], *PD*, June 13, 2002.

43. "邵阳特大涉黑团伙覆灭记" [The destruction of a mega criminal organization in Shaoyang].

44. "拿掉官方保护伞" [Take away official protection].

45. The gang was active during 1998–2007. "潼关公安局长等 20 多警察参与黑社会" [Police chief and more than twenty police officers in Tongguan participated in organized crime], *OL* (April 22, 2008).

46. "红与黑" [Red and black].

47. "沈阳公安局原副局长涉黑" [Former deputy police chief of Shenyang involved in organized crime].

48. "湖南耒阳明星公安局长肖强落马记" [The fall of Xiao Qiang, the former star police chief of Heyang in Hunan], *CYD*, August 26, 2008.

49. "来宾市原副市长李启亮违纪" [Li Qiliang, former deputy mayor of Laibin City, violates discipline], *CDID*, April 6, 2012; "来宾一国土干部领刑 5 年" [An official in the land bureau in Laibin receives a five-year prison term], 南国早报, May 25, 2012, http://www.ngzb.com.cn/thread-525103-1-1.html.

50. "东安县委副书记被公审" [A deputy party chief of Dong'an County stands trial], *PN*, January 26, 2002, http://www.people.com.cn/GB/other4788 /20020126/656255.html.

51. Wang served as the front man for Zhang Xiuwu, a local crime boss. "辽宁原人大副主任宋勇落马" [The fall of Song Yong, a deputy head of the people's congress in Liaoning], 小康, March 4, 2010, http://fanfu.people.com .cn/GB/145746/11070481.html; "被黑社会腐蚀掉的官员们" [Officials cor-

rupted by organized crime], *DAL* 30 (2012): 31–33; "凌源原市委书记宋久林受审, 被控包庇黑社会" [Song Jiulin, former party chief of Lingyuan City, on trial for protecting organized crime], *CNN*, May 18, 2010, http://fanfu.people.com.cn/GB/11631264.html.

52. "被金钱击倒的市委秘书长" [Chief secretary of the municipal party committee brought down by money], *PV* 9 (2004): 19.

53. 最高人民法院, "再审刘涌刑事判决书" [Verdict in the retrial of Liu Yong's criminal case] (2003): 刑提字第 5 号.

54. "茂名茂港区原公安分局局长杨强大肆受贿" [Yang Qiang, former police chief of Maogang District in Maoming, recklessly took bribes], *SD*, June 20, 2011.

55. "沈阳公安局原副局长涉黑" [Former deputy police chief of Shenyang involved in organized crime].

56. "茂名黑老大判 20 年" [Crime boss in Maoming gets a twenty-year sentence], 广州日报, December 20, 2011.

57. 最高人民法院, "再审刘涌刑事判决书" [Verdict in the retrial of Liu Yong's criminal case].

58. "湘中第一黑帮的穷途末路" [End of the road for the largest mafia group in central Hunan], *DAL* 11 (2006).

59. "青岛公检法多名涉黑老大聂磊案落马官员名单曝光" [List of several law enforcement officials in Qingdao arrested for involvement with crime boss Nie Lei revealed], 财新新世纪 (October 17, 2011).

60. "浙江温岭特大黑帮案开审" [Trial opens for the mega criminal gang in Wenling in Zhejiang], *CNN*, December 19, 2000, http://www.chinanews.com/2000-12-19/26/62306.html; "红与黑" [Red and Black].

61. "福州死囚富豪陈凯上诉" [Condemned Fuzhou tycoon Chen Kai appeals sentence], 法制早报, February 2, 2005; "福建大批高官因福州首富陈凯案被判重刑" [A large number of senior officials implicated in the case of Fuzhou's richest tycoon Chen Kai receive harsh sentences], 重庆晨报, December 17, 2004.

62. "陕西终审三秦打黑第一案" [Shaanxi ends trial in Sanqin's no. 1 case of fighting organized crime], *CYD*, March 13, 2002.

63. "云南西双版纳公安局原副局长受贿 12 万一审判 5 年" [Former deputy police chief in Yunnan's Xishuangbanna gets five years for taking 120,000

yuan in bribes], 中国法院网, June 4, 2008, http://cpc.people.com.cn/GB /64093/64371/7340671.html.

64. "吉林通化市公安局副局长涉黑受审" [Former deputy police chief of Tonghua on trial for involvement in organized crime], 新民网, November 12, 2009, http://news.163.com/09/1112/02/5NSSGDQ80001124J.html.

65. "茂名原茂港公安局长卖官纵容黑社会" [Former police chief of Maogang in Maoming sold public offices and connived with organized crime], *SD*, June 20, 2011.

66. "一个勇于惩腐除恶的老百姓" [An ordinary individual who dared to punish the corrupt and fight evil], *ACH* 4 (2001): 14–19.

67. "新化黑社会团伙调查" [An investigation into organized criminal groups in Xinhua].

68. "湖南耒阳明星公安局长肖强落马记" [The fall of Xiao Qiang, the former star police chief of Heyang in Hunan].

69. "山西涉黑屡犯被判死罪供出高官一串" [Sentenced to death, a repeat offender involved in organized crime in Shanxi reveals a list of senior officials], 新华社, November 17, 2005, http://news.sina.com.cn/o/2005-11-18 /06267470534s.shtml.

70. "与黑老大称兄道弟的公安厅副厅长" [A deputy provincial police chief who called a crime boss his brother], *DAL* 6 (2007): 24–25.

71. "青岛公检法多名涉黑老大聂磊案落马官员名单曝光" [List of several law enforcement officials in Qingdao arrested for involvement with crime boss Nie Lei revealed].

72. "茂名李振刚涉黑案" [The case of Li Zhengang's involvement in organized crime in Maoming], *LD*, June 23, 2011.

73. "福州高层大地震" [Major earthquake at the top of the Fuzhou government], *PV* 2 (2004): 14.

74. "茂名港区原公安分局局长杨强大肆受贿" [Yang Qiang, former police chief of Maogang District in Maoming, recklessly took bribes].

75. Hao Weicheng, a Changchun-based crime boss, had extensive business activities, one of which was forced eviction. Liu Yong of Shenyang also used violence to evict local residents to seize their land. "长春黑老大受审" [Changchun's crime boss stands trial], *CNN*, October 20, 2010, http://www

.chinanews.com/sh/2010/10-20/2598451.shtml; "最高人民法院, "再审刘涌刑事判决书" [Verdict in the retrial of Liu Yong's criminal case].

76. A deputy director of the Fujian provincial department of state security took more than 100,000 yuan from Chen Kai, Fuzhou's crime boss, and was sentenced to twelve years in jail. "福建大批高官因福州首富陈凯案被判重刑" [The large number of senior officials implicated in the case of Fuzhou's richest tycoon Chen Kai receive harsh sentences]. In 2002, the director of the Shaanxi provincial department of state security was sentenced to fifteen years for accepting a bribe of nearly 1 million yuan from the leader of a smuggling ring based in Fuzhou. The head of the bureau of state security in the city of Fuyang was sentenced to ten years in prison for accepting large bribes from unidentified individuals in 2005. http://blog.sina.com.cn/s/blog_425d3adf0100ve9m.html.

7. The Spread of Collusion

Epigraph: *习近平关于党风廉政建设和反腐败斗争论述摘编* [Selected speeches by Xi Jinping] (Beijing: 中央文献出版社, 2015): 19.

1. The contradiction between one-party rule and legal reform is explored in Stanley Lubman, ed., *The Evolution of Law Reform in China: An Uncertain Path* (Cheltenham: Edward Elgar, 2012).

2. 郑小楼, "法官腐败报告" [Report on corruption among judges], *Caijing* (August 5, 2013).

3. Data from the "Annual Work Reports of the Supreme People's Court to the National People's Congress," various years. Data for 2005 and 2015 are not included because the reports did not provide them. Prior to 1998, the reports contained the number of judges criminally prosecuted each year. In the period 1987–1992, forty-four judges were prosecuted; in the four-year period 1993–1997, 180 judges were prosecuted.

4. "司法不公窝案增加" [Increase in cases of *wo'an* in the judiciary], *新京报*, June 25, 2009; "司法人员职务犯罪窝案串案突出" [*Wo'an* and *chuan'an*: Striking characteristics of judicial officers who use their offices to commit crimes], *PD*, December 12, 2003. For earlier studies on judicial

corruption, see Ting Gong, "Dependent judiciary and unaccountable judges: Judicial corruption in contemporary China," *China Review* 4 (2004): 33–54; Ling Li, "Corruption in China's courts," in Randall Peerenboom, ed., *Judicial Independence in China: Lessons for Global Rule of Law Promotion* (New York: Cambridge University Press, 2010): 196–220; Yuhua Wang, "Court funding and judicial corruption in China," *China Journal* 69 (January 2013): 43–63; Zhou Keyuan, "Judicial reforms vs. judicial corruption: Recent developments in China," *Criminal Forum* 11 (2000): 232–351. Chinese literature on corruption in the judiciary has noted collective or collusive corruption, but there has been no systematic research. See 蒋超, "三十年来中国法官违法犯罪问题" [The problem of violation of law and criminal activity by Chinese judges in the last three decades], 宁夏社会科学 4 (2010): 9–16; 郑小楼, "法官腐败报告" [Report on corruption among judges].

5. The CCP launched its first major campaign against judicial corruption in 1998 and forbade judges from accepting gifts and meals from litigants or their lawyers. In 1998, a record 2,512 judicial officers were disciplined, 221 of whom were prosecuted. "最高人民法院工作报告 1999" [Work report of the Supreme People's Court 1999], http://www.court.gov.cn/qwfb/gzbg /201003/t20100310_2633.htm.

6. "西城法院原院长郭生贵死缓判决" [Former president of the Xicheng District Court Guo Shenggui gets suspended death sentence], *PN*, http:// politics.people.com.cn/GB/14562/8719971.html.

7. "茂名茂港区法院原院长严得犯五宗罪" [Yan De, former president of the Maogang District Court in Maoming, committed five criminal offenses], 广州日报, June 22, 2012.

8. "湖南高院原院长吴振汉落马记" [The fall of Wu Zhenhan, former president of the Hunan High Court], 荆楚网, http://news.sina.com.cn/c/l /2006-11-14/115611510751.shtml.

9. "深圳中院原副院长堕落轨迹" [A journey of corruption by a former vice president of the Shenzhen Intermediate Court], 东方网, http://news .xinhuanet.com/legal/2008-01/15/content_7427445.htm.

10. "140 万元贿赂法官" [1.4 million yuan in bribes for a judge], 新快报, December 15, 2010.

11. "详解张弢案" [A close analysis of the case of Zhang Tao], *新世纪* (March 2, 2011).

12. "究竟谁来监督法官?" [Who ultimately watches the judges?] *CNW* (April 19, 2004).

13. "透视武汉 13 名法官的腐败同盟" [Anatomy of a corrupt alliance of thirteen judges in Wuhan], *CNW* (April 19, 2004).

14. 郑小楼, "法官腐败报告" [Report on corruption among judges].

15. "究竟谁来监督法官" [Who ultimately watches the judges?].

16. 郑小楼, "法官腐败报告" [Report on corruption among judges].

17. "武汉市中级人民法院 13 名法官受贿" [Thirteen judges at the Wuhan Intermediate Court took bribes], *工人日报*, June 7, 2004.

18. "股权纠纷牵出法官窝案" [A dispute over share rights exposes a case of collusive judicial corruption], *XHN*, http://news.xinhuanet.com/legal/2012-06 /20/c_123309771.htm.

19. "剖析福州台江法官腐败窝案" [Anatomy of a case of collusive judicial corruption in Taijiang in Fuzhou], *CNN*, http://www.chinanews.com/fz/2014 /09-12/6585902.shtml.

20. "贿赂一串法官" [Bribing a group of judges], *福州晚报*, http://www .66163.com/fujian_w/news/fzwb/981229/5-1.htm.

21. "他把 25 名法官拉下水" [He bribed twenty-five judges], *SW*, April 30, 2009.

22. "沈阳 '慕马大案' 查处纪实" [The real story of investigating the mega scandal of Mu and Ma in Shenyang], *廉政在线*, http://jct.zj.gov.cn/fanfubai /detail.asp?id=97.

23. The president of the court, Yan De, was also in the pay of the mafia boss. "茂名 '黑老大' 李振刚重审" [Mafia boss Li Zhengang is retried], *南都数字报*, http://epaper.nandu.com/epaper/A/html/2014-09/20/content_3316738.htm ?div=-1.

24. "黑老大蹊跷出狱" [The strange release of a mafia boss], *SW*, November 7, 2007.

25. Donald Clarke, "Power and politics in the Chinese court system: The enforcement of civil judgments," *Columbia Journal of Asian Law* 10 (1996): 1–91.

26. Based on the press report, the incident likely occurred in 1999. "走向地狱之门" [The gate to hell], *DAL* (January 2002).

27. "剖析福州台江法官腐败窝案" [Anatomy of a case of collusive judicial corruption in Taijiang in Fuzhou].

28. "诉讼掮客放倒湛江 9 名法官" [Broker in litigation brought down nine judges in Zhanjiang], *SD,* April 27, 2011.

29. "尚军受贿落马" [Shang Jun arrested for taking bribes], *XHN,* http://news.xinhuanet.com/legal/2006-11/16/content_5337321_1.htm.

30. "茂名茂港区法院原院长严得犯五宗罪" [Yan De, former president of the Maogang District Court in Maoming, committed five criminal offenses].

31. "湖南高院原院长吴振汉落马" [The fall of Wu Zhenhan, former president of the Hunan High Court], *荆楚网,* http://www.cnhubei.com/200611/ca1205390.htm.

32. "辽宁高院原副院长陈长林被查" [Chen Changlin, former vice president of the Liaoning High Court, is investigated], *CXN,* http://china.caixin.com/2014-09-15/100728790.html.

33. "阜阳中院之痛" [The pain of the Fuyang Intermediate Court], *方圆法治* (September 2009): 14–19; "安徽阜阳中院腐败案审判" [Trial of the corruption case of the Fuyang Intermediate Court], *CYD,* March 31, 2008; "阜阳中级法院三任院长前腐后继" [Three presidents of the Fuyang Intermediate Court follow each other on a path of corruption], *法制与新闻* 10 (2006); "尚军受贿落马" [Shang Jun arrested for taking bribes].

34. In 1998, in an effort to crack down on judicial corruption, the Central Politics and Law Committee issued the "Four Prohibitions," one of which was against accepting meals, money, and gifts from litigants. 郑小楼, "法官腐败报告" [Report on corruption among judges].

35. "剖析福州台江法官腐败窝案" [Anatomy of a case of collusive judicial corruption in Taijiang in Fuzhou].

36. "公安局干警武装抗法案" [A case of armed policemen resisting judicial enforcement], *PV* 22 (2003): 28–29.

37. "Sanpei" services include drinking, eating, singing, dancing, and sleeping with clients. "贿赂一串法官" [Bribing a group of judges].

38. A private entrepreneur who lost a case overseen by one of the judges suspected that the judge was corrupt and followed him until he obtained evidence of the judge's corruption. "上海多名法官被曝参与集体招妓" [Several

judges in Shanghai shown patronizing prostitutes together], 腾讯网, http://news.qq.com/a/20130802/018022.htm.

39. "公安局干警武装抗法案" [A case of armed policemen resisting judicial enforcement].

40. "河南伊川矿难" [Mining disaster in Yichuan in Henan], *CXN*, http://china.caixin.com/2010-08-06/100167342.html.

41. "武汉法官犯罪触目惊心" [Shocking crimes committed by judges in Wuhan], *OO* (February 2, 2004).

42. "阜阳中院法官群体道德缺失" [Loss of collective morality by judges at the Fuyang Intermediate Court], *PN*, http://politics.people.com.cn/GB/1026/3362116.html.

43. Chinese Criminal Code, http://www.china.com.cn/policy/txt/2012-01/14/content_24405327_28.htm.

44. "温州市安监局原局长陈彩兴涉嫌受贿" [Former head of the Wenzhou bureau of work safety Chen Caixing suspected of taking bribes], 中国广播网, http://www.cnr.cn/2004news/internal/200810/t20081023_505131793.html; "温州纪委通报十大典型案件" [Wenzhou discipline committee publicizes ten major representative cases], 温州网, http://report.66wz.com/system/2008/12/19/101030146.shtml.

45. Twenty people were arrested in this case. "温州原环保局长涉嫌受贿法庭受审" [Former head of the Wenzhou bureau of environmental protection tried for bribery], *LD*, November 20, 2008; "温州纪委通报十大典型案件" [Wenzhou discipline committee publicizes ten major representative cases].

46. "广州海珠检察院屡查大案" [The Haizhu procuratorate in Guangzhou repeatedly uncovers major cases], 南方都市报, January 7, 2005; "为升官广州市环保局长李维宇拿脏款" [Li Weiyu, head of the Guangzhou municipal bureau of environmental protection, took bribes to seek promotion], 羊城晚报, December 28, 2004.

47. "介休环保局三名副局长落马" [The fall of three deputy directors of the Jiexiu bureau of environmental protection], *LD*, December 14, 2012.

48. "慈溪环保局原局长涉嫌严重违纪" [Former head of the Cixi bureau of environmental protection suspected of a serious violation of discipline], 钱江晚报, June 5, 2014. "浙江慈溪环保系统腐败窝案" [The *wo'an* inside the Cixi environmental protection system in Zhejiang], *PD*, June 18, 2009.

49. Zheng was the only vice minister executed for corruption in the post-Mao era. "药监局窝案里的小卒" [A pawn in the *wo'an* in the bureau of drug administration], *PV* 20 (2007).

50. "联手炮制假药的药监官员" [Officials in the bureau of drug administration who colluded in the production of counterfeit medicine], *PV* 21 (2007).

51. "郑筱萸受贿玩忽职守一审判决书" [Verdict in Zheng Xiaoyu's trial for accepting bribes and dereliction of duty], http://www.360doc.com/content/13/1204/10/3730583_334346626.shtml.

52. "郑筱萸腐败路线图" [Zheng Xiaoyu's map of corruption], *CNN*, http://www.chinanews.com/sh/news/2007/04-10/911752.shtml.

53. "出事故的安监局长" [Director of work safety bureau had an accident], *CDID*, March 15, 2013; "安徽省蚌埠市安监局原副局长调查事故收受贿赂" [Investigating an accident, former deputy head of Bengbu's bureau of work safety in Anhui took bribes], *XHN*, November 16, 2011, http://news.xinhuanet.com/legal/2011-11/16/c_111171422.htm.

54. "介休环保局三名副局长落马" [The fall of three deputy directors of the Jiexiu bureau of environmental protection].

55. This scandal implicated seven officials and over 200 mine owners. The government reportedly lost over 30 million yuan in income from mining rights. "吉林最大规模渎职腐败窝案" [Jilin's largest *wo'an* involving negligence and corruption], *JN*, April 8, 2008, http://www.jcrb.com/zhuanti/ffzt/hscwlfb/fbwa/200808/t20080815_63020.html.

56. "江苏南通环保腐败窝案" [The *wo'an* inside the bureau of environmental protection in Nantong, Jiangsu], *第一财经日报*, January 7, 2013.

57. "浙江海盐环保局现腐败窝案" [*Wo'an* exposed in the bureau of environmental protection in Haiyan, Zhejiang], *JN*, December 9, 2014, http://news.jcrb.com/jxsw/201412/t20141209_1457355.html.

58. "湖南药监领域腐败案调查" [Investigation into the corruption in Hunan's drug regulatory system], *CNN*, May 5, 2013, http://www.chinanews.com/gn/2013/05-05/4787754.shtml.

59. "两年内中国环评" [China's environmental assessment over the last two years], *CXN*, March 26, 2015, http://china.caixin.com/2015-03-26/100794908.html.

60. "被潜规则污染的环保局" [Bureau of environmental protection tainted by unspoken rules], *DAL* (October 19, 2007).

61. "广东江门环保窝案" [The *wo'an* in the bureau of environmental protection in Jiangmen, Guangdong], *SD,* January 11, 2010.

62. "别让腐败的水，脏了环保的门" [Do not let the water of corruption stain the door of environmental protection], *JN,* http://www.jcrb.com/n1 /jcrb499/ca267239.htm; "被污染的环保官员" [Tainted officials in the bureau of environmental protection], *三湘都市报,* October 18, 2004.

63. "环保局领导是怎样被'污染'的?" [How were the leaders of the bureau of environmental protection tainted?], *浙江廉政在线,* http://jct.zj.gov .cn/fanfubai/detail.asp?id=1793.

64. "湖南省安监局原局长谢光祥索贿" [Former head of the Hunan provincial bureau of work safety Xie Guangxiang sought bribes], *湖南日报,* March 31, 2010.

65. "湖南省安监局原局长谢光祥的阴阳人生" [The double life of Xie Guangxiang, former head of the Hunan provincial bureau of work safety], *LD,* April 8, 2010; "湖南安监局原局长谢光祥涉嫌受贿被纪委调查" [Xie Guangxiang, former head of the Hunan provincial bureau of work safety, investigated for bribery], *荆楚网,* December 18, 2008, http://news.eastday .com/c/20081218/u1a4052140.html.

66. "为升官广州市环保局长李维宇拿赃款" [Li Weiyu, head of the Guangzhou municipal bureau of environmental protection, took bribes to seek promotion].

67. "药监局窝案里的小卒" [A pawn in the *wo'an* in the bureau of drug administration].

68. "贪财局长 倒在 情人怀里" [Greedy bureau director falls for his mistress], *信息时报,* July 7, 2004.

69. "被潜规则污染的环保局" [Bureau of environmental protection tainted by unspoken rules].

70. "杭州彻查环保系统腐败" [Hangzhou thoroughly investigates corruption in the environmental protection sector], *SW,* April 4, 2008.

71. "浙江省海宁市安监局腐败窝案剖析" [Anatomy of *wo'an* in the bureau of work safety in Haining City of Zhejiang], *CDID,* November 24, 2014.

72. "会计自首揭药监系统贪腐窝案" [Accountant turns himself in and exposes collective corruption in the bureau of drug administration], *PD*, September 25, 2014.

73. "介休环保局三名副局长落马" [The fall of three deputy directors of the Jiexiu bureau of environmental protection].

74. "杭州彻查环保系统腐败" [Hangzhou thoroughly investigates corruption in the environmental protection sector]; "原广州市环保局局长受贿 68 万" [Former head of the Guangzhou municipal bureau of environmental protection took 680,000 yuan in bribes], *新快报*, December 28, 2004.

75. Wang Qishan, the CCP's anticorruption chief, used this phrase to describe the mega scandal in Shanxi. "王岐山谈塌方式腐败案" [Wang Qishan on cases of collapse-style corruption], *XHN*, March 11, 2015, http://news.xinhuanet.com/politics/2015-03/11/c_127567146.htm.

76. For details on collapse-style corruption in these jurisdictions, see "广西 8 年一正三副 4 名主席落马" [One governor and three deputy governors in Guangxi arrested for corruption in eight years], *CEH*, September 2, 2009; "内蒙 3 月内 12 名官员落马" [Twelve officials in Inner Mongolia arrested for corruption in three months], *新闻晨报*, September 19, 2014; "开封官场窝案" [The *wo'an* in the halls of power in Kaifeng], *民主与法制时报*, October 20, 2014.

77. "官场 大地震 未息" [The big earthquake in the halls of power has not quieted down], *Caijing* (May 1, 2005); "黑龙江政坛三年大地震" [Big earthquake in the government of Heilongjiang during the last three years], *新世纪周刊* (December 28, 2005).

78. "山西官员落马 加速度" [Fall of officials in Shanxi picks up speed], *CXN*, September 1, 2014, http://china.caixin.com/2014-09-01/100723645.html; "盘点山西反腐" [Summary of the anticorruption campaign in Shanxi], *新浪网*, http://shanxi.sina.com.cn/news/zt/luoma; "腐败重灾区主官" [Top leaders in areas hit hard by corruption], *CXN*, March 6, 2015, http://topics.caixin.com/2015-03-06/100789017.html.

79. "蘇榮" [Su Rong], *凤凰网*, http://news.ifeng.com/mainland/special/tgpzsr; "苏荣腐败案" [The corruption case of Su Rong], *JT*, March 6, 2015; "苏荣的权力场" [Su Rong's domain of power], *CNW* (October 9, 2014).

80. "云南落马官员名单" [A list of officials in Yunnan arrested for corruption], *广州生活网,* March 15, 2015, http://www.gzyeah.com/article/2015031532180.html; "继续追查外逃原书记高严" [Continuing the pursuit of the fugitive, former party chief Gao Yan], *观察网,* March 7, 2015, http://www.guancha.cn/FaZhi/2015_03_07_311411.shtml.

81. "福州死囚富豪陈凯上诉" [Condemned Fuzhou tycoon Chen Kai appeals his sentence], *BN,* January 23, 2005; "福建大批高官因福州首富陈凯案被判重刑" [A large number of senior officials in Fujian get long prison terms for involvement in the case of Fuzhou's richest tycoon, Chen Kai], *重庆晨报,* December17, 2004; "福州首富陈凯案" [The case of Fuzhou's richest tycoon, Chen Kai], *周末报,* August 18, 2004.

82. "沈阳 '慕马大案' 查处纪实" [The real story of the investigation of the mega scandal of Mu and Ma in Shenyang], *PN,* October 15, 2001, http://www.people.com.cn/GB/shehui/44/20011015/581373.html.

83. "安徽阜阳政府力图重塑形象" [The government of Fuyang in Anhui attempts to repair its image], *中国经济周刊* (May 28, 2007); 黄陵纪委, "王怀忠腐败案件" [The corruption case of Wang Huaizhong], http://www.ycjjw.gov.cn/WrzcNet_ReadNews.asp?NewsID=445.

84. "郴州腐败窝案" [A *wo'an* in Chenzhou], *CYD,* November 21, 2008.

85. "茂名官场窝案" [The *wo'an* in the halls of power in Maoming], *OMN,* March 30, 2014; "广东茂名官场又地震" [Another earthquake in the halls of power in Maoming], *CNN,* October 31, 2014, http://www.chinanews.com/gn/2014/10-31/6739256.shtml.

86. "王昭耀荣耀与耻辱" [The glory and shame of Wang Zhaoyao], *SW,* December 18, 2007; "安徽阜阳 '卖官' 市长肖作新受审" [Mayor Xiao Zuoxin of Fuyang in Anhui, seller of public office, stands trial], *东方网,* http://news.eastday.com/epublish/gb/paper134/3/class013400007/hwz186177.htm; "王怀忠腐败案件" [The corruption case of Wang Huaizhong]; "贫困县俩, 卖官书记" [Two office-selling party chiefs in a poor county], *XHN,* February 21, 2006, http://www.gxjjw.gov.cn/article/2006/0221/article_5841.html.

87. "广东省委原常委周镇宏判决书" [Verdict in the trial of Zhou Zhenhong, former member of the standing committee of the Guangdong CCP organization], http://www.thepaper.cn/newsDetail_forward_1295214; "茂名官场窝案" [The *wo'an* in the halls of power in Maoming]; "茂名原公安局长

倪俊雄落马" [Ni Junxiong, the former director of public security in Maoming, is arrested], *XHN,* June 28, 2012, http://news.xinhuanet.com/local/2012-06/28 /c_123340678.htm; "原茂名公安局长买官卖官" [The former director of public security in Maoming bought and sold public offices], *PN,* July 16, 2012, http://fanfu.people.com.cn/n/2012/0716/c64371-18521630.html.

88. "山西省原副省长杜善学" [Du Shanxue, former deputy governor of Shanxi province], *PN,* February 13, 2015, http://politics.people.com.cn/n /2015/0213/c1001-26563627.html; "山西省委原常委陈川平" [Chen Chuanping, former member of the standing committee of the Shanxi CCP organization department], *PN,* February 17, 2015, http://politics.people.com.cn/n /2015/0217/c1001-26580076.html; "苏荣腐败案" [The corruption case of Su Rong].

89. "苏荣的权力场" [Su Rong's domain of power].

90. "白恩培：一个省级政治山头的崩塌" [Bai Enpei: The collapse of a provincial political fiefdom], *凤凰网,* http://news.ifeng.com/mainland /special/tgpzbep/; "昆明落马书记张田欣" [Zhang Tianxin, the disgraced party chief of Kunming], *经济观察网,* July 23, 2014, http://business.sohu.com /20140723/n402624917.shtml; "揭秘落马官员仇和" [Exposing Qiu He, a disgraced official], *法制晚报,* May 4, 2015.

91. "安徽省原副省长王怀忠案" [The case of former deputy governor of Anhui, Wang Huaizhong], http://old.chinacourt.org/html/article/200402/13 /103600.shtml; "王怀忠腐败案件" [The corruption case of Wang Huaizhong]; "王怀忠走向死亡" [Wang Huaizhong marches to his death], *人民文摘* 3 (2004).

92. "湖南郴州市委书记李大伦落马波及 158 名官商" [The fall of Li Dalun, party chief of Chenzhou in Hunan, implicates 158 officials and businessmen], *秦风网,* August 31, 2012, http://www.ycjjw.gov.cn/WrzcNet_ReadNews.asp ?NewsID=444.

93. "沈阳慕马大案查处纪实" [The real story of investigating the mega scandal of Mu and Ma in Shenyang]; "解读沈阳刘涌黑帮发展过程" [Understanding the growth of Liu Yong's criminal organization in Shenyang], *CYD,* September 21, 2001.

94. "福州死囚陈凯上诉" [Condemned Fuzhou tycoon Chen Kai appeals his sentence].

95. "刘汉朋友圈" [Liu Han's circle of friends], *Caijing*, http://www.weixinyidu.com/n_17443.

96. "慕绥新、马向东与黑社会勾结实录" [Factual record of Mu Suixin and Ma Xiangdong's collusion with organized crime], 文摘报, November 29, 2001; "白恩培云南旧事" [Old stories about Bai Enpei in Yunnan], *CJN*, September 15, 2014, http://politics.caijing.com.cn/20140915/3698688.shtml; "起底白恩培" [Exposing Bai Enpei], 一财网, August 31, 2014, http://news.sina.com.cn/c/2014-08-31/175930772328.shtml.

97. "郴州腐败窝案" [A *wo'an* in Chenzhou].

98. "苏荣的权力场" [Su Rong's domain of power].

99. "王怀忠腐败案件" [The corruption case of Wang Huaizhong].

100. 大悟县纪律检查委员会, "慕绥新自供状" [Mu Suixin's confession], http://www.dwjwjc.com/info.aspx?id=34.

101. "沈阳慕马大案查处纪实" [The real story of investigating the mega scandal of Mu and Ma in Shenyang].

102. "福州首富陈凯案" [The case of Fuzhou's richest tycoon, Chen Kai].

Conclusion

Epigraph: 习近平关于党风廉政建设和反腐败斗争论述摘编 [Selected speeches by Xi Jinping] (Beijing: 中央文献出版社, 2015): 34.

1. Olivier Blanchard, Kenneth A. Froot, and Jeffrey D. Sachs, eds., *The Transition in Eastern Europe*, Vol. 2: *Restructuring* (Chicago: University of Chicago Press, 2007); Frank Schimmelfennig and Ulrich Sedelmeier, eds., *The Europeanization of Central and Eastern Europe* (Ithaca, NY: Cornell University Press, 2005).

2. Janos Kornai, "Transformational recession: The main causes," *Journal of Comparative Economics* 19 (1994): 39–63; Olivier Blanchard, *Reform in Eastern Europe* (Cambridge, MA: MIT Press, 1993).

3. Geoffrey Pridham and Tatu Vanhanen, *Democratization in Eastern Europe* (London: Routledge, 2002); Karen Dawisha and Bruce Parrott, *The Consolidation of Democracy in East-Central Europe*, Vol. 1 (Cambridge, UK: Cambridge University Press, 1997).

4. For a discussion on the predatory state, see Peter Evans, "Predatory, developmental, and other apparatuses: A comparative political economy perspective on the Third World state," *Sociological Forum* 4 (1989): 561–587.

5. Douglass North, *Institutions, Institutional Change and Economic Performance* (New York: Cambridge University Press, 1990).

6. Nicholas Lardy, *Markets over Mao: The Rise of Private Business in China* (Washington, DC: Peterson Institute for International Economics, 2014); Yasheng Huang, *Capitalism with Chinese Characteristics: Entrepreneurship and the State* (New York: Cambridge University Press, 2008).

7. See Bruce Dickson, *Red Capitalists in China: The Party, Private Entrepreneurs, and Prospects for Political Change* (Cambridge, UK: Cambridge University Press, 2003); Dickson, *Wealth into Power: The Communist Party's Embrace of China's Private Sector* (Cambridge, UK: Cambridge University Press, 2008).

8. Daron Acemoglu, "The form of property rights: Oligarchic vs. democratic societies," Working Paper No. 10037, National Bureau of Economic Research, 2003; Konstantin Sonin, "Why the rich may favor poor protection of property rights," *Journal of Comparative Economics* 31 (2003): 715–731.

9. The total net worth of the 137 dollar billionaires whose fortunes are based on real estate was estimated to be 36.902 trillion yuan in 2015. 胡润百富榜 [List of Hurun's one hundred richest people], http://www.hurun.net /CN/ArticleShow.aspx?nid=14677.

10. For a list of such flaws, see World Bank and Development Research Center of the State Council, *China 2030: Building a Modern, Harmonious, and Creative Society* (Washington, DC: World Bank, 2013).

11. As of July 2015, two bureau-level officials in the CCDI, five provincial CDI directors and three deputy directors, and ten prefecture-level CDI directors had been arrested for corruption.

12. "郭文贵围猎高官记" [Guo Wengui: A tale of trapping senior officials], *CXN*, March 25, 2015, http://china.caixin.com/2015-03-25/100794575 _all.html#page2.

13. "西藏首虎乐大克被查" [Le Dake, first tiger in Tibet, is being investigated], *BN*, June 27, 2015.

14. "全军查办案件，工程建设房产开发等占九成" [Ninety percent of corruption cases investigated by the PLA involve construction and real estate], *BYD*, December 1, 2014.

15. For representative works on this theory, see Sebastian Heilmann and Elizabeth J. Perry, eds., *Mao's Invisible Hand: The Political Foundations of Adaptive Governance in China* (Cambridge, MA: Harvard University Asia Center, 2011); David Shambaugh, *China's Communist Party: Atrophy and Adaptation* (Washington, DC: Woodrow Wilson Press; Berkeley: University of California Press, 2008); Andrew Nathan, "Authoritarian resilience," *Journal of Democracy* 14 (2003): 6–17.

16. Daron Acemoglu and James Robinson, *Why Nations Fail: The Origins of Power, Prosperity, and Poverty* (New York: Crown, 2012).

17. For brief surveys of democracy in Russia and Ukraine, see Steven Fish, *Democracy Derailed in Russia: The Failure of Open Politics* (Cambridge, UK: Cambridge University Press, 2005); Lucan Way, "Rapacious individualism and political competition in Ukraine, 1992–2004," *Communist and Post-Communist Studies* 38 (2005): 191–205.

Acknowledgments

I want to thank the Smith Richardson Foundation for its generous financial support. I am particularly grateful to Marin Strmecki and Allan Song of the foundation for their confidence in this project and their patience. During the research for the book, I benefited enormously from the support by the staff at the Universities Service Centre at the Chinese University of Hong Kong. In particular, I want to thank Jean Hung, Kim-min Chan, Gao Qi, and Celia Chan for their valuable assistance and hospitality during my frequent visits to the Centre. At Claremont McKenna College, I received indispensable research assistance from Fu Yu, Monica Wang, Xue Bai, Victoria Tang, and Wendy Sheng, who combed through Chinese sources to help gather data for the book. Desiree Gibson of the Keck Center for International Strategic Studies at Claremont McKenna also provided outstanding administrative assistance.

I greatly appreciate the helpful comments on the book from Ting Gong, Andrew Walder, and Xueguang Zhou. I also benefited from invaluable suggestions from the two anonymous reviewers. I am deeply indebted to Kathleen McDermott, my editor at Harvard University Press, for her encouragement and support. I am very grateful to Nancy Hearst for doing an outstanding proofreading job.

I also want to thank my wife, Meizhou, and my children, Alexander and Philip, for their love and patience during the research and writing of the book.

Finally, I wish to express my deep gratitude to Roderick MacFarquhar, my teacher, mentor, and lifelong friend. Rod's devotion to scholarship, intellectual integrity, personal generosity, and unwavering commitment to the values of justice and human decency have been a constant source of inspiration. To Rod this book is dedicated.

Index